Managing in a Time of Great Change

Books by Peter F. Drucker

Management
Managing in a Time of Great Change
Managing for the Future
Managing the Non Profit Organization
The Frontiers of Management
Innovation and Entrepreneurship
The Changing World of the Executive
Managing in Turbulent Times
Management: Tasks; Responsibilities; Practices
Technology, Management and Society
The Effective Executive
Managing for Results
The Practice of Management
Concept of the Corporation

Economics, politics, society
Post-Capitalist Society
The Ecological Vision
The New Realities
Towards the Next Economics
The Unseen Revolution
Men, Ideas and Politics
The Age of Discontinuity
Landmarks of Tomorrow
America's Next Twenty Years
The New Society
The Future of Industrial Man
The End of Economic Man

Fiction
The Temptation to Do Good
The Last of All Possible Worlds

Autobiography
Adventures of a Bystander

Managing in a Time of Great Change

Peter F. Drucker

BUTTERWORTH
HEINEMANN

Butterworth-Heinemann Ltd
Linacre House, Jordan Hill, Oxford OX2 8DP

 A member of the Reed Elsevier plc group

OXFORD LONDON BOSTON
MUNICH NEW DELHI SINGAPORE SYDNEY
TOKYO TORONTO WELLINGTON

First published 1995

British Library Cataloguing in Publication Data
Drucker, Peter F.
  Managing in a Time of Great Change
  I. Title
  658.406

ISBN 0 7506 2392 6

Printed in Great Britain by Clays, St Ives plc

Contents

Preface

All the pieces in this book – two interviews, one at the beginning and one at the end, and twenty-five chapters in between – have one common theme, despite their apparent diversity. They all deal with *changes that have already irreversibly happened*. They therefore deal with changes on which executives can – indeed must – take action. None of the pieces in this book attempts to predict the future. All deal with what executives can do – have to do – to make the future.

It is not so very difficult to predict the future. It is only pointless. Many futurologists have high batting averages – the way they measure themselves and are commonly measured. They do a good job foretelling *some* things. But what are always far more important are fundamental changes that happened though no one predicted them or could possibly have predicted them. Looking back ten years today, no one in 1985 predicted – or could have predicted – that the establishment of the European Economic Community would not release explosive economic growth in Europe but would, on the contrary, usher in a decade of economic stagnation and petty bickering. As a result, the unified Europe of 1995 is actually weaker in the world economy than was the fractured Europe of 1985. No one, ten years ago, predicted – or could have predicted – the explosive economic growth of mainland China, a growth that came despite

rather than because of its government policies. No one predicted the emergence of the 55 million overseas Chinese as the
new economic superpower. No one ten years ago could have
predicted that the biggest impact of the Information Revolution
on business would be a radical rethinking and restructuring of
the oldest information system – and one that apparently was
ossified in every joint and tissue – the accounting model of the
'bean counters'.

But equally important: one cannot make decisions for the
future. Decisions are commitments to action. And actions are
always in the present, and in the present only. But actions in the
present are also the one and only way to *make the future*.
Executives are paid to execute – that is, to take effective action.
That they can only do in contemplation of the present, and by
exploiting the changes that have already happened.

This book starts out with the executive's job, that is, with
management. What has already happened in the world of the
executive that puts into question – or perhaps even makes obsolete – the assumptions, rules, and practices which worked these
last forty years and which therefore have automatically been
taken for granted? The book then proceeds to look at the implications of one particular fundamental change in management,
economy, and society: the emergence of information as the
executive's key resource and as the organization's skeleton. The
premise of this part of the book is the old adage that either you
are the tool's master or you are its servant. What do executives
have to learn to be masters of the new tool? Then this book
moves out of the executive's job and organization into markets
and into a world economy in which there are new power centres,
new growth markets, new growth industries. In its last section
the book analyses the changes in society and government – the
biggest changes, perhaps, in this Century of Social Transformation, in which government has been both a great success and the
ultimate failure.

Only thirty – perhaps even only twenty – years ago it was often said that while there were a great many more managers and executives than there had been in the 1920s (let alone before the First World War), most of them were doing pretty much what their predecessors had done and in pretty much the same way. No one would say that anymore for today's managers and executives. But if there is one thing that is certain today it is that tomorrow's managers and executives will do things that are even more different from what today's managers and executives do. And they will do them quite differently. To enable today's executives to be ahead of this different tomorrow – indeed to make it their tomorrow – is the aim of this book.

Peter F. Drucker
Claremont, California
May 1995

Acknowledgements

From the very beginning, in 1991, every piece in this volume was written with this book in mind. But every single one was also prepublished, intentionally so. It is the reaction of readers – and especially of friends all over the world, former students, present and former clients – which ultimately determine whether a piece is worthy of being included in the final book. Prepublication is, so to speak, my market test.

For the most part, the pieces chosen appear as chapters in this book without any change other than perhaps a new title or a restoration of cuts that had to be made to fit a piece into a magazine or newspaper. But three long pieces in this book are substantially different from the version in which they were published originally – they are much longer. Chapter 21 ('A century of social transformation') was published only in an abridged version in *The Atlantic Monthly* and so was Chapter 25 ('Can the democracies win the peace?') Chapter 13 ('Trade lessons from the world economy') was similarly published only in an abridged version in *Foreign Affairs* magazine. The other long chapters – the two interviews which open and close the book; Chapters 1, 7 and 12 (all three first published in the *Harvard Business Review*); Chapter 18 (first published in *Foreign Affairs*); and Chapter 24 (first published in *The Atlantic Monthly*) – are published in this book the way they first appeared in print. Of the short pieces – reprinted virtually unchanged except for an occasional change in title – all but one first appeared in *The Wall Street Journal*. Chapter 16 first appeared in the *Asian Wall Street Journal* under the sponsorship of Citibank. The May 1955 epilogue to Chapter 24 was written especially for this book.

This is the fourth book of mine which owes its focus and structure to my friend, editor, and publisher M. Truman Talley, of Truman Talley Books. It was Mr Talley who fifteen years ago first had the idea that I might organize my articles and essays written over a period of years around a common idea and towards a common objective. Each piece was to be written separately and had to stand on its own. But eventually the pieces would form a unit – as does this book. Prepublication would test them, or rather would allow them to be tested by executives all over the world. Pieces that proved to contribute the most to their readers' effectiveness would be selected for republication in a book. The idea has proven extraordinarily productive. The three earlier books which resulted from it – published respectively in 1982 (*The Changing Work of the Executive*), 1986 (*The Frontiers of Management*), and 1992 (*Managing for the Future*) – have been extremely successful, both in their original English editions and in a large number of translations. They have also proven extremely effective as tools, guides, thought-starters, and action-starters for practising executives and managers worldwide. To M. Truman Talley my readers and I thus owe a large debt of gratitude. And I want to express my gratitude also to Mr Talley's associates, the managing editor and the production editor, who worked hard to turn a manuscript into a handsome book.

Interview: The post-capitalist executive
An interview with the *Harvard Business Review*
Conducted by T. George Harris

For half a century, Peter F. Drucker has been teacher and adviser to senior managers in business, human service organizations, and government. Sometimes called the godfather of modern management, he combines an acute understanding of socio-economic forces with practical insights into how leaders can turn turbulence into opportunity. With a rare gift for synthesis, Drucker nourishes his insatiable mind on a full range of intellectual disciplines, from Japanese art to network theory in higher mathematics. Yet he learns most from in-depth conversation with clients and students: a global network of men and women who draw their ideas from action and act on ideas.

Since 1946, when his book Concept of the Corporation *redefined employees as a resource rather than a cost, Drucker's works have become an ever-growing resource for leaders in every major culture, particularly among Japan's top decision makers in the critical stages of their rise to world business leadership. A goodly share of productive organizations worldwide are led by men and women who consider Drucker their intellectual guide, if not their personal mentor.*

Drucker's most productive insights have often appeared first in the Harvard Business Review. *He has written thirty HBR articles, more than any other contributor. In the September–*

October 1992 issue, he published core concepts from his major new work Post-Capitalist Society *(HarperCollins, 1993). HBR editors sent T. George Harris, a Drucker friend for twenty-four years, to the Drucker Management Center at the Claremont Graduate School in California for two days of intensive conversation about the book's practical implications for today's executives.*

HBR: Peter, you always bring ideas down to the gut level where people work and live. Now we need to know how managers can operate in the post-capitalist society.

Peter F. Drucker: You have to learn to manage in situations where you don't have command authority, where you are neither controlled nor controlling. That is the fundamental change. Management textbooks still talk mainly about managing subordinates. But you no longer evaluate an executive in terms of how many people report to him or her. That standard doesn't mean as much as the complexity of the job, the information it uses and generates, and the different kinds of relationships needed to do the work.

Similarly, business news still refers to managing subsidiaries. But this is the control approach of the 1950s or 1960s. The reality is that the multinational corporation is rapidly becoming an endangered species. Businesses used to grow in one of two ways: from grassroots up or by acquisition. In both cases, the manager had control. Today businesses grow through alliances, all kinds of dangerous liaisons and joint ventures, which, by the way, very few people understand. This new type of growth upsets the traditional manager, who believes he or she must own or control sources and markets.

How will the manager operate in a work environment free of the old hierarchies?
Would you believe that you're going to work permanently with people who work for you but are not your employees? Increas-

ingly, for instance, you outsource when possible. It is predict-able, then, that ten years from now a company will outsource all work that does not have a career ladder up to senior manage-ment. To get productivity, you have to outsource activities that have their *own* senior management. Believe me, the trend to-ward outsourcing has very little to do with economizing and a great deal to do with quality.

Can you give an example?
Take a hospital. Everybody there knows how important cleanli-ness is, but doctors and nurses are never going to be very concerned with how you sweep in corners. That's not part of their value system. They need a hospital maintenance company. One company I got to know in southern California had a clean-ing woman who came in as an illiterate Latina immigrant. She is brilliant. She figured out how to split a bedsheet so that the bed of a very sick patient, no matter how heavy, could be changed. Using her method, you have to move the patient about only six inches, and she cut the bed-making time from twelve minutes to two. Now she's in charge of the cleaning operations, but she is not an employee of the hospital. The hospital can't give her one single order. It can only say, 'We don't like this; we'll work it out'.

The point is, managers still talk about the people who 'report' to them, but that word should be stricken from management vocabulary. Information is replacing authority. A company treas-urer with outsourced information technology, IT, may have only two assistants and a receptionist, but his decisions on foreign exchange can lose or make more money in a day than the rest of the company makes all year. A scientist decides which research *not* to do in a big company lab. He doesn't even have a secretary or a title, but his track record means that he is not apt to be overruled. He may have more effect than the CEO. In the military, a lieutenant-colonel used to command a battalion, but today he may have only a receptionist and be in charge of liaison with a major foreign country.

Amid these new circumstances, everybody is trying to build the ideal organization, generally flat with few layers of bosses and driven directly by consumer satisfaction. But how do managers gear up their lives for this new world?

More than anything else, the individual has to take more responsibility for himself or herself, rather than depend on the company. In this country, and in Europe and even Japan, you can't expect that if you've worked for a company for five years you'll be there when you retire forty years from now. Nor can you expect that you will be able to do what you want to do at the company in forty years' time. In fact, if you make a wager on any big company, the chances of it being split within the next ten years are better than the chances of it remaining the way it is.

This is a new trend. Big corporations became stable factors before the First World War and in the 1920s were almost frozen. Many survived the Depression without change. Then there were thirty or forty years when additional stories were built onto skyscrapers or more wings added onto corporate centres. But now they're not going to build corporate skyscrapers. In fact, within the past ten years, the proportion of the workforce employed by *Fortune* 500 companies has fallen from 30 per cent to 13 per cent.

Corporations once built to last like pyramids are now more like tents. Tomorrow they're gone or in turmoil. And this is true not only of companies in the headlines like Sears or GM or IBM. Technology is changing very quickly, as are markets and structures. You can't design your life around a temporary organization.

Let me give you a simple example of the way assumptions are changing. Most men and women in the executive programme I teach are about forty-five years old and just below senior management in a big organization or running a mid-size one. When we began fifteen or twenty years ago, people at this stage were asking, 'How can we prepare ourselves for the next promotion?' Now they say, 'What do I need to learn so that I can decide where to go next?'

If a young man in a grey flannel suit represented the lifelong corporate type, what's today's image?

Taking individual responsibility and not depending on any particular company. Equally important is managing your own career. The stepladder is gone, and there's not even the implied structure of an industry's rope ladder. It's more like vines, and you bring your own machete. You don't know what you'll be doing next, or whether you'll work in a private office or one big amphitheatre or even out of your home. You have to take responsibility for knowing yourself, so you can find the right jobs as you develop and as your family becomes a factor in your values and choices.

That's a significant departure from what managers could expect in the past

Well, the changes in the manager's work are appearing everywhere, though on different timetables. For instance, I see more career confusion among the many Japanese students I've had over the years. They're totally bewildered. Though the Japanese are more structured than we ever were, suddenly they are halfway between being totally managed and having to take responsibility for themselves. What frightens them is that titles don't mean what they used to mean. Whether you were in India or France, if you were an assistant director of market research, everybody used to know what you were doing. That's no longer true, as we found in one multinational. A woman who had just completed a management course told me not long ago that in five years she would be an assistant vice president of her bank. I'm afraid I had to tell her that she might indeed get the title, but it would no longer have the meaning she thought it did.

Another rung in the ladder?

Yes. The big-company mentality. Most people expect the personnel department to be Pa or Ma Bell. When the AT&T personnel department was at its high point thirty years ago, it was the power behind the scenes. With all their testing and career planning, they'd know that a particular twenty-seven-year-old would be, by age forty-five, an assistant operating manager and no more. They didn't know whether he'd be in Nebraska or Florida. But unless he did something quite extraordinary, his career path until retirement was set.

Times have certainly changed. And, in fact, the Bell people have done better than most, because they could see that change coming in the antitrust decision. They couldn't ignore it. But most people still have a big-company mentality buried in their assumptions. If they lose a job with Sears, they hunt for one with K Mart, unaware that small companies create most of the new jobs and are about as secure as big companies.

Even today, remarkably few Americans are prepared to select jobs for themselves. When you ask, 'Do you know what you are good at? Do you know your limitations?' they look at you with a blank stare. Or they often respond in terms of subject knowledge, which is the wrong answer. When they prepare their resumés, they still try to list positions like steps up a ladder. It is time to give up thinking of jobs or career paths as we once did and think in terms of taking assignments one after the other.

How does one prepare for this new kind of managerial career?
Being an educated person is no longer adequate, not even educated in management. One hears that the government is doing research on new job descriptions based on subject knowledge. But I think that we probably have to leap right over the search for objective criteria and get into the subjective what I call *competencies*. Do you really like pressure? Can you be steady when things are rough and confused? Do you absorb information better by reading, talking, or looking at graphs and numbers? I asked one executive the other day, 'When you sit down with a person, a subordinate, do you know what to say?' Empathy is a practical competence. I have been urging this kind of self-knowledge for years, but now it is essential for survival.

People, especially the young, think that they want all the freedom they can get, but it is very demanding, very difficult to think through who you are and what you do best. In helping people learn how to be responsible, our educational system is more and more counterproductive. The longer you stay in school, the fewer decisions you have to make. For instance, the decision whether to take French II or Art History is really based on whether one likes to get up early in the morning. And graduate school is much worse.

Do you know why most people start with big companies? Because most graduates have not figured out where to place themselves, and companies send in the recruiters. But as soon as the recruits get through training and into a job, they have to start making decisions about the future. Nobody's going to do it for them.

And once they start making decisions, many of the best move to mid-size companies in three to five years, because there they can break through to top management. With less emphasis on seniority, a person can go upstairs and say, 'I've been in accounting for three years, and I'm ready to go into marketing'. Each year I phone a list of my old students to see what's happening with them. The second job used to be with another big company, often because people were beginning to have families and wanted security. But with two-career families, a different problem emerges. At a smaller organization, you can often work out arrangements for both the man and the woman to move to new jobs in the same city.

Some of the psychological tests being developed now are getting better at helping people figure out their competencies. But if the world economy is shifting from a command model to a knowledge model, why shouldn't education determine who gets each job?

Because of the enormous danger that we would not value the person in terms of performance, but in terms of credentials.

Strange as it may seem, a knowledge economy's greatest pitfall is in becoming a Mandarin meritocracy. You see creeping credentialism all around. Why should people find it necessary to tell me so-and-so is really a good researcher even though he or she doesn't have a PhD? It's easy to fall into the trap, because degrees are black and white. But it takes judgement to weigh a person's contribution.

The problem is becoming more serious in information-based organizations. When an organization re-engineers itself around information, the majority of management layers become redundant. Most turn out to have been just information relays. Now, each layer has much more information responsibility. Most large companies have cut the number of layers by 50 per cent, even in Japan. Toyota came down from twenty-odd to eleven. GM has streamlined from twenty-eight to perhaps nineteen, and even that number is decreasing rapidly. Organizations will become flatter and flatter.

As a result, there's real panic in Japan, because it's a vertical society based on subtle layers of status. Everybody wants to become a *kachō*, a supervisor or section manager. Still, the United States doesn't have the answer either. We don't know how to use rewards and recognition to move the competent people into the management positions that remain. I don't care for the popular theory that a generation of entrepreneurs can solve our problems. Entrepreneurs are monomaniacs. Managers are synthesizers who bring resources together and have that ability to 'smell' opportunity and timing. Today perceptiveness is more important than analysis. In the new society of organizations, you need to be able to recognize patterns to see what is there rather than what you expect to see. You need the invaluable listener who says, 'I hear us all trying to kill the new product to protect the old one.'

How do you find these people?
One way is to use small companies as farm clubs, as in baseball. One of my ablest friends is buying minority stakes in small

companies within his industry. When I said it didn't make sense, he said, 'I'm buying farm teams. I'm putting my bright young people in these companies so they have their own commands. They have to do everything a CEO does in a big company.'

And do you know the biggest thing these young executives have to learn in their new positions? My friend continued, 'We have more PhD's in biology and chemistry than we have janitors, and they have to learn that their customers aren't PhD's, and the people who do the work aren't'. In other words, they must learn to speak English instead of putting formulas on the blackboard. They must learn to listen to somebody who does not know what a regression analysis is. Basically, they have to learn the meaning and importance of respect.

A difficult thing to learn, let alone teach.
You have to focus on a person's performance. The individual must shoulder the burden of defining what his or her own contribution will be. We have to demand – and 'demand' is the word, nothing permissive – that people think through what constitutes the greatest contribution that they can make to the company in the next eighteen months or two years. Then they have to make sure that contribution is accepted and understood by the people they work with and for.

Most people don't ask themselves this question, however obvious and essential it seems. When I ask people what they contribute to an organization, they blossom and love to answer. And when I follow with 'Have you told other people about it?' the answer often is 'No, that would be silly, because they know'. But, of course, 'they' don't. We are one hundred years past the simple economy in which most people knew what others did at work. Farmers knew what most farmers did, and industrial workers knew what other factory workers did. Domestic servants understood each other's work, as did the fourth major group in that economy: small tradesmen. No one needed to explain. But now nobody knows what others do, even within the same organization. Everybody you work with needs to know your priorities. If you don't ask and don't tell, your peers and subordinates will guess incorrectly.

What's the result of this lack of communication?
When you don't communicate, you don't get to do the things you are good at. Let me give you an example. The engineers in my class, without exception, say they spend more than half their time editing and polishing reports – in other words, what they are least qualified to do. They don't even know that you have to write and rewrite and rewrite again. But there are any number of English majors around for that assignment. People seldom pay attention to their strengths. For example, after thinking for a long time, an engineer told me he's really good at the first design, at the basic idea, but not at filling in the details for the final product. Until then, he'd never told anybody, not even himself.

You're not advocating self-analysis alone, are you?
No. Not only do you have to understand your own competencies, but you also have to learn the strengths of the men and women to whom you assign duties, as well as those of your peers and boss. Too many managers still go by averages. They still talk about 'our engineers'. And I say, 'Brother, you don't have "engineers". You have Joe and Mary and Jim and Bob, and each is different.' You can no longer manage a workforce. You manage individuals. You have to know them so well you can go and say 'Mary, you think you ought to move up to this next job. Well, then you have to learn not to have that chip on your shoulder. Forget you are a woman; you are an engineer. And you have to be a little considerate. Do not come in at ten minutes to five on Friday afternoon to tell people they have to work overtime when you knew it at nine a.m.'

The key to the productivity of knowledge workers is to make them concentrate on the real assignment. Do you know why most promotions now fail? One-third are outright disasters, in my experience, while another third are a nagging backache. Not more than one in three works out. No fit. The standard case, of course, is the star salesman promoted to sales manager. That job can be any one of four things – a manager of salespeople, a market manager, a brand manager, or a supersalesman who opens up an entire new area. But nobody figures out what it is, so the man or woman who got the promotion just tries to do more of whatever led to the promotion. That's the surest way to be wrong.

Expand on your idea of information responsibility and how it fits into post-capitalist society.
Far too many managers think computer specialists know what information managers need to do their job and what information they owe to whom. Computer information tends to focus too much on inside information, not the outside sources and customers that count. In today's organization, you have to take responsibility for information because it is your main tool. But most don't know how to use it. Few are information-literate. They can play 'Mary Had a Little Lamb' but not Beethoven.

I heard today about a brand manager in a major OTC drug company who tried to get the scientific papers on the product he markets. But the corporate librarian complained to his superior. Under her rules, she gives hard science only to the company's scientists and lawyers. He had to get a consultant to go outside and use a computer database to pull up about twenty journal articles on his product, so he'd know how to develop honest advertising copy. The point of the story is that this brand manager is way ahead of the parade: ninety-nine out of a hundred brand managers don't know they need that kind of information for today's consumers and haven't a clue how to get it. The first step is to say 'I need it'.

And many people don't recognize the importance of this step. I work with an information manager at a large financial institution that has invested $1.5 billion in information. He and I talked all morning with his department's eight women and ten men. Very intelligent, but not one began to think seriously about what information they need in order to serve their customers. When I pointed this out, they said, 'Isn't the boss going to tell us?' We finally had to agree to meet a month later so that they could go through the hard work of figuring out what information they need and, more important, what they do not need.

So a manager begins the road to information responsibility first by identifying gaps in knowledge.
Exactly. To be information-literate, you begin with learning what it is you need to know. Too much talk focuses on the technology; even worse, on the speed of the gadget – always faster, faster. This kind of 'techie' fixation causes us to lose track of the fundamental nature of information in today's organization. To organize the way work is done, you have to begin with the specific job, then the information input, and finally the human relationships needed to get the job done.

The current emphasis on re-engineering essentially means changing an organization from the flow of things to the flow of information. The computer is merely a tool in the process. If you go to the hardware store to buy a hammer, you do not ask if you should do upholstery or fix the door. To put it in editorial terms, knowing how a typewriter works does not make you a writer. Now that knowledge is taking the place of capital as the driving force in organizations worldwide, it is all too easy to confuse data with knowledge and information technology with information.

What's the worst problem in managing knowledge specialists?
One of the most degenerative tendencies of the last forty years is the belief that if you are understandable, you are vulgar. When I was growing up, it was taken for granted that economists, physicists, psychologists – in fact leaders in any discipline – would make themselves understood. Einstein spent years with three different collaborators to make his theory of relativity accessible to the layman. Even John Maynard Keynes tried hard

to make his economics accessible. But just the other day, I heard a senior scholar seriously reject a younger colleague's work because more than five people could understand what he's doing. Literally.

We cannot afford such arrogance. Knowledge is power, which is why people who had it in the past often tried to make a secret of it. In post-capitalism, power comes from transmitting information to make it productive, not from hiding it.

That means you have to be intolerant of intellectual arrogance. And I mean *intolerant*. At whatever level, knowledge people must make themselves understood, and whatever field the manager comes from, he or she must be eager to understand others. This may be the main job of the manager of technical people. He or she must not only be an interpreter but also work out a balance between specialization and exposure.

Exposure is an important technique. For an exotic example, look at weather forecasting, where meteorologists and mathematicians and other specialists now work with teams of experts on satellite data. Europeans, on the one hand, have tried to connect these different disciplines entirely through information managers. On the other hand, Americans rotate people at an early stage. Suppose you put a PhD in meteorology on a team that is to work on the new mathematical model of hurricanes for three years. He isn't a mathematician, but he gets exposed to what mathematicians assume, what they eliminate, what their limitations are. With the combination of exposure and translation, the American approach yields forecasts that are about three times more accurate than the European ones, I'm told. And the exposure concept is useful in managing any group of specialists.

Is the fact that some teams provide exposure as well as interpreters a reason why the team has become such a hot topic?
There's a lot of nonsense in team talk, as if teams were something new. We have always worked in teams, and while sports give us hundreds of team styles, there are only a few basic

models to choose from. The critical decision is to select the right kind for the job. You can't mix soccer and doubles tennis. It's predictable that in a few years, the most traditional team will come back in fashion, the one that does research first, then passes the idea to engineering to develop, and then on to manufacturing to make. It's like a baseball team, and as you may know, I have done a little work with baseball-team management.

The great strength of baseball teams is that you can concentrate. You take Joe, who is a batter, and you work on batting. There is almost no interaction, nothing at all like the soccer team or the jazz combo, the implicit model of many teams today. The soccer team moves in unison but everyone holds the same relative position. The jazz combo has incredible flexibility because everyone knows each other so well that they all sense when the trumpet is about to solo. The combo model takes great discipline and may eventually fall out of favour, especially in Japanese car manufacturing, because we do not need to create new car models as fast as we have been.

I know several German companies that follow the baseball-team model, whether they know it or not. Their strength is clear: they are fantastic at exploiting and developing old knowledge, and Germany's mid-size companies may be better than their big ones simply because they concentrate better. On the other hand, when it comes to the new, from electronics to biotech, German scientists may do fine work, but their famous apprenticeship system discourages innovation.

So, beyond all the hype, teams can help the executive to navigate a post-capitalist society?
Thinking about teams helps us to highlight the more general problem of how to manage knowledge. In the production of fundamental new knowledge, the British groups I run into are way ahead of anybody. But they have never done much with their expertise, in part because many British companies don't value the technically oriented person enough. I don't know of a

single engineer in top management there. My Japanese friends are just the opposite. While they still do not specialize in scientific advances, they take knowledge and make it productive very fast. In the United States, on the other hand, we have not improved that much in existing industries. The automobile business, until recently, was perfectly satisfied doing what it did in 1939. But as we are discovering in computers and in biotech, we may be at our very best when it comes to groundbreaking technology.

Where is the lesson in all this for the manager?
The lesson is that the productivity of knowledge has both a qualitative and a quantitative dimension. Though we know very little about it, we do realize that executives must be both managers of specialists and synthesizers of different fields of knowledge – really of knowledges, plural. This situation is as threatening to the traditional manager, who worries about highfaluting highbrows, as it is to the intellectual, who worries about being too commercial to earn respect in his or her discipline. But in the post-capitalist world, the highbrow and the lowbrow have to play on the same team.

That sounds pretty democratic. Does a post-capitalist society based more on knowledge than capital become egalitarian?
No. Both of these words miss the point. *Democratic* bespeaks a narrow political and legal organization. Nor do I use the buzzword *participative*. Worse yet is the *empowerment* concept. It is not a great step forward to take power out at the top and put it in at the bottom. It's still power. To build achieving organizations, you must replace power with responsibility.

And while we're on the subject of words, I'm now not comfortable with the word *manager* because it implies subordinates. I find myself using *executive* more, because it implies responsibility for an area, not necessarily dominion over people. The word *boss*, which emerged in the First World War, is helpful in that it can be used to suggest a mentor's role, someone who can back you up on a decision. The new organizations need to go beyond senior–junior polarities to a blend with sponsor and mentor relations. In the traditional organization – the organization of the last one hundred years – the skeleton, or internal structure, was a combination of rank and power. In the emerging organization, it has to be mutual understanding and responsibility.

1993

Part One

Management

1
The theory of the business

Not in a very long time – not, perhaps, since the late 1940s or early 1950s – have there been as many new major management techniques as there are today: downsizing, outsourcing, total quality management, economic value analysis, benchmarking, re-engineering. Each is a powerful tool. But with the exceptions of outsourcing and re-engineering, these tools are designed primarily to do differently what is already being done. They are 'how-to-do' tools.

Yet *what* to do is increasingly becoming the central challenge facing managements, especially those of big companies that have enjoyed long-term success. The story is a familiar one: a company that was a superstar only yesterday finds itself stagnating and frustrated, in trouble and, often, in a seemingly unmanageable crisis. This phenomenon is by no means confined to the United States. It has become common in Japan and Germany, The Netherlands and France, Italy and Sweden. And it occurs just as often outside business – in labour unions, government agencies, hospitals, museums, and churches. In fact, it seems even less tractable in those areas.

The root cause of nearly every one of these crises is not that things are being done poorly. It is not even that the wrong things are being done. Indeed, in most cases, the *right* things are being done – but fruitlessly. What accounts for this apparent paradox? The assumptions on which the organization has been built and is being run no longer fit reality. These are the assumptions that shape any organization's behaviour, dictate its decisions about what to do and what not to do, and define what the organization considers meaningful results. These assumptions are about markets. They are about customers and competitors, their values and behaviour. They are about technology and its dynamics, about a company's strengths and weaknesses. These assumptions are about what a company gets paid for. They are what I call a company's *theory of the business*.

Every organization, whether a business or not, has a theory of the business. Indeed, a valid theory that is clear, consistent, and focused is extraordinarily powerful. In 1809, for instance, the German statesman and scholar Wilhelm von Humboldt founded the University of Berlin on a radically new theory of the university. And for more than one hundred years, until the rise of Hitler, his theory defined the German university, especially in scholarship and scientific research. In 1870, George Siemens, the architect and first CEO of Deutsche Bank, the first universal bank, had an equally clear theory of the business: to use entrepreneurial finance to unify a still rural and splintered Germany through industrial development. Within twenty years of its founding, Deutsche Bank had become Europe's premier financial institution, which it has remained to this day in spite of two world wars, inflation, and Hitler. And in the 1807s, Mitsubishi was founded on a clear and completely new theory of the business, which within ten years made it the leader in an emerging Japan and within another twenty years made it one of the first truly multinational businesses.

Similarly, the theory of the business explains both the success of companies like General Motors and IBM, which have dominated the US economy for the latter half of the twentieth century, and the challenges they now face. In fact, what underlies the current malaise of so many large and successful organizations worldwide is that their theory of the business no longer works.

Whenever a big organization gets into trouble – and especially if it has been successful for many years – people blame sluggishness, complacency, arrogance, mammoth bureaucracies. Plausible explanations? Yes. But rarely relevant or correct. Consider the two most visible and widely reviled 'arrogant bureaucracies' among large US companies that have recently been in trouble.

Since the earliest days of the computer, it had been an article of faith at IBM that the computer would go the way of electricity. The future, IBM knew and could prove with scientific rigour, lay with the central station, the ever more powerful mainframe into which a huge number of users could plug. Everything – economics, the logic of information, technology – led to that conclusion. But then, suddenly, when it seemed as if such a central-station, mainframe-based information system was actually coming into existence, two young men came up with the first personal computer. Every computer maker knew that the PC was absurd. It did not have the memory, the database, the speed, or the computing ability necessary to succeed. Indeed, every computer maker knew that the PC had to fail – the conclusion reached by Xerox only a few years earlier, when its research team had actually built the first PC. But when that misbegotten monstrosity – first the Apple, then the Macintosh – came on the market, people not only loved it, they bought it.

Every big, successful company throughout history, when confronted with such a surprise, has refused to accept it. 'It's a stupid fad and will be gone in three years,' said the CEO of Zeiss upon seeing the new Kodak Brownie in 1888, when the German company was as dominant in the world photographic market as IBM would be in the computer market a century later. Most mainframe makers responded in the same way. The list was long: Control Data, Univac, Burroughs, and NCR in the United States; Siemens, Nixdorf, Machines Bull, and ICL in Europe; Hitachi and Fujitsu in Japan. IBM, the overlord of mainframes with as much in sales as all the other computer makers put together and with record profits, could have reacted in the same way. In fact, it *should* have. Instead, IBM immediately accepted the PC as the new reality. Almost overnight, it brushed aside all its proven and time-tested policies, rules, and regulations and set up not one but two competing teams to design an even simpler PC. A couple of years later, IBM had become the world's largest PC manufacturer and the industry standard setter.

There is absolutely no precedent for this achievement in all of business history; it hardly argues bureaucracy, sluggishness, or arrogance. Yet despite unprecedented flexibility, agility, and humility, IBM was floundering a few years later in both the mainframe and the PC business. It was suddenly unable to move, to take decisive action, to change.

The case of GM is equally perplexing. In the early 1980s – the very years in which GM's main business, passenger cars, seemed almost paralysed – the company acquired two large businesses: Hughes Electronics and Ross Perot's Electronic Data Systems. Analysts generally considered both companies to be mature and chided GM for grossly overpaying for them. Yet within a few short years, GM had more than tripled the revenues and profits of the allegedly mature EDS. And ten years later, in 1994, EDS had a market value six times the amount that GM had paid for it and ten times its original revenues and profits.

Similarly, GM bought Hughes Electronics – a huge but profitless company involved exclusively in defence – just before the defence industry collapsed. Under GM management, Hughes has actually increased its defence profits and has become the only big defence contractor to move successfully into large-scale non-defence work. Remarkably, the same bean counters who had been so ineffectual in the car business – thirty-year GM veterans who had never worked for any other company or, for that matter, outside of finance and accounting departments – were the ones who achieved those startling results. And in the two acquisitions, they simply applied the policies, practices, and procedures that had always been used by GM.

This story is a familiar one at GM. Since the company's founding in a flurry of acquisitions eighty years ago, one of its core competencies has been to 'overpay' for well-performing but mature businesses – as it did for Buick, AC Spark Plug, and Fisher Body in those early years – and then turn them into world-class champions. Very few companies have been able to match GM's performance in making successful acquisitions, and GM surely did not accomplish those feats by being bureaucratic, sluggish, or arrogant. Yet what worked so beautifully in those businesses that GM knew nothing about failed miserably in GM itself.

What can explain the fact that at both IBM and GM the policies, practices, and behaviours that worked for decades – and in the case of GM are still working well when applied to something new and different – no longer work for the organization in which and for which they were developed? The realities that each organization actually faces have changed quite dramatically from those that each still assumes it lives with. Put another way, reality has changed, but the theory of the business has not changed with it.

Before its agile response to the new reality of the PC, IBM had once before turned its basic strategy around overnight. In 1950, Univac, then the world's leading computer company, showed the prototype of the first machine designed to be a multipurpose computer. All earlier designs had been for single-purpose machines. IBM's own two earlier computers, built in the late 1930s and 1946 respectively, performed astronomical calculations only. And the machine that IBM had on the drawing board in 1950, intended for the SAGE air defence system in the Canadian Arctic, had only one purpose: early identification of enemy aircraft. IBM immediately scrapped its strategy of developing advanced single-purpose machines; it put its best engineers to work on perfecting the Univac architecture and, from it, designing the first multipurpose computer able to be manufactured (rather than handcrafted) and serviced. Three years later, IBM had become the world's dominant computer maker and standard bearer. IBM did not create the computer. But in 1950, its flexibility, speed, and humility created the computer *industry*.

However, the same assumptions that had helped IBM prevail in 1950 proved to be its undoing thirty years later. In the 1970s, IBM assumed that there was such a thing as a 'computer', just as it had in the 1950s. But the emergence of the PC invalidated that assumption. Mainframe computers and PCs are, in fact, no more one entity than are generating stations and electric toasters. The latter, while different, are interdependent and complementary. In contrast, mainframe computers and PCs are primarily competitors. And in their basic definition of *information*, they actually contradict each other: for the mainframe, information means memory; for the brainless PC, it means software. Building generating stations and making toasters must be run as separate businesses, but they can be owned by the same corporate entity, as General Electric did for decades. In contrast, mainframe computers and PCs probably cannot co-exist in the same corporate entity.

IBM tried to combine the two. But because the PC was the fastest-growing part of the business, IBM could not subordinate it to the mainframe business. And because the mainframe was still the cash cow, IBM could not optimize the PC business. In the end, the assumption that a computer is a computer – or, more prosaically, that the industry is hardware driven – paralysed IBM.

GM had an even more powerful, and successful, theory of the business than IBM had, one that made GM the world's largest and most profitable manufacturing organization. The company did not have one setback in seventy years – a record unmatched in business history. GM's theory combined in one seamless web assumptions about markets and customers with assumptions about core competencies and organizational structure.

Since the early 1920s, GM assumed that the US car market was homogeneous in its values and segmented by extremely stable income groups. The resale value of the 'good' used car was the only independent variable under management's control. High trade-in values enabled customers to upgrade their new-car purchases to the next category – in other words, to cars with higher profit margins. According to this theory, frequent or radical changes in models could only depress trade-in values.

Internally, these market assumptions went hand in hand with assumptions about how production should be organized to yield the biggest market share and the highest profit. In GM's case, the answer was long runs of mass-produced cars with a minimum of changes each model year, resulting in the largest number of uniform yearly models on the market at the lowest fixed cost per car.

GM's management then translated these assumptions about market and production into a structure of semi-autonomous divisions, each focusing on one income segment and each arranged so that its highest-priced model overlapped with the next division's lowest-priced model, thus almost forcing people to trade up, provided that used-car prices were high.

For seventy years, this theory worked like a charm. Even in the depths of the Depression, GM steadily gained market share. But in the late 1970s, its assumptions about the market and about production became invalid. The market was fragmenting into highly volatile 'lifestyle' segments. Income became one factor among many in the buying decision, not the only one. At the same time, lean manufacturing created an economics of small scale. It made short runs and variations in models less costly and more profitable than long runs of uniform products.

GM knew all this but simply could not believe it. (GM's union still doesn't.) Instead, the company tried to patch things up. It maintained the existing divisions based on income segmentation, but each division now offered a 'car for every purse'. It tried to compete with lean manufacturing's economics of small scale by automating the large-scale, long-run mass production (losing some $30 billion in the process). Contrary to popular belief, GM patched things up with prodigious energy, hard work, and lavish investments of time and money. But patching only confused the customer, the dealer, and the employees and management of GM itself. In the meantime, GM neglected its *real* growth market, where it had leadership and would have been almost unbeatable: light trucks and minivans.

A theory of the business has three parts. First, there are assumptions about the environment of the organization: society and its structure, the market, the customer, and technology.

Second, there are assumptions about the specific mission of the organization. Sears, Roebuck and Company, in the years during and following the First World War, defined its mission as being the informed buyer for the American family. A decade later, Marks & Spencer in Great Britain defined its mission as being the change agent in British society by becoming the first classless retailer. AT&T, again in the years during and immediately after the First World War, defined its role as ensuring that every US family and business have access to a telephone. An organization's mission need not be so ambitious. GM envisioned a far more modest role – as the leader in 'terrestrial motorized transportation equipment', in the words of Alfred P. Sloan, Jr.

Third, there are assumptions about the core competencies needed to accomplish the organization's mission. For example, West Point, founded in 1802, defined its core competence as the ability to turn out leaders who deserve trust. Marks & Spencer, around 1930, defined its core competence as the ability to identify, design, and develop the merchandise it sold, instead of the ability to buy. AT&T, around 1920, defined its core competence as technical leadership that would enable the company to improve service continuously while steadily lowering rates.

The assumptions about environment define what an organization is paid for. The assumptions about mission define what an organization considers to be meaningful results; in other words, they point to how it envisions itself making a difference in the economy and in the society at large. Finally, the assumptions about core competencies define where an organization must excel in order to maintain leadership.

Of course, all this sounds deceptively simple. It usually takes years of hard work, thinking, and experimenting to reach a clear, consistent, and valid theory of the business. Yet to be successful, every organization must work one out.

What are the specifications of a valid theory of the business? There are four.

1 *The assumptions about environment, mission, and core competencies must fit reality.* When four penniless young men from Manchester, England – Simon Marks and his three brothers-in-law – decided in the early 1920s that a humdrum penny bazaar should become an agent of social change, the First World War had profoundly shaken their country's class structure. It had also created masses of new buyers for good-quality, stylish merchandise like lingerie, blouses, and stockings – Marks & Spencer's first successful product categories. Marks & Spencer then systematically set to work developing brand-new and unheard-of core competencies. Until then, the core competence of a merchant was the ability to buy well. Marks & Spencer decided that it was the merchant, rather than the manufacturer, who knew the customer. Therefore, the merchant, not the manufacturer, should design the products, develop them, and find producers to make the goods to his design, specifications, and costs. This new definition of the merchant took five to eight years to develop and to make acceptable to traditional suppliers, who had always seen themselves as 'manufacturers', not as 'subcontractors'.

2 *The assumptions in all three areas have to fit one another.* This was perhaps GM's greatest strength in the long decades of its ascendancy. Its assumptions about the market and about

the optimum manufacturing process were a perfect fit. GM decided in the mid-1920s that it also required new and as-yet-unheard-of core competencies: financial control of the manufacturing process and a theory of capital allocations. As a result, GM invented modern cost accounting and the first rational capital-allocation process.

3 *The theory of the business must be known and understood throughout the organization.* That is easy in an organization's early days. But as it becomes successful, an organization tends increasingly to take its theory for granted, becoming less and less conscious of it. Then the organization becomes sloppy. It begins to cut corners. It begins to pursue what is expedient rather than what is right. It stops thinking. It stops questioning. It remembers the answers but has forgotten the questions. The theory of the business becomes 'culture'. But culture is no substitute for discipline, and the theory of the business is a discipline.

4 *The theory of the business has to be tested constantly.* It is not graven on tablets of stone. It is a hypothesis. And it is a hypothesis about things that are in constant flux – society, markets, customers, technology. And so built into the theory of the business must be the ability to change itself.

Some theories of the business are so powerful that they last for a long time. But being human artifacts, they don't last forever, and, indeed, today they rarely last for very long at all. Eventually every theory of the business becomes obsolete and then invalid. That is precisely what happened to those on which the great US businesses of the 1920s were built. It happened to the GMs and the AT&Ts. It has happened to IBM. It is clearly happening today to Deutsche Bank and its theory of the universal bank. It is also clearly happening to the rapidly unravelling Japanese *keiretsu*.

The first reaction of an organization whose theory is becoming obsolete is almost always a defensive one. The tendency is to put one's head in the sand and pretend that nothing is happening.

The next reaction is an attempt to patch, as GM did in the early 1980s or as Deutsche Bank is doing today. Indeed, the sudden and completely unexpected crisis of one big German company after another for which Deutsche Bank is the 'house bank' indicates that its theory no longer works. That is, Deutsche Bank no longer does what it was designed to do: provide effective governance of the modern corporation.

But patching never works. Instead, when a theory shows the first signs of becoming obsolete, it is time to start thinking again, to ask again which assumptions about its environment mission, and core competencies reflect reality most accurately – with the clear premise that our historically transmitted assumptions, those with which all of us grew up, no longer suffice.

What, then, needs to be done? There is a need for preventive care – that is, for building into the organization systematic monitoring and testing of its theory of the business. There is a need for early diagnosis. Finally, there is a need to rethink a theory that is stagnating and to take effective action in order to change policies and practices, bringing the organization's behaviour into line with the new realities of its environment, with a new definition of its mission, and with new core competencies to be developed and acquired.

There are only two preventive measures. But if used consistently, they should keep an organization alert and capable of rapidly changing itself and its theory. The first measure is what I call *abandonment*. Every three years, an organization should challenge every product, every service, every policy, every distribution channel with the question, If we were not in it already, would we be going into it now? By questioning accepted policies and routines, the organization forces itself to think about its theory. It forces itself to test assumptions. It forces itself to ask: Why didn't this work, even though it looked so promising when we went into it five years ago? Is it because we made a mistake? Is it because we did the wrong things? Or is it because the right things didn't work?

Without systematic and purposeful abandonment, an organization will be overtaken by events. It will squander its best
resources on things it should never have been doing or should
no longer do. As a result, it will lack the resources, especially
capable people, needed to exploit the opportunities that arise
when markets, technologies, and core competencies change. In
other words, it will be unable to respond constructively to the
opportunities that are created when its theory of the business
becomes obsolete.

The second preventive measure is to study what goes on outside the business, and especially to study *non-customers*. Walk-
around management became fashionable a few years back. It *is*
important. And so is knowing as much as possible about one's
customers – the area, perhaps, where information technology is
making the most rapid advances. But the first signs of fundamental change rarely appear within one's own organization or
among one's own customers. Almost always they show up first
among one's non-customers. Non-customers always outnumber
customers. Wal-Mart, today's retail giant, has 14 per cent of the
US consumer-goods market. That means 86 per cent of the
market is non-customers.

In fact, the best recent example of the importance of the
non-customer in the US department store. At their peak some
twenty years ago, department stores served 30 per cent of the
US non-food retail market. They questioned their customers
constantly, studied them, surveyed them. But they paid no attention to the 70 per cent of the market who were not their
customers. They saw no reason why they should. Their theory of
the business assumed that most people who could afford to shop
in department stores did. Fifty years ago, that assumption fitted
reality. But when the baby boomers came of age, it ceased to be
valid. For the dominant group among baby boomers – women in
educated two-income families – it was not money that determined where to shop. Time was the primary factor, and this
generation's women could not afford to spend their time shop-

ping in department stores. Because department stores looked only at their own customers, they did not recognize this change until a few years ago. By then, business was already drying up. And it was too late to get the baby boomers back. The department stores learned the hard way that although being customer driven is vital, it is not enough. An organization must be market driven too.

To diagnose problems early, managers must pay attention to the warning signs. A theory of the business always becomes obsolete when an organization attains its original objectives. Attaining one's objectives, then, is not cause for celebration; it is cause for new thinking. AT&T accomplished its mission to give every US family and business access to the telephone by the mid-1950s. Some executives then said it was time to reassess the theory of the business and, for instance, separate local service – where the objectives had been reached – from growing and future businesses, beginning with long-distance service and extending into global telecommunications. Their arguments went unheeded, and a few years later AT&T began to flounder, only to be rescued by antitrust, which did by fiat what the company's management had refused to do voluntarily.

Rapid growth is another sure sign of crisis in an organization's theory. Any organization that doubles or triples in size within a fairly short period of time has necessarily outgrown its theory. Even Silicon Valley has learned that beer bashes are no longer adequate for communication once a company has grown so big that people have to wear name tags. But such growth challenges much deeper assumptions, policies, and habits. To continue in health, let alone grow, the organization has to ask itself again the questions about its environment, mission, and core competencies.

There are two more clear signals that an organization's theory of the business is no longer valid. One is unexpected success – whether one's own or a competitor's. The other is unexpected failure – again, whether one's own or a competitor's.

At the same time that Japanese car imports had Detroit's Big Three on the ropes, Chrysler registered a totally unexpected success. Its traditional passenger cars were losing market share even faster than GM's and Ford's were. But sales of its Jeep and its new minivans – an almost accidental development – skyrocketed. At the time, GM was the leader of the US light-truck market and was unchallenged in the design and quality of its products, but it wasn't paying any attention to its light-truck capacity. After all, minivans and light trucks had always been classified as commercial rather than passenger vehicles in traditional statistics, even though most of them are now being bought as passenger vehicles. However, had it paid attention to the success of Chrysler, its weaker competitor, GM might have realized much earlier that its assumptions about both its market and its core competencies were no longer valid. From the beginning, the minivan and light-truck market was not an income-class market and was little influenced by trade-in prices. And, paradoxically, light-trucks were the one area in which GM, fifteen years ago, had already moved quite far towards what we now call lean manufacturing.

Unexpected failure is as much a warning as unexpected success and should be taken as seriously as a sixty-year-old person's first 'minor' heart attack. Sixty years ago, in the midst of the Depression, Sears decided that car insurance had become an 'accessory' rather than a financial product and that selling it would therefore fit its mission as being the informed buyer for the American family. Everyone thought Sears was crazy. But car insurance became Sears' most profitable business almost instantly. Twenty years later, in the 1950s, Sears decided that diamond rings had become a necessity rather than a luxury, and the company became the world's largest – and probably most profitable – diamond retailer. It was only logical for Sears to decide in 1981 that investment products had become consumer goods for the American family. It bought Dean Witter and moved its offices into Sears stores. The move was a total disaster.

The US public clearly did not consider its financial needs to be 'consumer products'. When Sears finally gave up and decided to run Dean Witter as a separate business outside Sears stores, Dean Witter at once began to blossom. In 1992, Sears sold it at a tidy profit.

Had Sears seen its failure to become the American family's supplier of investments as a failure of its theory and not as an isolated incident, it might have begun to restructure and reposition itself ten years earlier than it actually did, when it still had substantial market leadership. For Sears might then have seen, as several of its competitors like J. C. Penney immediately did, that the Dean Witter failure threw into doubt the entire concept of market homogeneity – the very concept on which Sears and other mass retailers had based their strategy for years.

Traditionally, we have searched for the miracle worker with a magic wand to turn an ailing organization around. To establish, maintain, and restore a theory, however, does not require a Genghis Khan or a Leonardo da Vinci in the executive suite. It is not genius; it is hard work. It is not being clever; it is being conscientious. It is what CEOs are paid for.

There are indeed quite a few CEOs who have successfully changed the theory of their business. The CEO who built Merck into the world's most successful pharmaceuticals business by focusing solely on the research and development of patented, high-margin breakthrough drugs radically changed the company's theory by acquiring a large distributor of generic and non-prescription drugs. He did so without a 'crisis', while Merck was ostensibly doing very well. Similarly, a few years ago, the new CEO of Sony, the world's best-known manufacturer of consumer electronic hardware, changed the company's theory of the business. He acquired a Hollywood film production company and, with that acquisition, shifted the organization's centre of gravity from being a hardware manufacturer in search of software to being a software producer who creates a market demand for hardware.

But for every one of these apparent miracle workers, there are scores of equally capable CEOs whose organizations stumble. We can't rely on miracle workers to rejuvenate an obsolete theory of the business any more than we can rely on them to cure other types of serious illness. And when one talks to these supposed miracle workers, they deny vehemently that they act by charisma, vision, or, for that matter, the laying on of hands. They start out with diagnosis and analysis. They accept that attaining objectives and rapid growth demand a serious rethinking of the theory of the business. They do not dismiss unexpected failure as the result of a subordinate's incompetence or as an accident but treat it as a symptom of 'systems failure'. They do not take credit for unexpected success but treat it as a challenge to their assumptions.

They accept that a theory's obsolescence is a degenerative and, indeed, life-threatening disease. And they know and accept the surgeon's time-tested principle, the oldest principle of effective decision making: a degenerative disease will not be cured by procrastination. It requires decisive action.

1994

2
Planning for uncertainty

Uncertainty – in the economy, society, politics – has become so great as to render futile, if not counterproductive, the kind of planning most companies still practise: forecasting based on probabilities.

Unique events, such as the Perot phenomenon or the dissolution of the Soviet Empire, have no probability. Yet executives have to make decisions that commit to the future current resources of time and money. Worse, they have to make decisions *not* to commit resources – to forgo the future. The lengths of such commitments are steadily growing: in strategy and technology, marketing, manufacturing, employee development, in the time it takes to bring a new plant on stream or in the years until a commitment to a store location pays for itself. Every such commitment is based on assumptions about the future. To arrive at them, traditional planning asks 'What is most likely to happen?' Planning for uncertainty asks, instead, 'What has already happened that will create the future?'

The first place to look is in demographics. Nearly everybody who will be in the labour force of the developed countries in the year 2010 is already alive today. There have been two revolutionary changes in the workforce of developed countries: the explosion of advanced education and the rush of women into careers outside the home. Both are accomplished facts. The shift from blue-collar labour to knowledge and service workers as the centres of population gravity is irrevocable. But so is the ageing of both the workforce and population.

Business people need to ask: 'What do these accomplished facts mean for our business? What opportunities do they create? What threats? What changes do they demand – in the way the business is organized and run, in our goals, in our products, in our services, in our policies? And what changes do they make possible and likely to be advantageous?'

The next question is: 'What changes in industry and market structure, in basic values (e.g. the emphasis on the environment), and in science and technology have already occurred but have yet to have full impact?' It is commonly believed that innovations create changes – but very few do. Successful innovations exploit changes that have already happened. They exploit the time lag – in science, often twenty-five or thirty years – between the change itself and its perception and acceptance. During that time the exploiter of the change rarely faces much, if any, competition. The other people in the industry still operate on the basis of yesterday's reality. And once such a change has happened, it usually survives even extreme turbulence.

The First World War, the Depression, and the Second World War had no impact on such trends except to accelerate them. Examples are the shift of freight traffic from railways to roads, the shift to the telephone as a primary carrier of communications over distance, and the shift to the hospital as the centre of sickness care.

Closely related are the next questions: 'What are the trends in economic and societal structure? And how do they affect our business?' Since 1900, the unit of labour needed for an additional unit of manufacturing output has been going down steadily at a compound rate of about 1 per cent a year. Since the end of the Second World War the unit of raw materials needed for an additional unit of manufacturing output has been decreasing at the same rate. Since around 1950, the unit of energy needed for an additional unit of manufacturing output has also been going down steadily at that rate too. But from the 1880s, since the telephone and Frederick Winslow Taylor's *Principles of Scientific Management*, the amounts of information and knowledge needed for each additional unit of output have been going up steadily at a compound rate of 1 per cent a year – the rate at which businesses have added educated people to their payrolls.

Indeed, the computer may well have been a response to this information explosion rather than its cause. Similar structural trends can be found in most industries and markets. They do not make the 'weather' for an industry or a company – they create the 'climate'. Over any short-term period their effects are slight. But in the not-so-long run these structural trends are of far greater importance than the short-term fluctuations to which economists, politicians, and executives give all their attention.

Whoever exploits structural trends is almost certain to succeed. It is hard, however, to fight them in the short run and almost hopeless in the long run. When such a structural trend peters out or when it reverses itself (which is fairly rare), those who continue as before face extinction and those who change fast face opportunity.

The most important structural trends are those that many executives have never heard of: the distribution of consumers' disposable income. They are particularly important in a time of uncertainty like today's. At such a time, these trends tend to change – and to change fast.

For the past one hundred years most of the tremendous increase in wealth-producing capacity and personal incomes – a fiftyfold increase in the developed countries – has been spent on greater leisure, on health care, and on education. These three, in other words, were the dominant growth areas of the twentieth century.

Will they continue in that role? For leisure the answer is almost certainly 'no'. Health-care spending as a percentage of consumer income is more than likely to be capped in the next decade despite the increase in the number of old people and the advances in medicine. Education should continue its growth – but primarily as education of already well-educated adults, while changing from the most labour-intensive of major industries to one of the most highly capital-intensive ones. What challenges – to a company's policies, products, markets, goals – do such changes present? What opportunities?

These are macroeconomic trends. But similar structural trends shape the microeconomies of individual industries and markets; they are equally important. For three hundred years, since the colonial days, the floor space per family, and with it the percentage of consumers' income spent on housing, has steadily grown in the United States (in contrast to Europe and Japan). Has this trend now come to an end with the drastic changes in family size and composition?

Since the Second World War, the share of consumers' disposable income spent on entertainment electronics – radio, TV, audio cassettes, video cassettes, and so on – has grown steadily, a trend the Japanese understood and exploited. Has it plateaued? The share of consumers' disposable income spent on telecommunications has been growing for a century, it may be poised to explode.

Economic wisdom has it that older people do not save. Is this still true? The growth of mutual funds would argue the opposite. And what would such a shift in the distribution of disposable income by people over fifty or fifty-five – the fastest-growing segment of the developed countries' population – mean for financial institutions, their products, services, and marketing? These are not particularly arcane matters. Most executives know the answers or how to get them. It's just that they rarely ask the questions.

The answers to the question 'What has already happened that will make the future?' define the potential of opportunities for a given company or industry. To convert this potential into reality requires matching the opportunities with the company's strengths and competence. It requires what I first (in my 1964 book *Managing for Results*) presented as 'strength analysis' and what now – thanks mainly to the work of Professors C. K. Prahalad and Gary Hamel – is coming to be known as the analysis of 'core competence'.

'What is this company good at? What does it do well? What strengths, in other words, give it a competitive edge? Applied to what?' Strength analysis also shows where there is need to improve or to upgrade existing strengths and where new strengths have to be acquired. It shows both what the company *can* do and what it *should* do. Matching a company's strengths to the changes that have already taken place produces, in effect, a plan of action. It enables a business to turn the unexpected into advantage. Uncertainty ceases to be a threat and becomes an opportunity.

There is, however, one condition: that the business create the resources of knowledge and of people to respond when opportunity knocks. This means developing a separate futures budget.

The 10 per cent or 12 per cent of annual expenditures needed to create and maintain the resources for the future – in research and technology, in market standing and service, in people and their development – must be put into a constant budget maintained in good years and bad. These are investments, even though accountants and tax collectors consider them operating expenses. They enable a business to make its future – and that, in the last analysis, is what planning for uncertainty means.

1992

3
The five deadly business sins

The past few years have seen the downfall of one once-dominant business after another: General Motors, Sears, and IBM, to name just a few. But in every case the main cause has been at least one of the five deadly business sins – avoidable mistakes that will harm the mightiest business.

The first and easily the most common sin is *the worship of high profit margins and of 'premium pricing'*. The prime example of what this leads to is the near-collapse of Xerox in the 1970s. Having invented the copier – and few products in industrial history have had greater success faster – Xerox soon began to add feature after feature to the machine, each priced to yield the maximum profit margin and each driving up the machine's price. Xerox's profits soared and so did the stock price. But the vast majority of consumers who need only a simple machine became increasingly ready to buy from a competitor. And when Japan's Canon brought out such a machine, it immediately took over the US market. Xerox barely survived.

GM's troubles – and those of the entire US car industry – are, in large measure, also the result of the fixation on profit margin. By 1970, the Volkswagen Beetle had taken almost 10 per cent of the American market, showing there was US demand for a small and fuel-efficient car. A few years later, after the first 'oil crisis', that market had become very large and was growing fast. Yet the US car makers were quite content for many years to leave it to the Japanese, as small-car profit margins appeared to be so much lower than those for big cars.

This soon turned out to be a delusion – it usually is. GM, Chrysler and Ford increasingly had to subsidize their big-car buyers with discounts, rebates, cash bonuses. In the end, the Big Three probably gave away more in subsidies than it would have cost them to develop a competitive (and profitable) small car.

The lesson: the worship of premium pricing always creates a market for the competitor. And high profit margins do not equal maximum profits. Total profit is profit margin multiplied by turnover. Maximum profit is thus obtained by the profit margin that yields the largest *total* profit flow, and that is usually the profit margin that produces optimum market standing.

Closely related to this first sin is the second one: *mispricing a new product by charging 'what the market will bear.'* This, too, creates a risk-free opportunity for the competition. It is the wrong policy even if the product has patent protection. Given enough incentive, a potential competitor will find a way around the strongest patent.

The Japanese have the world's fax-machine market today because the Americans who invented the machine, developed it, and first produced it, charged what the market would bear – the highest price they could get. The Japanese, however, priced the machine in the United States two or three years down the learning curve – a good 40 per cent lower. They had the market virtually overnight; only one small US fax-machine manufacturer, which makes a speciality product in tiny quantities, survives.

By contrast, DuPont has remained the world's largest producer of synthetic fibres because, in the mid-1940s, it offered its new and patented nylon on the world market for the price at which it would have to be sold five years hence to maintain itself against competition. This was some two-fifths lower than the price DuPont could then have obtained from the manufacturers of women's hosiery and underwear.

DuPont's move delayed competition by five or six years. But it also immediately created markets for nylon that nobody at the company had even thought about (for example, in car tyres), and these markets soon became both bigger and more profitable than the women's-wear market could ever have been. This strategy thus produced a much larger total profit for DuPont than charging what the traffic would bear could have done. And DuPont kept the markets when the competitors did appear, after five or six years.

The third deadly sin is *cost-driven pricing*. The only thing that works is price-driven costing. Most American and practically all European companies arrive at their prices by adding up costs and then putting a profit margin on top. And then, as soon as they have introduced the product, they have to start cutting the price, have to redesign the product at enormous expense, have to take losses – and, often, have to drop a perfectly good product because it is priced incorrectly. Their argument? 'We have to recover our costs and make a profit.'   This is true but irrelevant: customers do not see it as their job to ensure that manufacturers make a profit. The only sound way to price is to start out with what the market is willing to pay – and thus, it must be assumed, what the competition will charge – and design to that price specification.

Cost-driven pricing is the reason there is no longer an American consumer-electronics industry. It had the technology and the products. But it operated on cost-led pricing – and the Japanese practised price-led costing. Cost-led pricing also nearly destroyed the US machine-tool industry and gave the Japanese, who again used price-led costing, their leadership in the world market. The US industry's recent (and still quite modest) comeback is the result of that industry's finally having switched to price-led costing.

If Toyota and Nissan succeed in pushing the German luxury car makers out of the US market, it will be the result of their using price-led costing. To be sure, to start out with price and then whittle down costs is more work *initially*. But in the end it is much less work than to start out wrong and then spend loss-making years bringing costs into line – let alone far cheaper than losing a market.

The fourth of the deadly business sins is *slaughtering tomorrow's opportunity on the altar of yesterday*. It is what derailed IBM. IMB's downfall was paradoxically caused by unique success: IBM's catching up, almost overnight, when Apple brought out the first PC in the mid-1970s. But then when IBM had gained leadership in the new PC market, it subordinated this new and growing business to the old cash cow, the mainframe computer.

Top management practically forbade the PC people to sell to potential mainframe customers. This did not help the mainframe business – it never does. But it stunted the PC business. All it did was create sales for the IBM 'clones' and thereby guarantee that IBM would not reap the fruits of its achievement.

This is actually the second time that IBM has committed this sin. Forty years ago, when IBM first had a computer, top management decreed that it must not be offered where it might interfere with the possible sale of punch cards, then the company's cash cow. The company was saved by the Justice Department's bringing an antitrust suit against IBM's domination of the punch-card market, which forced management to abandon the cards – and saved the fledgling computer. The second time Providence did not come to IBM's rescue, however.

The last of the deadly sins is *feeding problems and starving opportunities*. For many years I have been asking new clients to tell me who their best-performing people are. And then I ask: 'What are they assigned to?' Almost without exception, the performers are assigned to problems – to the old business that is sinking faster than has been forecast; to the old product that is being outflanked by a competitor's new offering; to the old technology – for example, analogue switches, when the market has already switched to digital. Then I ask: 'And who takes care of the opportunities?' Almost invariably, the opportunities are left to fend for themselves.

All one can get by 'problem-solving' is damage containment. Only opportunities produce results and growth. And opportunities are actually every bit as difficult and demanding as problems are. First draw up a list of the opportunities facing the business and make sure that each is adequately staffed (and adequately supported). Only then should you draw up a list of the problems and worry about staffing them.

I suspect that Sears has been doing the opposite – starving the opportunities and feeding the problems – in its retail business these past few years. This is also, I suspect, what is being done by the major European companies that have steadily been losing ground on the world market (e.g. Siemens in Germany). The right thing to do has been demonstrated by GE, with its policy to get rid of all businesses – even profitable ones – that do not offer long-range growth and the opportunity for the company to be number one or number two worldwide. And then GE places its best-performing people in the opportunity businesses, and pushes and pushes.

Everything I have been saying in this *article* has been known for generations. Everything has been amply proved by decades of experience. There is thus no excuse for managements to indulge in the five deadly sins. They are temptations that must be resisted.

1993

4
Managing the family business

The majority of businesses everywhere – including the United States and all other developed countries – are family-controlled and family-managed. And family management is by no means confined to small and medium-sized firms – families run some of the world's largest companies. Levi Strauss, for instance, has been family-controlled and family-managed since its inception a century and a half ago. DuPont, controlled and managed by family members for 170 years (since its founding in 1802 until professional management took over in the mid-1970s), grew into the world's largest chemical company. And two centuries after a still obscure coin dealer began to send out his sons to establish banks in Europe's capitals, financial firms bearing the Rothschild name and run by Rothschilds are still among the world's premier private bankers.

Yet management books and management courses deal almost entirely with the publicly owned and professionally managed company – they rarely as much as mention the family-managed business. Of course, there is no difference whatever between professionally managed and family-managed businesses in respect to all functional work: research or marketing or accounting. But with respect to *management*, the family business requires its own and very different rules. These rules have to be stringently observed. Otherwise, the family-managed business will not survive, let alone prosper.

The first rule is that family members do not work in the business unless they are at least as able as any non-family employee, and work at least as hard. It is much cheaper to pay a lazy nephew not to come to work than to keep him on the payroll. In a family-managed company family members are always 'top management' whatever their official job or title. For on Saturday evening they sit at the boss's dinner table and call him 'Dad' or 'Uncle'. Mediocre or, worse, lazy family members allowed to work in the family-managed business are rightly resented by non-family co-workers. They are an affront to their self-respect. If mediocre or lazy family members are kept on the payroll, respect for top management and for the business altogether rapidly erodes within the entire workforce. Capable non-family people will not stay. And the ones who do soon become courtiers and toadies.

Most CEOs of family businesses know this, of course. But still, far too many try to be 'clever'. For example, the mediocre or lazy family member gets the title 'Director of Research'. And a highly competent, non-family professional is brought in at a lush salary as 'Deputy Director of Research', and is told by the CEO 'My cousin Jim's title is a mere formality, and only meant to keep his mother off our backs – she's our second-largest shareholder, after all. Everybody else, including Jim, knows that *you* are in charge of research. And you'll work directly with me and need not pay attention to Jim.' But this only makes things worse. With a mediocre Jim actually in charge, the company might still get mediocre research. With a deeply resentful and jealous Jim having the official authority but no real responsibility, and an equally resentful and totally cynical outsider having the responsibility but no real authority, the company will get no research at all. All it will get are intrigues and politicking.

DuPont survived and prospered as a family business because it faced up to the problem. All male DuPonts were entitled to an entrance job in the company. Five or six years after a DuPont had started, his performance would be carefully reviewed by four or five family seniors. And if this review concluded that the young family member was not likely to be top management material ten years later, he was eased out.

The second rule is equally simple: no matter how many family members are in the company's management, and how effective they are, one top job is always filled by an outsider who is not a member of the family. Typically, this is either the financial executive or the head of research – the two positions in which technical qualifications are most important. But I also know successful family companies in which this outsider serves as the head of marketing or as the head of personnel. And while the CEO of Levi Strauss is a family member and a descendant of the founder, the president and COO is a non-family professional.

The first such 'inside outsider' I knew, almost sixty years ago, was the chief financial officer of a very large and completely family-managed business in the United Kingdom. Though otherwise on the closest terms of friendship with his family-member colleagues, he never attended a family party or a family wedding. He did not even play golf at the country club where the family members played. 'The only family affairs I attend,' he once said to me, 'are funerals. But *I* chair the monthly top-management meeting.'

There is need in the family company, in other words, for one senior person – and a highly respected one – who is not family and who never mixes business and family.

The world's oldest 'family business', the Mafia, follows this rule faithfully – in its native Sicily as well as in the United States. As anyone knows who has seen a *Godfather* film or has read a *Godfather* book, in a Mafia family the *consigliere*, the lawyer, who is the second most powerful person, might even be a non-Sicilian.

Rule three is that family-managed businesses, except perhaps for the very smallest ones, increasingly need to staff key positions with non-family professionals. The knowledge and expertise needed, whether in manufacturing or in marketing, in finance, in research, in human resource management have become far too great to be satisfied by any but the most competent family member no matter how well-intentioned he or she may be. And then, these non-family professionals have to be treated as equals. They have to have 'full citizenship' in the firm. Otherwise they simply will not stay.

The first of the great business families to realize that certain outsiders need to be granted 'full citizenship' was the tightest of all business clans, the Rothschilds. Until the Second World War they admitted only family members to partnership in their banks. During the nineteenth and early twentieth centuries, the non-family general manager who reached his late forties was given a huge severance pay – in one case a million dollars – so that he could set up his own banking firm. Since the Second World War, however, non-family members have been admitted to a partnership in a Rothschild firm – the best known of them being Georges Pompidou, who later succeeded Charles de Gaulle as president of France.

Even the family-managed business that faithfully observes the preceding three rules tends to get into trouble – and often breaks up – over *management succession*. It is then that what the business needs and what the family wants tend to collide. Here are two brothers who have built a successful manufacturing business. Now that they are nearing retirement age, each pushes his own son as the next CEO. Thus, though they have worked together harmoniously for twenty years, they become adversaries and eventually sell out rather than compromise. Here is the widow of one of a company's founders who, in order to save her daughter's floundering marriage, pushes her moderately endowed son-in-law to be the next CEO and successor to her ageing brother-in-law. Here is the founder of the fair-sized high-tech company who forces an unwilling son to give up his career as a university scientist in order to take over the management of the firm – only to have the son sell out to a big conglomerate within six months after his father's death. Anyone who has worked with family companies could forever add to the list.

There is only one solution: entrust the succession decision to an outsider who is neither part of the family nor part of the business.

Benjamin Disraeli, the great Tory prime minister, played this role for the Rothschilds in the 1880s, when the 'cousins', the third generation of the family, began to die off. He persuaded the entire family to accept the youngest – but ablest – of the next generation, the Viennese Leopold, as the effective head of all three Rothschild banks, the one in London, the one in Paris, and the one in Vienna. On a much smaller scale, I have seen this role being played successfully by a CPA who had been the outside auditor of a medium-sized food retailer since the business was started twenty years earlier. A university professor, who for ten years had been its scientific adviser, saved a fair-sized high-tech company – and the owning family – by persuading two brothers and two cousins and the wives of all four to accept as the new CEO the daughter of one of the cousins who was the youngest but also the ablest of the next generation.

But it is usually much too late to bring in the outsider when the succession problem becomes acute. By that time the family members have committed themselves to this or that candidate. Furthermore, succession planning in the family business needs to be integrated with financial and tax planning, an integration which cannot be done overnight. More and more family-managed businesses, therefore, now try to find the right outside arbitrator long before the decision has to be made and, ideally, long before the family members have begun to disagree on the succession.

Sixth- or seventh-generation family businesses, like Levi Strauss, DuPont, the Rothschilds, are rare. Few businesses remain family-managed into, let alone beyond, the fourth generation. The biggest family-managed business around today, Fiat in Italy, is run by the third generation of Agnellis, who are now in their sixties and seventies. Few people in the company, I am told, expect Fiat still to be family-managed twenty years hence. The fourth generation of a family owning a successful business is sufficiently well off, as a rule, for the ablest of them to want to pursue their own interests and their own careers rather than dedicate themselves to the business. Also, by that time there are often so many family members that ownership has become splintered. For the members of the fourth generation, their share in the company is thus no longer 'ownership'; it has become 'investment'. They will want to diversify rather than to keep all their financial eggs in the family-company basket, and they therefore want the business to be sold or to go public. But for the second and even for the third generation, maintaining the family company may be the most advantageous course. Often it is the only course, as the business is not big enough to be sold or to go public. And to make family succession possible is surely also in the public interest. The growth dynamics in the economy are shifting fast from the giants to the medium-sized businesses, and these latter tend to be owner-controlled and owner-managed. Therefore, to encourage entrepreneurship requires encouraging the family-managed business and to make possible its continuation. So far, however, the family-managed businesses that survive the founder – let alone those that still prosper under the third generation of family management – are the exception rather than the rule. Far too few family-managed businesses and their owners accept the four management rules and the one *basic precept* which underlies all of them: both the business and the family will only survive and do well if the family serves the business. Neither will do well if the business is run to serve the family. The controlling word in 'family-managed business' is not 'family'. It has to be 'business'.

1994

5
Six rules for presidents

It's hard to imagine a more diverse group than Bill Clinton's predecessors in the American presidency – in abilities, personalities, values, styles, and achievements. But even the weakest of them had considerable effectiveness as long as they observed six management rules. And even the most powerful lost effectiveness as soon as they violated these rules.

What needs to be done? is the first thing the president must ask. He must not stubbornly do what he wants to do, even if it was the focus of his campaign.

Harry Truman came to the presidency in April 1945 convinced – as were most Americans – that with the end of the war in sight, the country could and should focus again on domestic problems. He was passionately committed to reviving the New Deal. What made him an effective president was his accepting within a few weeks that international affairs, especially the containment of Stalin's worldwide aggression, had to be given priority whether he liked it or not (and he didn't). There seems to be a law of American politics that the world always changes between Election Day and Inauguration Day. To refuse to accept this – as Jimmy Carter tried to do – is not to be 'principled'. It is to deny reality and condemn oneself to being ineffectual.

Concentrate, don't splinter yourself is the second rule. There are usually half a dozen right answers to 'What needs to be done?' Yet unless a president makes the risky and controversial choice of only one, he will achieve nothing.

Franklin Roosevelt snubbed the outside world during his first five years in office, despite the rise of Hitler in Europe and the Japanese invasion in China. By early 1938 we were still in deepest Depression, and the country was highly isolationist in mood. But practically overnight, FDR switched his priority to international affairs, all but neglecting domestic issues. Lyndon Johnson, thirty years later, tried to fight the war in Vietnam and the war on poverty simultaneously. We lost both.

The president's top priority has to be something that truly needs to be done. If it is not highly controversial, it is likely to be the wrong priority. It has to be doable – and doable fairly fast – which means that it has to be a limited objective. But it also has to be important enough to make a difference if done successfully.

Ronald Reagan applied these guidelines when he decided in 1981 to make stopping inflation his first priority and to do so by raising interest rates sky-high. Any second-year economics student could have told Mr Reagan that this would cause a massive recession – and indeed unemployment jumped within a few months from an already high $7\frac{1}{2}$ per cent to 10 per cent, a rate not seen since the Depression. Yet stopping inflation was surely something that needed to be done. It was quickly doable, and it did make a difference.

Mr Reagan's action laid the foundation for the subsequent expansion in employment – the greatest in US history. And it earned Mr Reagan the public's trust, which he enjoyed to the end of his tenure. Mr Clinton might have gained similar success if he had made insuring the 37 million Americans who lack health coverage his first priority. Instead he shrank from the likely political battle, miring this limited (and doable) objective in the morass of comprehensive health-care reform.

Don't ever bet on a sure thing is rule three. It always misfires. If any president since George Washington ever had a popular mandate it was FDR at his second inauguration in 1937 – re-elected with the largest majority in US history and in full control of Congress.

President Roosevelt had every reason to believe that his plan to 'pack' the Supreme Court and thereby to remove the last obstacle to the New Deal reforms would be a sure thing. He never even tested the plan before announcing it. It immediately blew up in his face – so much so that he never regained control of Congress. Mr Clinton too must have thought that removing the ban on gays in the military would be a sure thing – he too never tested the proposal before announcing it. It immediately led to the sharpest drop in public opinion ratings ever suffered by a new president.

Packing the Supreme Court was not perceived by the American public as a way to promote the highly popular New Deal but as a subversion of the Founders' America. President Clinton's proposal was perceived to have far less to do with gay rights than with the combat-readiness of the armed forces. Such differences in perception are always 'obvious' in retrospect, but in retrospect only. An effective president knows, therefore, that there is no risk-free politics.

An effective president does not micromanage is rule four. The tasks that a US president must do himself are already well beyond what any but the best-organized and most energetic person can possibly accomplish. Whatever the president does not have to do he therefore *must* not do.

Presidents are much too far away from the scene of action, much too dependent on what other people tell them or choose not to tell them, and much too busy to study the fine print and to micromanage successfully. As Lyndon Johnson and Jimmy Carter have proved, there is no quicker way for a president to discredit himself than to be his own chief operating executive.

Yet in the American system the president, and no one else, is ultimately accountable for the government's performance. And in carrying out the work of government, 'God is in the details'. An effective president has to say no to the temptation to micromanage but he has to make sure operations are being taken care of. A president needs a small team of highly disciplined people, each with clear operating responsibility for one area.

The model might be FDR's cabinet. Nine of its ten members (all but the secretary of state) were what we now would call technocrats – competent specialists in one area. 'I make the decision,' Roosevelt said, 'and then turn the job over to a cabinet member and leave him or her alone.' That the operating team delivered an exceptional performance – not one financial scandal, for instance, despite unprecedented government spending – explains in large measure Roosevelt's own unprecedented hold on power and office.

Later presidents tried to get the same effectiveness by having one chief of staff, a chief operating officer. It has never worked. But the other alternative, the one Mr Clinton has chosen – to have dozens and dozens of deputy secretaries, undersecretaries, assistant secretaries, special assistants and so on – only converts government into a perpetual mass meeting.

A president has no friends in the administration was Lincoln's maxim and is rule five. Any president who has disregarded it has lived to regret it.

No one can trust 'friends of the president'. Whom do they work for? Whom do they speak for? To whom do they really report? At best, they are suspected of running around their official superiors and to their Great Friend; at worst, they are known as the president's spies. Above all, they are always tempted to abuse their position as a friend and the power that goes with it. If they do so by taking a bribe or otherwise enriching themselves or their families, the resulting 'financial scandal' makes the headlines. Non-financial abuses (e.g. obtaining special treatment for this or that interest group) are usually hushed up. Yet such abuses can do even more damage than the financial misdeeds to the president's effectiveness, his policies, his reputation.

Presidents are human beings, and their job is a lonely one. Being politicians, they tend to be gregarious people who crave company, companionship, sympathy. This explains both why presidents are so prone to bring friends into their administrations and why they are usually extremely reluctant to get rid of a friend who has proved incompetent or betrayed their trust. But effective presidents should emulate the most gregarious man ever to occupy the White House: Teddy Roosevelt. Even as president he led a hectic social life, but not one of his half-dozen 'intimates' worked in his administration.

Many presidents' wives, the prime example being Bess Truman, were their husband's main advisers and confidantes. But prior to Hillary Rodham Clinton not one held a position in an administration.

And the sixth rule? It is the advice Harry Truman gave the newly elected John F. Kennedy: *'Once you're elected you stop campaigning.'*

1993

6
Managing in the network society

For well over a hundred years all developed countries were moving steadily towards an *employee society of organizations*. Now this trend is reversing itself. The developed countries, with the United States in the lead, are fast moving towards a *network society* – in respect to the relationship between organizations and individuals who work for them, and in respect to the relationships between different organizations.

There were, of course, plenty of employed people before 1860 and 1870 when Big Business and Big Civil Service emerged as the first modern organizations. There were domestic servants and hired hands on the farm; sales clerks in the small store; journeymen and apprentices in the craftsman's shop. But these people did not work for an 'organization': they worked for a 'master' or a 'mistress'. In 1913 – the year before the First World War – fewer than a fifth of the labour force worked for an organization – primarily as blue-collar workers in industry. And most of these still worked in small family-owned enterprises rather than in big businesses. Forty years later, in the 1950s, employees of large organizations dominated every developed economy – as blue-collar workers and managers in industry; as civil servants in giant government agencies; as nurses in rapidly growing hospitals; as teachers in even faster-growing universities. The best-selling books of those years were jeremiads about the 'Organization Man' who immerses himself into grey conformity and puts loyalty to the organization above everything else. Few people then doubted that by 1990 almost everyone in the workforce would be an employee of an organization, and probably of a big one.

A substantially larger proportion of adults now participate in the US labour force than did thirty or forty years ago. Most of them – and especially the great majority of educated people – do indeed work *for* an organization. But increasingly they are not *employees* of that organization. They are contractors, part-timers, temporaries ('temps'). Recently I ran a three-day seminar for some 300 alumni of one of the major US graduate business schools – mostly people in their late thirties or early forties, and highly successful. Practically every one of them worked for an organization – but barely half of them as employees. Fewer still expected to spend their entire working life as employees of an organization. One participant – a forty-five-year old metallurgist – only five years ago was an executive of a *Fortune* 500 Company. Today he is on his own and retained by five different companies, one of them his former employer. 'There simply wasn't enough for me to *do* in the old company' he said. 'It has a serious metallurgical problem only three or four times a year. The rest of the time I wrote memoranda. Now, when that company has a metallurgical problem I dive right in – not as a consultant but as a full-time member of the team and as its leader. But I stay only until we've licked the problem. I work the same way for my other four clients.' Then there was the thirty-eight-year-old information specialist who similarly works as a 'permanent temp' for a number of state agencies in the Midwest. There was the woman executive of an 'outsourcing' firm who described herself as an 'itinerant member of top management' in the twenty large hospitals for which her company keeps the books and does housekeeping and maintenance. Among the participants there were also an engineer on the payroll of a 'temporary-help' firm who works as plant manager for large companies – usually on a three-year contract – whenever such a company builds and runs in a new plant; the woman physician who similarly works as a 'temp' in setting up emergency departments in hospitals; and a former college dean who works as a 'full-time temp' – for a year at a time – setting up and running fund-raising campaigns for small and medium-sized colleges.

Temporary and part-time work emerged some thirty-five years ago to supply typists, receptionists, and checkers in the supermarket – people of relatively low skill. At first the temps filled in whenever a regular employee was sick or went on vacation. Increasingly temps do high-skill and high-status work. And increasingly temps work for the same organization for long periods of time. In the United States the number of temporary-employment agencies *doubled* in the five years 1989–1994: from 3500 firms to 7000. A good deal of this growth, perhaps half if not more, is in agencies providing professionals – all the way up to senior managers – rather than low-skill people or people to fill entry positions.

Relations between organizations are changing just as fast as relations between organizations and the people who work for them. The most visible example is 'outsourcing', in which a company, a hospital, a government agency, turns over an entire activity to an independent firm that specializes in that kind of work. Hospitals – first in the United States and now, increasingly, in Japan as well – have been turning over maintenance and housekeeping to outsourcing firms for many years now; increasingly they are now outsourcing their data processing and their business management. Outsourcing the information system has become routine – for businesses, for government agencies, for universities, for hospitals. In only one recent day (13 March 1995) two such outsourcing ventures were announced. The largest hospital company in the United States, Columbia/HCA Healthcare, announced that it had outsourced the purchasing and maintenance of all diagnostic instruments in its 300 hospitals to the Medical-Electronics Group of the General Electric Company, the world's largest manufacturer of such instruments. Yet these diagnostic instruments are the core of a modern hospital. They are its biggest investment – amounting at Columbia/HCA Healthcare to many *billions* of dollars; its biggest revenue producer; but also the key to a hospital's medical performance. On the same day IBM, still the world's largest computer maker, announced the formation of a new business (called Network Station Management) to purchase, maintain, and manage the many thousands of PCs in large companies – by now the largest single investment in the office of the typical US big company.

In another ten or fifteen years, organizations may have outsourced all work that is 'support' rather than 'revenue producing' and all activities which do not offer career opportunities into senior management. This would mean that in many organizations a majority of people who work for it might not be its employees but employees of an outsourcing contractor.

More important even may be the trend towards *Alliances* as the vehicle for business growth. Downsizing, divestments, mergers, acquisitions – these dominate the headlines. But the greatest change in corporate structure – and in the way business is being conducted – may be the largely unreported growth of relationships which are based not on *ownership* but on *partnership*: joint ventures; minority investments cementing a joint-marketing agreement or an agreement to do joint research; semi-formal alliances of all sorts. Japanese computer makers are gaining access to software technology by buying minority stakes in high-tech Silicon Valley firms. Large pharmaceuticals companies – both American and European – gain access to research in genetics, in medical electronics, in biotechnology, by similarly buying minority stakes in start-up firms in these new disciplines, or by going into partnership with university research labs. Banks gain access to new investment markets by going into partnership with small, independent asset managers – with or without putting in any money. And there are any number of even less formal 'alliances' – most of them unreported – like the one between the world's leading designer of microchips, Intel, and Sharp, a major Japanese manufacturer. Intel will do the research and design; Sharp the manufacturing. Each company will separately then market the resulting new products – and, apparently neither firm is investing a penny in the other one. In telecommunications there are the 'consortia' in which three or more big established telephone companies – one American, one English, one Swedish, for instance – team up to obtain licences for cellular-phone services all over the world, or for cable television, or to buy together into an old government monopoly system about to be privatized. Like outsourcing, the trend towards alliances of this sort in which nobody has control – that is, toward partnerships – is accelerating. One reason is that no one company, not even the telephone giants, has enough money to swing the deal alone. A more important one is that no one company has by itself the needed technology. And in many parts of the world, especially in 'emerging countries' like Coastal China or Malaysia, business cannot be done except through a joint venture or an alliance with a local partner. 'Today,' the CEO of a major pharmaceuticals company said recently, '80 per cent of our sales and profits come from products we make in plants we own a hundred per cent and sell through wholly owned subsidiaries. In ten years more than half of all we sell – and we plan on doubling in volume during that period – will come from joint ventures, licences, alliances, and from products made by companies in which we have either no investment or only a minority stake but for which we are the research and/or marketing partner. It is simply impossible for us – and we are among the world's research leaders – to have enough scientific expertise in all the new fields. It is equally impossible for us – and we pride ourselves on our marketing organization – to serve all the new channels through which health-care products will be marketed as the health-care systems of the world are re-engineering themselves.'

Not quite thirty years ago, in 1967, the world's business-best-seller was *Le Défi Américain* (*The American Challenge*) by Jean-Jacques Servan-Schreiber, a French journalist. It predicted that by 1985 or 1990 the world's economies would be owned and run by a mere dozen or so huge American multinationals whose plants would produce some 90 per cent of the world's manufactured goods. Even earlier, in 1955, the *Fortune* 500 had made bigness the measurement of business success. Bigger was better, whether in business, in government, in the hospital, in the university. And in that big organization – as in Servan-Schreiber's giant American multinational – one top management controlled everything and ran everything. Everyone who worked for or with that big company was its full-time employee. By the time Servan-Schreiber published his book the tide in the world economy had already turned: both the Europeans and the Japanese were giving the Americans a run for their money. A few years later the growth dynamics in the US economy (and soon thereafter in the European economies as well) were beginning to shift towards the medium-sized company. But still, the basic structures of organizations and of employment seemed to remain what they had been for a century. *Now both are changing rapidly.*

Even if twenty years hence the majority of managers and professionals will still be employees of the organization they work for, the psychology of the workforce – and especially of the knowledge workforce – will largely be determined by the large minority who are not employees of that organization, whether they are employees of an outsourcing firm, of a partnership organization or half-independent contractors. For the organizations and their top managements this means that they had better stop talking about 'loyalty'. They will have to *earn the trust* of the people who work for them, whether these people are its own employees or not. Even the professional or executive who has no intention of leaving the company's employ will know that there are opportunities outside – they already know that, even in Japan. And even professionals or executives who would much prefer to stay with the company they now work for will know that there is now no such thing as 'lifetime employment' – such as was the rule in the big US or European company only a few years ago and is still considered the rule (though with great doubts) in the big Japanese company. Even in government service where lifetime tenure has been the rule for a century or longer, radical downsizing, privatization, shutting down whole agencies is surely going to occur in all developed (and in most emerging) countries. Conversely, individual professionals and executives will have to learn that they must take responsibility for *placing* themselves – both within their organization and outside of it. This means, above all, that they must know their strengths. Most résumés I get – and I get several from former students every day – list the jobs the person *has* held. A few then describe the job the person would like to get. Very, very few even mention what the person has done well and can do well. Even fewer state what a future employer can and should expect from that person. Very, very few, in other words, yet look upon themselves as a 'product' that has to be *marketed*.

Equally novel are the demands partnerships and alliances make on managing a business and its relationships. Executives are used to *command*. They are used to think through what they want and then to get acceptance of it by subordinates. Even Japanese 'consensus management' is a way to get acceptance by the organization of whatever the higher-ups have decided should be done – and so is the much-touted 'participative management'. But in a partnership – whether with an outsourcing contractor, with a joint-venture partner, with a company in which one holds a minority stake – one cannot command. One can only gain trust. Specifically, that means that one must not start out with the question 'What do we want to do?' The right question is 'What do *they* want to do? What are *their* objectives? *Their* values? *Their* ways of doing things?' Again, these are *marketing* relationships – and in marketing one starts with the customer rather than with one's own product.

I asked the participants in that alumni seminar a few months ago what to call this new organization and its society. At first they said 'Call it free-form'. But then they reconsidered and said 'Call it the *Network society*'.

1995

Part Two

The Information-based Organization

7
The new society of organizations

Every few hundred years throughout Western history a sharp transformation has occurred. In a matter of decades, society altogether rearranges itself – its worldview, its basic values, its social and political structures, its arts, its key institutions. Fifty years later a new world exists. And the people born into that world cannot even imagine the world in which their grandparents lived and into which their own parents were born.

Our age is such a period of transformation. Only this time the transformation is not confined to Western society and Western history. Indeed, one of the fundamental changes is that there is no longer a 'Western' history or a 'Western' civilization. There is only world history and world civilization.

Whether this transformation began with the emergence of the first non-Western country, Japan, as a great economic power or with the first computer – that is, with information – is moot. My own candidate would be the GI Bill of Rights, which gave every American soldier returning from the Second World War the money to attend a university, something that would have made absolutely no sense only thirty years earlier at the end of the First World War. The GI Bill of Rights and the enthusiastic response to it on the part of America's veterans signalled the shift to a knowledge society.

In this society, knowledge is *the* primary resource for individuals and for the economy overall. Land, labour, and capital – the economist's traditional factors of production – do not disappear, but they become secondary. They can be obtained, and obtained easily, provided there is specialized knowledge. At the same time, however, specialized knowledge by itself produces nothing. It can become productive only when it is integrated into a task. And that is why the knowledge society is also a society of organizations: the purpose and function of every organization, business and non-business alike, is the integration of specialized knowledges into a common task.

If history is any guide, this transformation will not be completed until 2010 or 2020. Therefore, it is risky to try to foresee in every detail the world that is emerging. But what new questions will arise and where the big issues will lie we can, I believe, already discover with a high degree of probability.

In particular, we already know the central tensions and issues that confront the society of organizations: the tension created by the community's need for stability and the organization's need to destabilize; the relationship between individual and organization and the responsibilities of each to the other; the tension that arises from the organization's need for autonomy and society's stake in the Common Good; the rising demand for socially responsible organizations; the tension between specialists with specialized knowledges and the organization's need for these specialists to perform as a team. All these will be central concerns, especially in the developed world, for years to come. They will not be resolved by pronunciamento or philosophy or legislation. They will be resolved where they originate: in the individual organization and in the manager's office.

Society, community, and family are all conserving institutions. They try to maintain stability and to prevent, or at least to slow, change. But the modern organization is a destabilizer. It must be organized for innovation, and innovation, as the great Austrian–American economist Joseph Schumpeter said, is 'creative

destruction'. And it must be organized for the systematic abandonment of whatever is established, customary, familiar, and
comfortable, whether that is a product, a service, or a process; a
set of skills; human and social relationships; or the organization
itself. In short, it must be organized for constant change. The
organization's function is to put knowledge to work – on tools,
products, and processes; on the design of work; on knowledge
itself. It is the nature of knowledge that it changes fast and that
today's certainties always become tomorrow's absurdities.

Skills change slowly and infrequently. If a stonecutter of
ancient Greece came back to life today and went to work in a
stonemason's yard, the only change of significance would be the
design he was asked to carve on the tombstones. The tools he
would use are the same, only now they have electric batteries in
the handles. Throughout history, the craftsman who had learned
a trade after five or seven years of apprenticeship had learned,
by age eighteen or nineteen, everything he would ever need to
use during his lifetime. In the society of organizations, however,
it is safe to assume that anyone with any knowledge will have to
acquire new knowledge every four or five years or become
obsolete.

This is doubly important because the changes that affect a
body of knowledge most profoundly do not, as a rule, come out
of its own domain. After Gutenberg first used movable type,
there was practically no change in the craft of printing for 400
years – until the steam engine came in. The greatest challenge
to the railways came not from changes in railways but from the
car, the truck, and the airplane. The pharmaceuticals industry is
being profoundly changed today by knowledge coming from
genetics and microbiology, disciplines that few biologists had
heard of forty years ago.

It is by no means only science or technology that creates new
knowledge and makes old knowledge obsolete. Social innovation
is equally important and often more important than scientific
innovation. Indeed, what triggered the present worldwide crises

in that proudest of nineteenth-century institutions, the commercial bank, was not the computer or any other technological change. It was the discovery by non-bankers that an old but hitherto rather obscure financial instrument, commercial paper, could be used to finance companies and would thus deprive the banks of the business on which they had held a monopoly for 200 years and which gave them most of their income: the commercial loan. The greatest change of all is probably that in the last forty years, purposeful innovation – both technical and social – has itself become an organized discipline that is both teachable and learnable.

Nor is rapid knowledge-based change confined to business, as many still believe. No organization in the fifty years since the Second World War has changed more than the US military. Uniforms have remained the same. Titles of rank have remained the same. But weapons have changed completely, as the Gulf War of 1991 dramatically demonstrated; military doctrines and concepts have changed even more drastically, as have the armed services' organizational structures, command structures, relationships, and responsibilities.

Similarly, it is a safe prediction that in the next fifty years, schools and universities will change more and more drastically than they have since they assumed their present form more than 300 years ago, when they reorganized themselves around the printed book. What will force these changes is in part new technology, such as computers, videos, and telecasts via satellite; in part the demands of a knowledge-based society in which organized learning must become a lifelong process for knowledge workers; and in part new theory about how human beings learn.

For managers, the dynamics of knowledge impose one clear imperative: every organization has to build the management of change into its very structure. On the one hand, this means that every organization has to prepare for the abandonment of everything it does. Managers have to learn to ask every few years of every process, every product, every procedure, every policy: 'If we did not do this already, would we go into it now, knowing what we now know?' If the answer is no, the organization has to ask, 'So what do we do now?' And it has to *do* something, and not say, 'Let's make another study'. Indeed, organizations increasingly will have to *plan* abandonment rather than try to prolong the life of a successful product, policy, or practice – something that so far only a few large Japanese companies have faced up to.

On the other hand, every organization must devote itself to creating the new. Specifically, every management has to draw on three systematic practices. The first is continuing improvement of everything the organization does, the process the Japanese call *kaizen*. Every artist throughout history has practised *kaizen*, or organized, continuous self-improvement. But so far only the Japanese – perhaps because of their Zen tradition – have embodied it in the daily life and work of their business organizations (although not in their singularly change-resistant universities). The aim of *kaizen* is to improve a product or service so that it becomes a truly different product or service in two or three years' time.

Second, every organization will have to learn to exploit its knowledge, that is, to develop the next generation of applications from its own successes. Again, Japanese businesses have done the best with this endeavour so far, as demonstrated by the success of the consumer electronics manufacturers in developing one new product after another from the same American invention, the tape recorder. But successful exploitation of their successes is also one of the strengths of the fast-growing American pastoral churches.

Finally, every organization will have to learn to innovate – and innovation can now be organized – and must be organized – as a systematic process. And then, of course, one comes back to abandonment, and the process starts all over. Unless this is done, the knowledge-based organization will very soon find itself obsolescent, losing performance capacity and with it the ability to attract and hold the skilled and knowledgeable people on whom its performance depends.

The need to organize for change also requires a high degree of decentralization. That is because the organization must be structured to make decisions quickly. And those decisions must be based on closeness – to performance, to the market, to technology, and to all the many changes in society, the environment, demographics, and knowledge that provide opportunities for innovation if they are seen and utilized.

All this implies, however, that the organization of the post-capitalist society must constantly upset, disorganize, and destabilize the community. They must change the demand for skills and knowledges: just when every technical university is geared up to teach physics, organizations need geneticists. Just when bank employees are most proficient as loan officers they must become investment counsellors. But also, businesses must be free to close factories on which local communities depend for employment or to replace grizzled model makers who have spent years learning their craft with twenty-five-year-old whiz kids who know computer simulation.

Similarly, hospitals must be able to move the delivery of babies into a free-standing birthing centre when the knowledge base and technology of obstetrics change. And we must be able to close a hospital altogether when changes in medical knowledge, technology, and practice make a hospital with fewer than 200 beds both uneconomical and incapable of giving first-rate care. For a hospital – or a school or any other community organization – to discharge its social function we must be able to close it down, no matter how deeply rooted in the local community it is and how much beloved, if changes in demographics, technology, or knowledge set new prerequisites for performance.

But every one of such changes upsets the community, disrupts it, deprives it of continuity. Every one is 'unfair'. Every one destabilizes.

Equally disruptive is another fact of organizational life: the modern organization must be *in* a community but cannot be *of* it. An organization's members live in a particular place, speak its language, send their children to its schools, vote, pay taxes, and need to feel at home there. Yet the organization cannot submerge itself in the community or subordinate itself to the community's ends. Its 'culture' has to transcend community.

It is the nature of the task, not the community in which the task is being performed, that determines the culture of an organization. The American civil servant, though totally opposed to Communism, will understand immediately what a Chinese colleague tells him about the bureaucratic intrigues in Beijing. But he would be totally baffled in his own Washington, DC, if he were to sit in on a discussion of next week's advertising promotions by the managers of the local grocery chain.

To perform its task the organization has to be organized and managed the same way as others of its type. For example, we hear a great deal about the differences in management between Japanese and American companies. But a large Japanese company functions very much like a large American company; and both function very much like a large German or British company. Likewise, no one will ever doubt that he or she is in a hospital, no matter where the hospital is located. The same holds true for schools and universities, for labour unions and research labs, for museums and opera houses, for astronomical observatories and large farms.

In addition, each organization has a value system that is determined by its task. In every hospital in the world, health care is considered the ultimate good. In every school in the world, learning is considered the ultimate good. In every business in the world, production and distribution of goods or services is considered the ultimate good. For the organization to perform to a high standard, its members must believe that what it is doing is, in the last analysis, the one contribution to community and society on which all others depend.

In its culture, therefore, the organization will always transcend the community. If an organization's culture and the values of its community clash, the organization must prevail – or else it will not make its social contribution. 'Knowledge knows no boundaries' says an old proverb. There has been a 'town and gown' conflict ever since the first university was established more than 750 years ago. But such a conflict – between the autonomy the organization needs in order to perform and the claims of the community, between the values of the organization and those of the community, between the decisions facing the organization and the interests of the community – is inherent in the society of organizations.

The issue of social responsibility is also inherent in the society of organizations. The modern organization has and must have social power – and a good deal of it. It needs power to make decisions about people: whom to hire, whom to fire, whom to promote. It needs power to establish the rules and disciplines required to produce results: for example, the assignment of jobs and tasks and the establishment of working hours. It needs power to decide which factories to build where and which factories to close. It needs power to set prices, and so on.

And non-businesses have the greatest social power – far more, in fact, than business enterprises. Few organizations in history were ever granted the power the university has today. Refusing to admit a student or to a grant a student a diploma is tantamount to debarring that person from careers and opportunities. Similarly, the power of the American hospital to deny a physician admitting privileges is the power to exclude that physician from the practice of medicine. The labour union's power over admission to apprenticeship or its control of access to employment in a 'closed shop', where only union members can be hired, gives the union tremendous social power.

The power of the organization can be restrained by political power. It can be made subject to due process and to review by the courts. But it must be exercised by individual organizations rather than by political authorities. This is why post-capitalist society talks so much about social responsibilities of the organization.

It is futile to argue, as Milton Friedman, the American economist and Nobel Laureate does, that a business has only one responsibility: economic performance. Economic performance is the *first* responsibility of a business. Indeed, a business that does not show a profit at least equal to its cost of capital is irresponsible; it wastes society's resources. Economic performance is the base without which a business cannot discharge any other responsibilities, cannot be a good employee, a good citizen, a good neighbour. But economic performance is not the *only* responsibility of a business any more than educational performance is the only responsibility of a school or health care the only responsibility of a hospital.

Unless power is balanced by responsibility, it becomes tyranny. Furthermore, without responsibility, power always degenerates into non-performance, and organizations must perform. So the demand for socially responsible organizations will not go away; rather, it will widen.

Fortunately, we also know, if only in rough outline, how to answer the problem of social responsibility. Every organization must assume full responsibility for its impact on employees, the environment, customers, and whomever and whatever it touches. That is its social responsibility. But we also know that society will increasingly look to major organizations, for-profit and non-profit alike, to tackle major social ills. And there we had better be watchful, because good intentions are not always socially responsible. It is irresponsible for an organization to accept – let alone to pursue – responsibilities that would impede its capacity to perform its main task and mission or to act where it has no competence.

Organization has become an everyday term. Everybody gives a nod of understanding when somebody says 'In our organization, everything should revolve around the customer' or 'In this organization, they never forget a mistake'. And most, if not all, social tasks in every developed country are performed in and by an organization of one kind or another. Yet no one in the United States – or anywhere else – talked of 'organizations' until after the Second World War. *The Concise Oxford Dictionary* did not even list the term in its current meaning in the 1950 edition. It is only the emergence of management since the Second World War, what I call the 'Management Revolution', that has allowed us to see that the organization is discrete and distinct from society's other institutions.

Unlike communities, societies, or families, organizations are purposefully designed and always specialized. Communities and societies are defined by the bonds that hold their members together, whether they be language, culture, history, or locality. An organization is defined by its task. The symphony orchestra does not attempt to cure the sick; it plays music. The hospital takes care of the sick but does not attempt to play Beethoven.

Indeed, an organization is effective only if it concentrates on one task. Diversification destroys the performance capacity of an organization, whether it is a business, a labour union, a school, a hospital, a community service, or a house of worship. Society and community must be multidimensional; they are environments. An organization is a tool. And as with any other tool, the more specialized it is, the greater its capacity to perform its given task.

Because the modern organization is composed of specialists, each with his or her own narrow area of expertise, its mission must be crystal clear. The organization must be single-minded, or its members will become confused. They will follow their own speciality rather than apply it to the common task. They will each define 'results' in terms of their own speciality and impose its values on the organization. Only a focused and common mission will hold the organization together and enable it to produce. Without such a mission, the organization will soon lose credibility and consequently its ability to attract the very people it needs to perform.

It can be all too easy for managers to forget that joining an organization is always voluntary. *De facto* there may be little choice. But even where membership is all but compulsory – as membership in the Catholic Church was in all the countries of Europe for many centuries for all but a handful of Jews and gypsies – the fiction of voluntary choice is always carefully maintained: the godfather at the infant's baptism pledges the child's voluntary acceptance of membership in the Church.

Likewise, it may be difficult to leave an organization – the Mafia, for instance, a big Japanese company, the Jesuit order. But it is always possible. And the more an organization becomes an organization of knowledge workers, the easier it is to leave it and move elsewhere. Therefore, an organization is always in competition for its most essential resource: qualified, knowledgeable people.

All organizations now say routinely 'People are our greatest asset'. Yet few practise what they preach, let alone truly believe it. Most still believe, though perhaps not consciously, what nineteenth-century employers believed: people need us more than we need them. But in fact, organizations have to market membership as much as they market products and services – and perhaps more. They have to attract people, hold people, recognize and reward people, motivate people, and serve and satisfy people.

The relationship between knowledge workers and their organizations is a distinctly new phenomenon, one for which we have no good term. For example, an employee, by definition, is someone who gets paid for working. Yet the largest single group of 'employees' in the United States consists of the millions of men and women who work several hours a week without pay for one or another non-profit organization. They are clearly 'staff' and consider themselves as such, but they are unpaid volunteers. Similarly, many people who work as employees are not employed in any legal sense because they do not work for someone else. Fifty or sixty years ago, we would have spoken of these people (many, if not most, of whom are educated professionals) as 'independent'; today we speak of the 'self-employed'.

These discrepancies – and they exist in just about every language – remind us why new realities often demand new words. But until such a word emerges, this is probably the best definition of employees in the post-capitalist society: people whose ability to make a contribution depends on having access to an organization.

As far as the employees who work in subordinate and menial occupations are concerned – the salesclerk in the supermarket, the cleaning woman in the hospital, the delivery-truck driver – the consequences of this new definition are small. For all practical purposes, their position may not be too different from that of the wage earner, the 'worker' of yesterday, whose direct descendants they are. In fact, this is precisely one of the central social problems modern society faces.

But the relationship between the organization and knowledge workers, who already number at least one-third and more likely two-fifths of all employees, is radically different, as is that between the organization and volunteers. They can work only because there is an organization, thus they too are dependent. But at the same time, they own the 'means of production' – their knowledge. In this respect, they are independent and highly mobile.

Knowledge workers still need the tools of production. In fact, capital investment in the tools of the knowledge employee may already be higher than the capital investment in the tools of the manufacturing worker ever was. (And the social investment, for example, the investment in a knowledge worker's education, is many times the investment in the manual worker's education.) But this capital investment is unproductive unless the knowledge worker brings to bear on it the knowledge that he or she owns and that cannot be taken away. Machine operators in the factory did as they were told. The machine decided not only what to do but how to do it. The knowledge employee may well need a machine, whether it be a computer, an ultrasound analyser, or a telescope. But the machine will not tell the knowledge worker what to do, let alone how to do it. And without this knowledge, which belongs to the employee, the machine is unproductive.

Further, machine operators, like all workers throughout history, could be told what to do, how to do it, and how fast to do it. Knowledge workers cannot be supervised effectively. Unless they know more about their speciality than anybody else in the organization, they are basically useless. The marketing manager may tell the market researcher what the company needs to know about the design of a new product and the market segment in which it should be positioned. But it is the market researcher's job to tell the president of the company what market research is needed, how to set it up, and what the results mean.

During the traumatic restructuring of American business in the 1980s, thousands, if not hundreds of thousands, of knowledge employees lost their jobs. Their companies were acquired, merged, spun off, or liquidated. Yet within a few months, most of them found new jobs in which to put their knowledge to work. The transition period was painful, and in about half the cases, the new job did not pay quite as much as the old one and may not have been as enjoyable. But the laid-off technicians, professionals, and managers found they had the 'capital', the knowledge: they owned the means of production. Somebody else, the organization, had the tools of production. The two needed each other.

One consequence of this new relationship – and it is another new tension in modern society – is that loyalty can no longer be obtained by the paycheque. The organization must earn loyalty by proving to its knowledge employees that it offers them exceptional opportunities for putting their knowledge to work. Not so long ago we talked about 'labour'. Increasingly we are talking about 'human resources'. This change reminds us that it is the individual, and especially the skilled and knowledgeable employee, who decides in large measure what he or she will contribute to the organization and how great the yield from his or her knowledge will be.

Because the modern organization consists of knowledge specialists, it has to be an organization of equals, of colleagues and associates. No knowledge ranks higher than another; each is judged by its contribution to the common task rather than by any inherent superiority or inferiority. Therefore, the modern organization cannot be an organization of boss and subordinate. It must be organized as a team.

There are only three kinds of teams. One is the sort of team that plays together in tennis doubles. In that team – and it has to be small – each member adapts himself or herself to the personality, the skills, the strengths, and the weaknesses of the other member or members. Then there is the team that plays soccer. Each player has a fixed position; but the whole team moves together (except for the goalie) while individual members retain their relative positions. Finally, there is the American baseball team – or the orchestra – in which all the members have fixed positions.

At any given time, an organization can play only one kind of game. And it can use only one kind of team for any given task. Which team to use or game to play is one of the riskiest decisions in the life of an organization. Few things are as difficult in an organization as transforming one kind of team in to another.

Traditionally, American industry has used a baseball-style team to produce a new product or model. Research did its work and passed it on to manufacturing. Manufacturing did its work and passed it on to marketing. Accounting usually came in at the manufacturing phase. Personnel usually came in only when there was a true crisis – and often not even then.

Then the Japanese reorganized their new product development into a soccer team. In such a team, each function does its own work, but from the beginning they work together. They move with the task, so to speak, the way a soccer team moves with the ball. It took the Japanese at least fifteen years to learn how to do this. But once they had mastered the new concept, they cut development time by two-thirds. Where traditionally it has taken five years to bring out a new car model, Toyota, Nissan, and Honda now do it in eighteen months. This, as much as their quality control, has given the Japanese the upper hand in both the American and European car markets.

Some American manufacturers have been working hard to reorganize their development work according to the Japanese model. Ford Motor Company, for instance, began to do so in the early 1980s. Ten years later, in the early 1990s, it has made considerable progress – but not nearly enough to catch up with the Japanese. Changing a team demands the most difficult learning imaginable: unlearning. It demands giving up hard-earned skills, habits of a lifetime, deeply cherished values of craftsmanship and professionalism, and – perhaps the most difficult of all – it demands giving up old and treasured human relationships. It means abandoning what people have always considered 'our community' or 'our family'.

But if the organization is to perform, it must be organized as a team. When modern organizations first arose in the closing years of the nineteenth century, the only model was the military. The Prussian army was as much a marvel of organization for the world of 1870 as Henry Ford's assembly line was for the world of 1920. In the army of 1870, each member did much the same thing, and the number of people with any knowledge was infinitesimally small. The army was organized by command-and-control, and business enterprise as well as most other institutions copied that model. This is now rapidly changing. As more and more organizations become information-based, they are transforming themselves into soccer or tennis teams, that is, into responsibility-based organizations in which every member must act as a responsible decision maker. All members, in other words, have to see themselves as 'executives'.

Even so, an organization must be managed. The management may be intermittent and perfunctory, as it is, for instance, in the parent–teacher association at a US suburban school. Or management may be a full-time and demanding job for a fairly large group of people, as it is in the military, the business enterprise, the labour union, and the university. But there have to be people who make decisions or nothing will ever get done. There have to be people who are accountable for the organization's mission, its spirit, its performance, its results. Society, community, and family may have 'leaders', but only organizations know a 'management'. And while this management must have considerable authority, its job in the modern organization is not to command. It is to inspire.

The society of organizations is unprecedented in human history. It is unprecedented in its performance capacity both because each of its constituent organizations is a highly specialized tool designed for one specific task and because each bases itself on the organization and deployment of knowledge. It is unprecedented in its structure. But it is also unprecedented in its tensions and problems. Not all of these are serious. In fact, some of them we already know how to resolve – issues of social responsibility, for example. But there are other areas where we do not know the right answer and where we may not even be asking the right questions yet.

There is, for instance, the tension between the community's need for continuity and stability and the organization's need to be an innovator and destabilizer. There is the split between 'literati' and 'managers'. Both are needed: the former to produce knowledge, the latter to apply knowledge and make it productive. But the former focus on words and ideas, the latter on people, work, and performance. There is the threat to the very basis of the society of organizations – the knowledge base – that arises from ever greater specialization, from the shift from knowledge to *knowledges*. But the greatest and most difficult challenge is that presented by society's new pluralism.

For more than 600 years no society has had as many centres of power as the society in which we now live. The Middle Ages indeed knew pluralism. Society was composed of hundreds of competing and autonomous power centres: feudal lords and knights, exempt bishoprics, autonomous monasteries, 'free' cities. In some places, the Austrian Tyrol, for example, there were even 'free peasants', beholden to no one but the Emperor. There were also autonomous craft guilds and transnational trading leagues like the Hanseatic Merchants and the merchant bankers of Florence, toll and tax collectors, local 'parliaments' with legislative and tax-raising powers, private armies available for hire, and myriads more.

Modern history in Europe – and equally in Japan – has been the history of the subjugation of all competing centres of power by one central authority, first called the 'prince', then the 'state'. By the middle of the nineteenth century the unitary state had triumphed in every developed country except the United States, which remained profoundly pluralistic in its religious and educational organizations. Indeed, the abolition of pluralism was the 'progressive' cause for nearly 600 years.

But just when the triumph of the state seemed assured, the first new organization arose – the large business enterprise. (This, of course, always happens when the 'end of history' is announced.) Since then, one new organization after another has sprung up. And old organizations like the university, which in Europe seemed to have been brought safely under the control of central governments, have become autonomous again. Ironically, twentieth-century totalitarianism, especially Communism, represented the last desperate attempt to save the old and once progressive creed in which there is only one centre of power and one organization rather than a pluralism of competing and autonomous organizations.

That attempt failed, as we know. But the failure of central authority, in and of itself, does nothing to address the issues that follow from a pluralistic society. To illustrate, consider a story that many people have heard of or, more accurately, misheard.

During his lifetime, Charles E. Wilson was a prominent personality in the United States, first as president and chief executive officer of General Motors, at that time the world's largest and most successful manufacturer, then as Secretary of Defence in the Eisenhower administration. But if Wilson is remembered at all today it is for something he did *not* say: 'What is good for General Motors is good for the United States.' What Wilson actually said in his 1953 confirmation hearings for the Defense Department job was 'What is good for the United States is good for General Motors'.

Wilson tried for the remainder of his life to correct the misquote. But no one listened to him. Everyone argued that 'if he didn't say it, he surely believes it – in fact he *should* believe it'. For as has been said, executives in an organization – whether business or university or hospital or the Boy Scouts – must believe that its mission and task are society's most important mission and task as well as the foundation for everything else. If they do not believe this, their organization will soon lose faith in itself, its self-confidence, its pride, and the ability to perform.

The diversity that is characteristic of a developed society and that provides its great strength is only possible because of the specialized, single-task organizations that we have developed since the Industrial Revolution and, especially, during the last fifty years. But the feature that gives them the capacity to perform is precisely that each is autonomous and specialized, informed only by its own narrow mission and vision, its own narrow values, and not by any consideration of society and community.

Therefore, we come back to the old – and never resolved – problem of the pluralistic society: who takes care of the common good? Who defines it? Who balances the separate and often competing goals and values of society's institutions? Who makes the trade-off decisions and on what basis should they be made?

Medieval feudalism was replaced by the unitary sovereign state precisely because it could not answer these questions. But the unitary sovereign state has now itself been replaced by a new pluralism – a pluralism of function rather than one of political power – because it could neither satisfy the needs of society nor perform the necessary tasks of community. That, in the final analysis, is the most fundamental lesson to be learned from the failure of socialism, the failure of the belief in the all-embracing and all-powerful state. The challenge that faces us now, and especially in the developed, free-market democracies such as the United States, is to make the pluralism of autonomous, knowledge-based organizations redound both to economic performance and to political and social cohesion.

1992

8
There's three kinds of teams

'Team-building' has become a buzzword in American business. The results are not overly impressive.

The Ford Motor Company began more than ten years ago to build teams to design its new models. It now reports 'serious problems', and the gap in development time between Ford and its Japanese competitors has hardly narrowed. General Motors' Saturn Division was going to replace the traditional assembly line with teamwork in its 'factory of the future'. But the plant has been steadily moving back toward the Detroit-style assembly line. Procter & Gamble launched a team-building campaign with great fanfare several years ago. Now P&G is moving back to individual accountability for developing and marketing new products.

One reason – perhaps the major one – for these near-failures is the all-but-universal belief among executives that there is just one kind of team. There actually are three – each different in its structure, in the behaviour it demands from its members, in its strengths, its vulnerabilities, its limitations, its requirements, but above all, in what it can do and should be used for.

The first kind of team is the baseball team. The surgical team that performs an open-heart operation and Henry Ford's assembly line are both 'baseball teams'. So is the team Detroit traditionally sets up to design a new car.

The players play *on* the team; they do not play *as* a team. They have fixed positions they never leave. The second baseman never runs to assist the pitcher; the anaesthesiologist never comes to the aid of the surgical nurse. 'Up at bat, you're totally alone' is an old baseball saying. In the traditional Detroit design team, marketing people rarely saw designers and were never consulted by them. Designers did their work and passed it on to the development engineers, who in turn did their work and passed it on to manufacturing, which in turn did its work and passed it on the marketing people.

The second kind of team is the football team. The hospital unit that rallies round a patient who goes into shock at 3 a.m. is a 'football team', as are Japanese car makers' design teams. The players on the football team, like those on the baseball team, have fixed positions. But on the football team players play as a team. The Japanese car makers' design teams, which Detroit and P&G rushed to imitate, are football-type teams. To use an engineering term, the designers, engineers, manufacturing people, and marketing people work 'in parallel'. The traditional Detroit team worked 'in series'.

Third, there is the tennis doubles team – the kind Saturn management hoped would replace the traditional assembly line. It is also the sort of team that plays in a jazz combo, the team of senior executives who form the 'president's office' in big companies, or the team that is most likely to produce a genuine innovation like the personal computer fifteen years ago.

On the doubles team, players have a primary rather than a fixed position. They are supposed to 'cover' their team-mates, adjusting to their team-mates' strengths and weaknesses and to the changing demands of the 'game'.

Business executives and the management literature have little good to say these days about the baseball-style team, whether in the office or on the factory floor. There is even a failure to recognize such teams as teams at all. But this kind of team has enormous strengths. Each member can be evaluated separately, can have clear and specific goals, can be held accountable, can be measured – as witness the statistics a true aficionado reels off about every major-leaguer in baseball history. Each member can be trained and developed to the fullest extent of the individual's strengths. And because the members do not have to adjust to anybody else on the team, every position can be staffed with a 'star', no matter how temperamental, jealous, or limelight-hogging each of them might be.

But the baseball team is inflexible. It works well when the game has been played many times and when the sequence of its actions is thoroughly understood by everyone. That is what made this kind of team right for Detroit in the past.

As recently as twenty years ago, to be fast and flexible in car design was the last thing Detroit needed or wanted. Traditional mass production required long runs with minimum changes. And since the resale value of the 'good used car' – one less than three years old – was a key factor for the new-car buyer, it was a serious mistake to bring out a new design (which would depreciate the old car) more than every five years. Sales and market share took a dip on several occasions when Chrysler prematurely introduced a new, brilliant design.

The Japanese did not invent 'flexible mass production'; IBM was probably the first to use it, around 1960. But when the Japanese car industry adopted it, it made possible the introduction of a new car model in parallel with a successful old one. And then the baseball team did indeed become the wrong team for Detroit, and for mass-production industry as a whole. The design process then had to be restructured as a football team.

The football team does have the flexibility Detroit now needs. But it has far more stringent requirements than the baseball team. It needs a 'score' – such as the play the coach signals to the huddle on the field. The specifications with which the Japanese begin their design of a new car model – or a new consumer-electronics product – are far more stringent and detailed than anything Detroit is used to in respect to style, technology, performance, weight, price and so on. And they are far more closely adhered to.

In the traditional 'baseball' design team, every position – engineering, manufacturing, marketing – does its job its own way. The word of the coach is law. Players are beholden to this one boss alone for their orders, their rewards, their appraisals, their promotions.

The individual engineer on the Japanese design team is a member of his company's engineering department. But he is on the design team because the team's leader has asked for him – not because the chief engineer sent him there. He can consult engineering and get advice. But his orders come from the design-team chief, who also appraises his performance. If there are stars on these teams, they are featured only if the team leaders entrusts them with a 'solo'. Otherwise they subordinate themselves to the team.

Even more stringent are the requirements of the doubles team – the kind that GM's Saturn Division hoped to develop in its 'flexible-manufacturing' plant, and a flexible plant does indeed need such a team. The team must be quite small, with five to seven members at most. The members have to be trained together and must work together for quite some time before they fully function as a team. There must be one clear goal for the entire team yet considerable flexibility with respect to the individual member's work and performance. And in this kind of team only the team 'performs'; individual members 'contribute'.

All three of these kinds of teams are true teams. But they are so different – in the behaviour they require, in what they do best, and in what they cannot do – that they cannot be hybrids. One kind of team can play only one way. And it is very difficult to change from one kind of team to another.

Gradual change cannot work. There has to be a total break with the past, however traumatic it may be. This means that people cannot report to both their old boss and to the new coach, or team leader. And their reward, their compensation, their appraisals, and their promotions must be totally dependent on their performance in their new roles on their new teams. But this is so unpopular that the temptation to compromise is always great.

At Ford, for instance, the financial people have been left under the control of the financial staff and report to them rather than to the new design teams. GM's Saturn Division has tried to maintain the authority of the traditional bosses – the first-line supervisors and the shop stewards – rather than hand decision-making power over to the work teams. This, however, is like playing baseball and a tennis doubles match with the same people, on the same field, and at the same time. It can only result in frustration and non-performance. And a similar confusion seems to have prevailed at P&G.

Teams, in other words, are tools. As such, each team design has its own uses, its own characteristics, its own requirements, its own limitations. Teamwork is neither 'good' nor 'desirable' – it is a fact. Wherever people work together or play together they do so as a team. Which team to use for what purpose is a crucial, difficult, and risky decision that is even harder to unmake. Managements have yet to learn how to make it.

1992

9
The information revolution in retail

Wherever I went in Europe in 1993 – Britain, France, Germany, Italy, Belgium, Austria, Switzerland – I heard the same lament: European economic unification is at a standstill in manufacturing and finance. But in retailing, where no one expected it, economic unification is galloping across Europe.

Ten years ago, Aldi, a food discounter, was still purely German; now it is in seven European countries with some 3300 stores. Other food discounters – German, French, Danish – are expanding with similar speed across Europe, from Spain to Norway. Sweden-based Ikea now dominates Western Europe's furniture business and is opening stores in the former Russian satellites. Italy-based Benetton (women's fashions) and Britain-based The Body Shop (toiletries) are becoming market leaders in one European country after the other.

The internationalization of retailing is by no means confined to Europe. Japanese retailers, both food and non-food, are rapidly expanding in China. Ikea and Benetton have nearly as much market penetration in the United States as they have in Europe. America's Wal-Mart is set to cover Mexico with Sam's Clubs, while Toys 'R' Us is pushing aggressively into Japan.

Most of the earlier retailers who went multinational tried to improve slightly on what retailers in their 'host' countries were already doing quite well. This was true of Sears building traditional Sears stores in Latin America in the 1950s or German Tengelmann and Dutch Ahold buying established supermarket chains in the United States in the 1970s and early 1980s. But the new multinationals are revolutionaries, rejecting the very assumptions that most retailers still consider holy writ.

During the past half-century, 'shopping centre' has become almost synonymous with 'successful retailing'. And the bigger, the better. But the new retailers shun shopping centres. They build freestanding stores or go into 'minimalls' that contain only a handful of shops. 'The shopping centre,' a top executive of one of the fastest-growing European discount retailers said to me, 'submerges the personality of the individual store into the anonymity of the parking lot.' And the new retailers aim at a sharply profiled personality and a clear market niche.

The new retailers rarely speak of 're-engineering' – to them it sounds too much like manufacturing. But they constantly redesign operations. Indeed, many redefine the entire business.

Wal-Mart's success, for example, rests in large measure on its redefining retailing as the *moving* of merchandise, rather than its sale. This led to the integration of the entire process – all the way from the manufacturer's machine to the selling floor – on the basis of 'real-time' information about customer purchases. As a result, Wal-Mart could cut out three tiers of warehouses and a full third of the costs of traditional retailing. But Wal-Mart still carries a full assortment of goods, and that means thousands of items.

Aldi has re-engineered operations in much the same way. But it also has cut its assortment to the 600 items that, its research showed, are all a household buys regularly. Each item has been designed by Aldi, is made to its specifications, and is sold under its own brand name. As a result, it has doubled or tripled sales per square foot of shelf space – a retailer's basic capital and cost centre.

Spar, another German deep-discounter, is going further still. It will carry only the 200 items a household buys every week.

Another fast-growing European retailer will apply the same principle a different way. Its deep-discount 'clubs' will carry only the 200 items needed for special occasions – and absolutely nothing people buy regularly or often.

Ikea can sell at a low price because it realized that half the cost of finished furniture is final assembly. Provided that parts are meticulously engineered and instructions crystal-clear, even mechanical morons can do the final assembly at home.

Everybody in retailing talks of 'service' as the key to success, if not to survival. So do the new retailers. But they mean something different.

For traditional merchants, service means salespeople who personally take care of an individual customer. But the new retailers employ very few salespeople. Service to them means that customers do not need a salesperson, do not have to spend time trying to find one, do not have to ask, do not have to wait. It means that the customers know where goods are the moment they enter the store, in what colours and sizes, and at what price. It means providing *information*.

But service for the new retailers also means getting customers out of the store as fast as possible once they have made their purchases. A European superdiscounter is studying a technology that eliminates the checkout counter. When a customer has decided to buy an item, she puts her credit card into a slot on the shelf and does so as many times as she wants packages or bottles of a particular item. There is no shopping cart. Her purchasers are packed and waiting when she is ready to leave. All she has to do is to check the goods and sign a prepared credit-card slip.

Ray Kroc, the founder of McDonald's – the first, the most successful, and the most multinational of the new retailers – is reputed to have said 'A mother with two small children does not come to our store because the hamburgers are delicious. She comes because the restrooms are clean.' This is often considered pure whimsy. But it was meant to express a radically new concept of what 'shopping' means. What customers – at least a good many of them – want is not shopping that is enjoyable but shopping that is painless.

The retail store was invented in the late seventeenth century – first in Japan, shortly thereafter in Western Europe. From its very early days it has been based on three assumptions: shopping offers the customer – especially the housewife – perhaps the only way to have a little choice, to make a few decisions, to have a little say and a little power. Second, it offers the housewife the only break from the monotonous and dreary routine that the Germans call 'The Three K's': *Kinder, Kirche, Küche* (children, church, kitchen). And, finally, the retail store offers access to the world to people whose information otherwise consists of inane chats over the back fence or at the sewing circle.

The retail store has, of course, changed many times over the past 300 years of its existence. But traditional retailers – department stores, shopping centres, hardware stores, supermarkets, shoe stores – by and large still accept the traditional assumptions, if only subconsciously.

The new retailers, however, reject them. Their prototypical customer has a paying job, if not a career. She has many occasions to choose and to make decisions, and most of them more interesting than what to cook for dinner. And even if she never leaves the house, she has unlimited access to the outside world through the telephone and TV screen. Shopping is no longer a satisfaction to her, it is a chore.

The department store – the success story of the early twentieth century – is slipping everywhere. Shopping centres and supermarkets – the success stories of the past half-century – are, at best, holding their own. The new retailers are rapidly expanding. Still, there are signs that theirs, too, may be a fairly short-lived success.

Retailers now talk of 'shopping without a store' through interactive TV. They talk of 'virtual reality' in which the customer in her own living room 'walks' through a simulated shopping centre on her computer screen, 'tries on' a blouse, and orders by pushing a few buttons.

The technology for all this is available and is increasingly less expensive. And there are quite a few signs that a substantial number of customers are becoming receptive to it. There is the upsurge in catalogue sales in all developed countries – 'non-tech' shopping without a store. In the United States direct selling over cable TV has been successful for costume jewellery, for instance; in some affluent suburbs interactive TV also works for selling ready-to-heat 'gourmet' meals. In more and more beauty parlours women 'try on' and 'adjust' different haircuts on a TV monitor, deciding which style suits them best.

Shopping without a store is thus no longer science fiction. But it is still speculation (and a lot of hype). But even without any new technology, retailing has already changed. The changes are having profound effects on advertising, on consumer-goods manufacturers, and on the structure of the economy. Retailing – rather than manufacturing or finance – may be where the action is now.

1993

10
Be data literate; know what to know

Executives have become computer-literate. The younger ones, especially, know more about the way the computer works than they know about the mechanics of the car or the telephone. But not many executives are information-literate. They know how to *get* data. But most still have to learn how to *use* data.

Few executives yet know how to ask 'What information do I need to do my job? When do I need it? In what form? And from whom should I be getting it?' Still fewer ask 'What new tasks can I tackle now that I get all these data? Which old tasks should I abandon? Which tasks should I do differently?' Practically no one asks 'What information do I owe? To whom? When? In what form?'

A 'database', no matter how copious, is not information. It is information's ore. For raw material to become information, it must be organized for a task, directed towards specific performance, applied to a decision. Raw material cannot do that itself. Nor can information specialists. They can cajole their customers, the data users. They can advise, demonstrate, teach. But they can no more manage data for users than a personnel department can take over the management of the people who work with an executive.

Information specialists are tool makers. The tool users, whether executive or professional, have to decide what information to use, what to use it for, and how to use it. They have to make themselves information-literate. This is the first challenge facing information users now that executives have become computer-literate.

But the organization, too, has to become information-literate. It, too, needs to learn to ask 'What information do we need in this company? When do we need it? In what form? And where do we get it?' So far, such questions are being asked primarily by the military, and even there mainly for tactical, day-to-day decisions. In business, such questions have been asked only by a few multinationals, foremost among them the Anglo-Dutch Unilever, a few oil companies (such as Shell) and the large Japanese trading companies.

The moment these questions are asked, it becomes clear that the information a business most depends on is available, if at all, only in a primitive and disorganized form. For what a business needs the most for its decisions – especially its strategic ones – are data about what goes on outside of it. It is only outside the business where there are results, opportunities, and threats.

So far, the only data from the outside that have been integrated into most companies' information systems and into their decision-making processes are day-to-day market data: what existing customers buy, where they buy, how they buy. Few businesses have tried to get information about their non-customers, let alone have integrated such information into their databases. Yet no matter how powerful a company is in its industry or market, non-customers almost always outnumber customers.

American department stores had a very large customer base, perhaps 30 per cent of the middle-class market, and they had far more information about their own customers than any other industry. Yet their failure to pay attention to the 70 per cent who were not customers largely explains why they are today in a severe crisis. Their non-customers increasingly were the young, affluent, double-earner families who were the growth market of the 1980s.

The commercial banks, for all their copious statistics about their customers, similarly did not realize until very late that more and more of their potential customers had become non-customers. Many potential customers had turned to commercial paper to finance themselves instead of borrowing from the banks.

When it comes to non-market information – demographics; the behaviour and plans of actual and potential competitors; technology; economics; the shifts signalling foreign-exchange fluctuations to come and capital movements – there are either no data at all or only the broadest of generalizations. Few attempts have been made to think through the bearing that such information has on the company's decisions. How to obtain these data; how to test them; how to put them together with the existing information system to make them effective in a company's decision process – this is the second major challenge facing information users today.

It needs to be tackled soon. Companies today rely for their decisions either on inside data, such as costs, or on untested assumptions about the outside. In either case they are trying to fly on one wing.

Finally, the most difficult of the new challenges: we will have to bring together the two information systems that businesses now run side by side – computer-based data processing and the accounting system. At least we will have to make the two compatible.

People usually consider accounting to be 'financial'. But that is valid only for the past, going back 700 years, that deals with assets, liabilities, and cash flows; it is only a small part of modern accounting. Most of accounting deals with operations rather than with finance, and for operational accounting, money is simply a notation and the language in which to express non-monetary events. Indeed, accounting is being shaken to its very roots by reform movements aimed at moving it away from being financial and towards becoming operational.

There is the new 'transactional' accounting that attempts to relate operations to their expected results. There are attempts to change asset values from historical cost to estimates of expected future returns. Accounting has become the most intellectually challenging area in the field of management, and the most turbulent one. All these new accounting theories aim at turning accounting data into information for management decision making. In other words, they share the goals of computer-based data processing.

Today these two information systems operate in isolation from each other. They do not even compete, as a rule. In the business schools we keep the two apart with separate departments of accounting and of computer science, and separate degrees in each.

The practitioners have different backgrounds, different values, different career ladders. They work in different departments and for different bosses. There is a 'chief information officer' for computer-based data processing, usually with a background in computer technology. Accounting typically reports to a 'chief financial officer', often with a background in financing the company and in managing its money. Neither boss, in other words, is information-focused as a rule.

The two systems increasingly overlap. They also increasingly come up with what look like conflicting – or at least incompatible – data about the same event; for the two look at the same event quite differently. Until now this has created little confusion. Companies tended to pay attention to what their accountants told them and to disregard the data of their information system, at least for top-management decisions. But this is changing as computer-literate executives are moving into decision-making positions.

One development can be considered highly probable: managing money – what we now call the 'treasury function' – will be divorced from accounting (that is, from its information component) and will be set up, staffed, and run separately. How we will otherwise manage the two information systems is up for grabs. But that we will bring them together within the next ten years, or at least sort out which system does what, can be predicted.

Computer people still are concerned with greater speed and bigger memories. But the challenges increasingly will be not technical; rather they will be to convert data into information that is actually being used.

1992

11
We need to measure, not count

Quantification has been the rage in business and economics these past fifty years. Accountants have proliferated as fast as lawyers. Yet we do not have the measurements we need.

Neither our concepts nor our tools are adequate for the control of operations or for managerial control. And, so far, there are neither the concepts nor the tools for business control – that is, for economic decision making. In the past few years, however, we have become increasingly aware of the need for such measurements. And in one area, the operational control of manufacturing, the needed work has actually been done.

Traditional cost accounting in manufacturing – now seventy-five years old – does not record the cost of non-producing, such as the cost of faulty quality, or of a machine being out of order, or of needed parts not being on hand. Yet these unrecorded and uncontrolled costs in some plants run as high as the costs that traditional accounting does record. By contrast, a new method of cost accounting developed in the past ten years – called 'activity-based' accounting – records all costs. And it relates them, as traditional cost accounting cannot, to value added. Within the next ten years it should be in general use. And then we will have operational control in manufacturing.

But this control will be in manufacturing only. We still will not have cost control in services: schools, banks, government agencies, hospitals, hotels, retail stores, research labs, architectural firms, and so on. We know how much a service takes in, how much it spends and on what. But we do not know how the spending relates to the work the service organization does and to its results – one of the reasons the costs of hospitals, colleges, and the post office are out of control. Yet in every developed country, two-thirds to three-quarters of total output, employment, and costs are in services.

A few big banks are just beginning to implement cost accounting for services. Though results so far are quite spotty, we have found out a few important things. In contrast to cost accounting in manufacturing, cost accounting for services will have to be top-down, starting with the cost of the entire system over a given period. How the work is organized matters far more than it does in manufacturing. Quality and productivity are as important to cost in services as is quantity of output. In most services, teams are the cost centre rather than individuals or machines. And in services, the key is not 'cost' but 'cost-effectiveness'. But these are still only beginnings.

Even if we had the measurements we need for manufacturing and for services, we would still not have true operational control. We would still treat the individual organization – the manufacturer, the bank, the hospital – as *the* cost centre. But the costs that matter are the costs of the entire economic process in which the individual manufacturer, bank, or hospital is only a link in the chain. The costs of the entire process are what the ultimate customer (or the taxpayer) pays and what determines whether a product, a service, an industry, or an economy is competitive. A large part of these costs are 'interstitial' – incurred between, say, the parts supplier and manufacturer, or between the manufacturer and distributor, and recorded by neither.

The cost advantage of the Japanese derives in considerable measure from their control of these costs within a *keiretsu*, the 'family' of suppliers and distributors clustered around a manufacturer. Treating the *keiretsu* as one cost stream led, for instance, to 'just-in-time' parts delivery. It also enabled the *keiretsu* to shift operations to where they are most cost-effective.

Process-costing from the machine in the supplier's plant to the checkout counter in the store also underlies the phenomenal rise of Wal-Mart. It resulted in the elimination of a whole slew of warehouses and of reams of paperwork, which slashed costs by a third. But process-costing requires a redesign of relationships and changes in habits and behaviour. It requires compatible accounting systems where organizations now pride themselves on having their own unique method. It requires choosing what is cost-effective rather than what is cheapest. It requires joint decisions within the entire chain as to who does what.

Similarly drastic are the changes needed for effective managerial control. Balance sheets were designed to show what a business would be worth if liquidated today. Budgets are meant to ensure that money is spent only where authorized. What managements need, however, are balance sheets that relate the enterprise's current condition to its future wealth-producing capacity, both short term and long term. Managements need budgets that relate proposed expenditures to future results but also provide follow-up information that shows whether promised results have actually been achieved.

So far, we have only bits and pieces: the cash-flow forecast, for example, or the analysis of proposed capital investments. Now, however, for the first time, some large multinational companies – American and European – are beginning to put these pieces together into 'going-concern' balance sheets and 'going-concern' budgets.

But most needed – and totally lacking – are measurements to give us business control. Financial accounting, balance sheets, profit-and-loss statements, allocation of costs, and so forth are an X-ray of the enterprise's skeleton. But much as the diseases we most commonly die from – heart disease, cancer, Parkinson's – do not show up in a skeletal X-ray, a loss of market standing or a failure to innovate does not register in the accountant's figures until the damage has been done.

We need new measurements – call them a 'business audit' – to give us effective business control. We need measurements for a company or industry that are akin to the 'leading indicators' and 'lagging indicators' that economists have developed during the past half-century to predict the direction in which the economy is likely to move and for how long. For the first time, big institutional investors, including some of the very large pension funds, are working on such concepts and tools to measure the business performance of the companies in which they invest.

These are only beginnings. And so far, each of these areas is being worked on separately. Indeed, the people working in one field – for example, pension funds – may not even be aware of the work done in other areas.

It may take many years, decades perhaps, until we have the measurements we need in all these areas. But at least we know now that we need new measurements, and we know what they have to be. Slowly, and still gropingly, we are moving from counting to measuring.

1993

12
The information executives need today

Ever since the new data-processing tools first emerged thirty or forty years ago, businesspeople have both over- and under-rated the importance of information in the organization. We – and I include myself – over-rated the possibilities to the point where we talked of computer-generated 'business models' that could make decisions and might even be able to run much of the business. But we also grossly under-rated the new tools; we saw in them the means to do better what executives were already doing to manage their organizations.

Nobody talks of business models making economic decisions any more. The greatest contribution of our data-processing capacity so far has not even been to management. It has been to operations – in the form of such things as computer-assisted design or the marvellous software that architects now use to solve structural problems in the buildings they design.

Yet even as we both over- and under-estimated the new tools, we failed to realize that they would drastically change the *tasks* to be tackled. Concepts and tools, history teaches again and again, are mutually interdependent and interactive. One changes the other. That is now happening to the concept we call a business and to the tools we call information. The new tools enable us – indeed, may force us – to see our businesses differently, to see them as

- Generators of resources, that is, as the organizations that convert costs into yields
- Links in an economic chain, which managers need to understand as a whole in order to manage their costs
- Society's organs for the creation of wealth
- Both creators and creatures of a material environment, which is the area outside the organization in which opportunities and results lie but in which the threats to the success and survival of every business also originate.

This chapter deals with the tools executives require to generate the information they need. And it deals with the concepts underlying those tools. Some of the tools have been around for a long time, but rarely, if ever, have they been focused on the task of managing a business. Some have to be refashioned; in their present form they no longer work. For some tools that promise to be important in the future, we have so far only the briefest specifications. The tools themselves still have to be designed.

Even though we are just beginning to understand how to use information as a tool, we can outline with high probability the major parts of the information system executives need to manage their businesses. So, in turn, can we begin to understand the concepts likely to underlie the business – call it the redesigned corporation – that executives will have to manage tomorrow.

From cost accounting to yield control

We may have gone furthest in redesigning both business and information in the most traditional of our information systems: accounting. In fact, many businesses have already shifted from traditional cost accounting to activity-based costing. Activity-based costing represents both a different concept of the business process, especially for manufacturers, and different ways of measuring.

Traditional cost accounting, first developed by General Motors seventy years ago, postulates that total manufacturing cost is the sum of the costs of individual operations. Yet the cost that matters for competitiveness and profitability is the cost of the total process, and that is what the new *activity-based costing* records and makes manageable. Its basic premise is that manufacturing is an integrated process that starts when supplies, materials, and parts arrive at the plant's loading dock and continues even after the finished product reaches the end user. Service is still a cost of the product, and so is installation, even if the customer pays.

Traditional cost accounting measures what it costs to *do* something, for example to cut a screw thread. Activity-based costing also records the cost of *not doing*, such as the cost of machine downtime, the cost of waiting for a needed part or tool, the cost of inventory waiting to be shipped, and the cost of reworking or scrapping a defective part. The costs of not doing, which traditional cost accounting cannot and does not record, often equal and sometimes even exceed the costs of doing. Activity-based costing therefore gives not only much better cost control but, increasingly, it also gives *result control*.

Traditional cost accounting assumes that a certain operation – for example, heat treating – has to be done and that it has to be done where it is being done now. Activity-based costing asks 'Does it have to be done? If so, where is it best done?' Activity-based costing integrates what were once several activities – value analysis, process analysis, quality management, and costing – into one analysis.

Using that approach, activity-based costing can substantially lower manufacturing costs – in some instances by a full third or more. Its greatest impact, however, is likely to be in services. In most manufacturing companies, cost accounting is inadequate.

But service industries – banks, retail stores, hospitals, schools, newspapers, and radio and television stations – have practically no cost information at all.

Activity-based costing shows us why traditional cost accounting has not worked for service companies. It is not because the techniques are wrong. It is because traditional cost accounting makes the wrong assumptions. Service companies cannot start with the cost of individual operations, as manufacturing companies have done with traditional cost accounting. They must start with the assumption that there is only *one* cost: that of the total system. And it is a fixed cost over any given time period. The famous distinction between fixed and variable costs, on which traditional cost accounting is based, does not make much sense in services. Neither does another basic assumption of traditional cost accounting: that capital can be substituted for labour. In fact, in knowledge-based work especially, additional capital investment will likely require more rather than less labour. For example, a hospital that buys a new diagnostic tool may have to add four or five people to run it. Other knowledge-based organizations have had to learn the same lesson. But that all costs are fixed over a given time period and that resources cannot be substituted for one another, so that the *total* operation has to be costed – those are precisely the assumptions with which activity-based costing starts. By applying them to services, we are beginning for the first time to get cost information and yield control.

Banks, for instance, have been trying for several decades to apply conventional cost-accounting techniques to their business – that is, to figure the costs of individual operations and services – with almost negligible results. Now they are beginning to ask 'Which one *activity* is at the centre of costs and of results?' The answer: serving the customer. The cost per customer in any major area of banking is a fixed cost. Thus it is the *yield* per customer – both the volume of services a customer uses and the mix of those services – that determines costs and profitability.

Retail discounters, especially those in Western Europe, have known that for some time. They assume that once a unit of shelf space is installed, the cost is fixed and management consists of maximizing the yield thereon over a given time span. Their focus on yield control has enabled them to increase profitability despite their low prices and low margins.

Services are still only beginning to apply the new costing concepts. In some areas, such as research labs, where productivity is nearly impossible to measure, we may always have to rely on assessment and judgement rather than on measurement. But for most knowledge-based and service work, we should, within ten to fifteen years, have developed reliable tools to measure and manage costs and to relate those costs to results.

Thinking more clearly about costing in services should yield new insights into the costs of getting and keeping customers in businesses of all kinds. If GM, Ford, and Chrysler had had activity-based costing, for example, they would have realized early on the utter futility of their competitive blitzes of the past few years, which offered new-car buyers spectacular discounts and hefty cash rewards. Those promotions actually cost the Big Three carmakers enormous amounts of money and, worse, enormous numbers of potential customers. In fact, every one resulted in a nasty drop in market standing. But neither the costs of the special deals nor their negative yields appeared in the companies' conventional cost-accounting figures, so management never saw the damage. Conventional cost accounting shows only the costs of individual manufacturing operations in isolation, and those were not affected by the discounts and rebates in the marketplace. Also, conventional cost accounting does not show the impact of pricing decisions on such things as market share. Activity-based costing shows – or at least attempts to show – the impact of changes in the costs and yields of every activity on the results of the whole. Had it been used, it soon would have shown the damage done by the discount blitzes. In fact, because the Japanese already use a form of activity-based costing – though still a fairly primitive one – Toyota, Nissan, and Honda knew better than to compete with US carmakers through discount blitzes and thus maintained both their market share and their profits.

From legal fiction to economic reality

Knowing the cost of your operations, however, is not enough. To compete successfully in an increasingly competitive global market, a company has to know the costs of its entire economic chain and has to work with other members of the chain to manage costs and maximize yield. Companies are therefore beginning to shift from costing only what goes on inside their own organizations to costing the entire economic process, in which even the biggest company is just one link.

The legal entity, the company, is a reality for shareholders, for creditors, for employees, and for tax collectors. But *economically*, it is fiction. Thirty years ago the Coca-Cola Company was a franchisor. Independent bottlers manufactured the product. Now the company owns most of its bottling operations in the United States. But Coke drinkers – even those few who know that fact – could not care less. What matters in the marketplace is the economic reality, the costs of the entire process, regardless of who owns what.

Again and again in business history, an unknown company has come from nowhere and in a few short years overtaken the established leaders without apparently even breathing hard. The explanation always given is superior strategy, superior technology, superior marketing, or lean manufacturing. But in every single case, the newcomer also enjoys a tremendous cost advantage, usually about 30 per cent. The reason is always the same: the new company knows and manages the costs of the entire economic chain rather than its costs alone.

Toyota is perhaps the best-publicized example of a company that knows and manages the costs of its suppliers and distributors; they are all, of course, members of its *keiretsu*. Through that network, Toyota manages the total cost of making, distributing, and servicing its cars as one cost stream, putting work where it costs the least and yields the most.

Managing the economic cost stream is not a Japanese invention, however, but an American one. It began with the man who designed and built General Motors, William Durant. In about 1908, Durant began to buy small, successful car companies – Buick, Oldsmobile, Cadillac, Chevrolet – and merged them into his new General Motors Corporation. In 1916, he set up a separate subsidiary called United Motors to buy small, successful parts companies. His first acquisitions included Delco, which held Charles Kettering's patents to the automotive self-starter.

Durant ultimately bought about twenty supplier companies; his last acquisition – in 1919, the year before he was ousted as GM's CEO – was Fisher Body. Durant deliberately brought the parts and accessories makers into the design process of a new car model right from the start. Doing so allowed him to manage the total costs of the finished car as one cost stream. In fact, Durant invented the *keiretsu*.

However, between 1950 and 1960, Durant's *keiretsu* became an albatross around the company's neck. Unionization imposed higher labour costs on GM's parts divisions than on their independent competitors. The outside customers, the independent car companies such as Packard and Studebaker, which had bought 50 per cent of the output of GM's parts divisions, disappeared one by one. And GM's control over both the costs and quality of its main suppliers disappeared with them. But for forty years or more, GM's systems costing gave it an unbeatable advantage over even the most efficient of its competitors, which for most of that time was Studebaker.

Sears, Roebuck and Company was the first to copy Durant's system. In the 1920s it established long-term contracts with its suppliers and bought minority interests in them. Sears was then able to consult with suppliers as it designed the product and to understand and manage the entire cost stream. That gave the company an unbeatable cost advantage for decades.

In the early 1930s, London-based Marks & Spencer copied Sears, with the same result. Twenty years later, the Japanese, led by Toyota, studied and copied both Sears and Marks & Spencer. Then in the 1980s, Wal-Mart Stores adapted the approach by allowing suppliers to stock products directly on store shelves, thereby eliminating warehouse inventories and with them nearly one-third of the cost of traditional retailing.

But those companies are still rare exceptions. Although economists have known the importance of costing the entire economic chain since Alfred Marshall wrote about it in the late 1890s, most businesspeople still consider it theoretical abstraction. Increasingly, however, managing the economic cost chain will become a necessity. Indeed, executives need to organize and manage not only the cost chain but also everything else – especially corporate strategy and product planning – as one economic whole, regardless of the legal boundaries of individual companies.

A powerful force driving companies toward economic-chain costing will be the shift from cost-led pricing to price-led costing. Traditionally, Western companies have started with costs, put a desired profit margin on top, and arrived at a price. They practised cost-led pricing. Sears and Marks & Spencer long ago switched to price-led costing, in which the price the customer is willing to pay determines allowable costs, beginning with the design stage. Until recently, those companies were the exceptions. Now price-led costing is becoming the rule. The Japanese first adopted it for their exports. Now Wal-Mart and all the discounters in the United States, Japan, and Europe are practising price-led costing. It underlies Chrysler's success with its recent models and the success of GM's Saturn. Companies can practise price-led costing, however, only if they know and manage the *entire* cost of the economic chain.

The same ideas apply to outsourcing, alliances, and joint ventures – indeed, to any business structure that is built on partnership rather than control. And such entities, rather than the traditional model of a parent company with wholly owned subsidiaries, are increasingly becoming the models for growth, especially in the global economy.

Still, it will be painful for most businesses to switch to economic-chain costing. Doing so requires uniform or at least compatible accounting systems at companies along the entire chain. Yet each one does its accounting in its own way, and each is convinced that its system is the only possible one. Moreover, economic-chain costing requires information sharing across companies, yet even within the same company, people tend to resist information sharing. Despite those challenges, companies can find ways to practise economic-chain costing now, as Procter & Gamble is demonstrating. Using the way Wal-Mart develops close relationships with suppliers as a model, P&G is initiating information sharing and economic-chain management with the 300 large retailers that distribute the bulk of its products worldwide.

Whatever the obstacles, economic-chain costing is going to be done. Otherwise, even the most efficient company will suffer from an increasing cost disadvantage.

Information for wealth creation

Enterprises are paid to create wealth, not to control costs. But that obvious fact is not reflected in traditional measurements. First-year accounting students are taught that the balance sheet portrays the liquidation value of the enterprise and provides creditors with worst-case information. But enterprises are not normally run to be liquidated. They have to be managed as going concerns, that is, for *wealth creation*. To do that requires information that enables executives to make informed judgements. It requires four sets of diagnostic tools: foundation information, productivity information, competence information, and information about the allocation of scarce resources. Together, they constitute the executive's tool kit for managing the current business.

Foundation information

The oldest and most widely used set of diagnostic management tools are cash-flow and liquidity projections and such standard measurements as the ratio between dealers' inventories and sales of new cars; the earnings coverage for the interest payments on a bond issue; and the ratios between receivables outstanding more than six months, total receivables, and sales. Those may be likened to the measurements a doctor takes at a routine physical: weight, pulse, temperature, blood pressure, and urine analysis. If those readings are normal, they do not tell us much. If they are abnormal, they indicate a problem that needs to be identified and treated. Those measurements might be called foundation information.

Productivity information

The second set of tools for business diagnosis deals with the productivity of key resources. The oldest of them – of Second World War vintage – measures the productivity of manual labour. Now we are slowly developing measurements, though still quite primitive ones, for the productivity of knowledge-based and service work. However, measuring only the productivity of workers, whether blue or white collar, no longer gives us adequate information about productivity. We need data on *total-factor productivity*.

That explains the popularity of economic value-added analysis. EVA is based on something we have known for a long time: what we generally call profits, the money left to service equity, is usually not profit at all. Until a business returns a profit that is greater than its cost of capital, it operates at a loss. Never mind that it pays taxes as if it had a genuine profit. The enterprise still returns less to the economy than it devours in resources. It does not cover its full costs unless the reported profit exceeds the cost of capital. Until then, it does not create wealth; it destroys it. By that measurement, incidentally, few US businesses have been profitable since the Second World War.

By measuring the value added over *all* costs, including the cost of capital, EVA measures, in effect, the productivity of *all* factors of production. It does not, by itself, tell us why a certain product or a certain service does not add value or what to do about it. But it shows us what we need to find out and whether we need to take remedial action. EVA should also be used to find out what works. It does show which product, service, operation, or activity has unusually high productivity and adds unusually high value. Then we should ask ourselves, what can we learn from those successes?*

The most recent of the tools used to obtain productivity information is benchmarking – comparing one's performance with the best performance in the industry or, better yet, with the best anywhere in business. Benchmarking assumes correctly that what one organization does, any other organization can do as well. And it assumes, also correctly, that being at least as good as the leader is a prerequisite to being competitive. Together, EVA and benchmarking provide the diagnostic tools to measure total-factor productivity and to manage it.

Competence information

A third set of tools deals with competences. Ever since C. K. Prahalad and Gary Hamel's pathbreaking article 'The core competence of the corporation' (*Harvard Business Review*, May-June 1990), we have known that leadership rests on being able to do something others cannot do at all or find difficult to do

---

*I discussed EVA at considerable length in my 1964 book *Managing for Results*, but the last generation of classical economists, Alfred Marshall in England and Eugen Böhm-Bawerk in Austria, were already discussing it in the late 1890s.

even poorly. It rests on core competencies that meld market or customer value with a special ability of the producer or supplier.

Some examples: the ability of the Japanese to miniaturize electronic components, which is based on their 300-year-old artistic tradition of putting landscape paintings on a tiny lacquered box, called an *inro*, and of carving a whole zoo of animals on the even tinier button, called a *netsuke*, that holds the box on the wearer's belt; or the almost unique ability GM has had for eighty years to make successful acquisitions; or Marks & Spencer's also unique ability to design packaged and ready-to-eat gourmet meals for middle-class purses. But how does one identify both the core competencies one has already and those the business needs in order to take and maintain a leadership position? How does one find out whether one's core competence is improving or weakening? Or whether it is still the right core competence and what changes it might need?

So far, the discussion of core competencies has been largely anecdotal. But a number of highly specialized mid-size companies – a Swedish pharmaceuticals producer and a US producer of speciality tools, to name two – are developing the methodology to measure and manage core competencies. The first step is to keep careful track of one's own and one's competitors' performances, looking especially for unexpected successes and for unexpected poor performance in areas where one should have done well. The successes demonstrate what the market values and will pay for. They indicate where the business enjoys a leadership advantage. The non-successes should be viewed as the first indication either that the market is changing or that the company's competencies are weakening.

That analysis allows for the early recognition of opportunities. For example, by carefully tracking an unexpected success, a US tool maker found that small Japanese machine shops were buying its high-tech, high-priced tools, even though it had not designed the tools with them in mind or even called on them. That allowed the company to recognize a new core competence:

the Japanese were attracted to its products because they were easy to maintain and repair despite their technical complexity. When that insight was applied to designing products, the company gained leadership in the small-plant and machine-shop markets in the United States and Western Europe, huge markets where it had done practically no business before.

Core competencies are different for every organization; they are, so to speak, part of an organization's personality. But every organization – not just businesses – needs one core competence: *innovation*. And every organization needs a way to record and appraise its *innovative performance*. In organizations already doing that – among them several top-flight pharmaceuticals manufacturers – the starting point is not the company's own performance. It is a careful record of the innovations in the entire field during a given period. Which of them were truly successful? How many of them were ours? Is our performance commensurate with our objectives? With the direction of the market? With our market standing? With our research spending? Are our successful innovations in the areas of greatest growth and opportunity? How many of the truly important innovation opportunities did we miss? Why? Because we did not see them? Or because we saw them but dismissed them? Or because we botched them? And how well do we convert an innovation into a commercial product? A good deal of that, admittedly, is assessment rather than measurement. It raises rather than answers questions, but it raises the right questions.

Resource-allocation information

The last area in which diagnostic information is needed to manage the current business for wealth creation is the allocation of scarce resources: capital and performing people. Those two convert into action whatever information management has about its business. They determine whether the enterprise will do well or poorly.

GM developed the first systematic capital-appropriations process about seventy years ago. Today practically every business has a capital-appropriations process, but few use it correctly. Companies typically measure their proposed capital appropriations by only one or two of the following yardsticks: return on investment, payback period, cash flow, or discounted present value. But we have known for a long time – since the early 1930s – that none of those is *the* right method. To understand a proposed investment, a company needs to look at *all four*. Sixty years ago that would have required endless number-crunching. Now a laptop computer can provide the information within a few minutes. We also have known for sixty years that managers should never look at just one proposed capital appropriation in isolation but should instead choose the projects that show the best ratio between opportunity and risks. That requires a capital-appropriations *budget* to display the choices – again, something far too many businesses do not do. Most serious, however, is that most capital-appropriations processes do not even ask for two vital pieces of information:

- What will happen if the proposed investment fails to produce as promised as do three out of every five? Would it seriously hurt the company, or would it be just a flea bite?
- If the investment is successful – and especially if it is more successful than we expect – what will it commit us to?

No one at GM seemed to have asked what Saturn's success would commit the company to. As a result, the company may end up killing its own success because of its inability to finance it.

In addition, a capital-appropriations request requires specific deadlines: when should we expect what results? Then the results – successes, near-successes, near-failures, and failures – need to be reported and analysed. There is no better way to improve an organization's performance than to measure the results of capital appropriations against the promises and expectations that led to their authorization. How much better off the United States would be today had such feedback on government programmes been standard practice for the past fifty years.

Capital, however, is only one key resource of the organization, and it is by no means the scarcest one. The scarcest resources in any organization are performing people. Since the Second World War, the US military – and so far no one else – has learned to test its placement decisions. It now thinks through what it expects of senior officers before it puts them into key commands. It then appraises their performance against those expectations. And it constantly appraises its own process for selecting senior commanders against the successes and failures of its appointments. In business, by contrast, placement with specific expectations as to what the appointee should achieve and systematic appraisal of the outcome are virtually unknown. In the effort to create wealth, managers need to allocate human resources as purposefully and as thoughtfully as they do capital. And the outcomes of those decisions ought to be recorded and studied as carefully.

Where the results are

Those four kinds of information tell us only about the current business. They inform and direct *tactics*. For *strategy*, we need organized information about the environment. Strategy has to be based on information about markets, customers, and non-customers; about technology in one's own industry and others; about worldwide finance; and about the changing world economy. For that is where the results are. Inside an organization there are only cost centres. The only profit centre is a customer whose cheque has not bounced.

Major changes also start outside an organization. A retailer may know a great deal about the people who shop at its stores. But no matter how successful it is, no retailer ever has more than a small fraction of the market as its customers; the great majority are non-customers. It is always with non-customers that basic changes begin and become significant.

At least half the important new technologies that have transformed an industry in the past fifty years came from outside the industry itself. Commercial paper, which has revolutionized finance in the United States, did not originate with the banks. Molecular biology and genetic engineering were not developed by the pharmaceuticals industry. Though the great majority of businesses will continue to operate only locally or regionally, they all face, at least potentially, global competition from places they have never even heard of before.

Not all the needed information about the outside is available, to be sure. There is no information – not even unreliable information – on economic conditions in most of China, for instance, or on legal conditions in most of the successor states to the Soviet Empire. But even where information is readily available, many businesses are oblivious to it. Many US companies went into Europe in the 1960s without even asking about labour legislation. European companies have been just as blind and ill-informed in their ventures into the United States. A major cause of the Japanese real estate investment debacle in California during the 1990s was the failure to find out elementary facts about zoning and taxes.

A serious cause of business failure is the common assumption that conditions – taxes, social legislation, market preferences, distribution channels, intellectual property rights, and many others – *must* be what we think they are or at least what we think they *should* be. An adequate information system has to include information that makes executives question that assumption. It must lead them to ask the right questions, not just feed them the information they expect. That presupposes first that executives know what information they need. It demands further that they obtain that information on a regular basis. It finally requires that they systematically integrate the information into their decision making.

A few multinationals – Unilever, Coca-Cola, Nestlé, the Japanese trading companies, and a few big construction companies – have been working hard on building systems to gather and organize outside information. But in general, the majority of enterprises have yet to start the job.

Even big companies, in large part, will have to hire outsiders to help them. To think through what the business needs requires somebody who knows and understands the highly specialized information field. There is far too much information for any but specialists to find their way around. The sources are totally diverse. Companies can generate some of the information themselves, such as information about customers and non-customers or about the technology in one's own field. But most of what enterprises need to know about the environment is obtainable only from outside sources – from all kinds of data banks and data services, from journals in many languages, from trade associations, from government publications, from World Bank reports and scientific papers, and from specialized studies.

Another reason why there is need for outside help is that the information has to be organized so as to question and challenge a company's strategy. To supply data is not enough. The data have to be integrated with strategy, they have to test a company's assumptions, and they must challenge a company's current outlook. One way to do that may be a new kind of software, information tailored to a specific group – say, to hospitals or to casualty insurance companies. The Lexis database supplies such information to lawyers, but it only gives answers; it does not ask questions. What we need are services that make specific suggestions about how to use the information, ask specific questions regarding the user's business and practices, and perhaps provide interactive consultation. Or we might 'outsource' the outside-information system. Perhaps the most popular provider of the outside-information system, especially for smaller enterprises, will be the 'inside outsider', the independent consultant.

Whichever way we satisfy it, the need for information on the environment where the major threats and opportunities are likely to arise will become increasingly urgent.

It may be argued that few of those information needs are new, and that is largely true. Conceptually, many of the new measurements have been discussed for many years and in many places. What is new is the technical data-processing ability. It enables us to do quickly and cheaply what, only a few short years ago, would have been laborious and very expensive. Seventy years ago, the time-and-motion study made traditional cost accounting possible. Computers have now made activity-based cost accounting possible; without them, it would be practically impossible.

But that argument misses the point. What is important is not the tools. It is the concepts behind them. They convert what were always seen as discrete techniques to be used in isolation and for separate purposes into one integrated information system. That system then makes possible business diagnosis, business strategy, and business decisions. That is a new and radically different view of the meaning and purpose of information: as a measurement on which to base future action rather than as a post-mortem and a record of what has already happened.

The command-and-control organization that first emerged in the 1870s might be compared to an organism held together by its shell. The corporation that is now emerging is being designed around a skeleton: *information*, both the corporation's new integrating system and its articulation.

Our traditional mindset – even if we use sophisticated mathematical techniques and impenetrable sociological jargon – has always somehow perceived business as buying cheap and selling dear. The new approach defines a business as the organization that adds value and creates wealth.

1995

Part Three

The Economy

13
Trade lessons from the world economy

There are opinions galore about international trade policy, especially for the United States. All are argued with passion but rarely with much evidence. The world economy has actually been growing faster for forty years than at any time since the eighteenth-century 'Commercial Revolution', which created both the first modern economies and the discipline of economics. And though all developed economics have been stagnant and in recession these last few years, the world economy is still expanding at a good clip. But no one asks, *What are the facts? What do they teach us? What are the lessons, above all, for domestic economic policy?*

There are important lessons in four areas: the structure of the world economy; the changed meaning of trade and investment; the relationship between world economy and domestic economy; and trade policy. In each of these areas the lessons are quite different from what practically everybody believes and asserts, whether 'free trader', 'managed trader', or 'protectionist'.

I

Twenty years ago no one talked of the 'world economy'. The term then was 'international trade'. The change in term – and everybody now talks of the world economy – bespeaks a profound change in economic reality. Twenty or thirty years ago the economy outside the borders of a nation – and especially outside the borders of a middle-sized or large nation – could still be seen as different, as separate, as something that could be safely ignored in dealing with the domestic economy and in domestic economic policy. That, as the evidence makes unambiguously clear, is sheer delusion today – but it is still very much the basic position of economists, of politicians, and of the public at large, especially in the United States.

The 'international economy' traditionally had two parts: foreign trade and foreign investment. The world economy also has two parts – but they are different from those of international trade. The first part consists of flows of money and information; the second, trade and investment, rapidly merging into one transaction, and actually only different dimensions of the same phenomenon, namely, the new integrating force of the world economy, cross-border alliances. While both of these segments are growing fast, money and information flows are growing the fastest. They deserve to be looked at first.

The centre of world money flows, the London Interbank market, handles more money in one day than would be needed in many months – perhaps an entire year – to finance the 'real economy' of international trade and international investment. Similarly, the trades during one day on the main currency markets – London, New York, Zurich, and Tokyo – exceed by several orders of magnitude what would be needed to finance the international transactions of the real economy.

The information flows – conferences, meetings, and seminars; telecommunications, whether by telephone, teleconference, fax, electronic mail; computer transmissions; software; magazines and books; films and videos; and many other communications by new (and largely electronic) technologies – may already exceed money flows in the fees, royalties, and profits they generate. They are also probably growing faster than any category of transactions ever grew before in economic history.

Transnational money flows can be seen as the successor to what bankers call 'portfolio investments', that is, investments made for the sake of (usually short-term) financial income such as dividends or interest. But today's money flows are not only vastly larger than portfolio investments ever were, they are almost totally autonomous and uncontrollable by any national agency or in large measure by any national policy. Above all, their economic impact is different. The money flows of traditional portfolio investment were the *stabilizers* of the international economy. They flowed from countries of low short-term returns – low because of low interest rates, overvalued stock prices, or overvalued currency – into countries of higher short-term returns, thus restoring equilibrium. And they *reacted* to a country's financial policy or economic condition. Today's world money flows have become the great *destabilizers*. They force a country into 'crash' programmes – into raising interest rates to astronomical levels, for instance, which throttle business activity, or into devaluing a currency overnight way below its trade parity or its purchasing-power parity – thus generating inflationary pressures. And today's money flows are not driven, by and large, by the expectation of greater income but by the expectation of immediate speculative profits. They are a pathological phenomenon bespeaking the fact that neither fixed foreign-exchange rates nor flexible foreign-exchange rates really work, though they are the only two known systems so far. Because money flows are a symptom, it is futile for governments to try to restrict them, for instance by taxing money-flow profits; the trading just moves elsewhere. They are a fever, to be sure; but they are not the disease. All that can be done – and it needs to be included in the specifications for an effective trade policy – is to build resistance into the economy against the impacts of money flows.

In contrast to money flows, the economic impacts of information flows are benign. Few things, in fact, so stimulate economic growth as rapid development of information, whether telecommunications, computer data, computer networks, or access (however distorted) to the outside world provided by the entertainment media. In the United States, information flows and the goods needed to carry them have become the largest single source of foreign-currency income. But just as we do not view the medieval cathedral as an economic phenomenon – although it was for several centuries Europe's biggest economic activity next to farming, and its biggest non-military employer – information flows are primarily a *social* phenomenon. Their impacts are primarily cultural and social. Economic factors, such as high costs, are a restraint on information flows rather than motivators. Yet information flows are an increasingly dominant factor in the world economy.

The first lesson of the world economy is thus that the two most significant phenomena – money flows and information flows – do not fit into any theory or policy we have. They are not even 'transnational'; they are outside altogether, and 'nonnational'.

II

For practically everybody, *international* trade means merchandise trade, that is, imports and exports of manufactured goods, farm products, and raw materials such as petroleum, iron ore, copper, and timber. And *merchandise* trade is what the newspaper reports on every month. But increasingly, international trade is *services* trade – little reported and largely unnoticed. But even merchandise trade is no longer what practically everybody, including economists and policy makers, assumes it to be. Increasingly it is not a 'transaction' that is a sale or a purchase of individual goods. Increasingly it is a 'relationship' – either structural trade or institutional trade – in which the individual transaction is only a 'shipment' and an accounting entry. And both services trade and relationship trade behave differently from transactional merchandise trade.

As everybody knows, the United States has a large and intractable trade deficit. Actually, though, US trade is more or less in balance and may yield a small surplus. The trade deficit that is daily bewailed by US newspapers, our business executives and economists, our government officials, and our politicians is a deficit in *merchandise* trade (caused primarily by (1) an appalling waste of petroleum in the United States (2) the steady decline in both the volume of and the world market prices for US farm exports). The United States has, however, a very large surplus in *services* trade. It is being generated by financial services and retailing; by higher education and Hollywood; by tourism; by hospital companies; by royalties on books, software, and videos; by consulting firms; by fees and royalties on technology; and by a host of other businesses and professions. According to the official figures – published only every three months and then in a little-read government bulletin – the US services surplus amounts to two-thirds of the merchandise trade deficit. But as is acknowledged even by the government statisticians who collect the figures, US services exports are grossly underreported. They may be some 50 per cent higher than the official statistics tell us – and services exports are still growing fast.

The United States has the largest single share of the world's services trade followed by the United Kingdom, with Japan at the bottom of the list among developed countries. But in every developed country, services trade is growing as fast as merchandise trade, and probably a good deal faster. Within ten years it may equal, if not exceed, merchandise trade, at least for highly advanced countries.

Only one major component of services trade is at all susceptible to the 'factors' that govern international trade according to trade theory and trade policy: tourism. It responds immediately to foreign-exchange fluctuations and, sluggishly, to changes in labour costs. The rest – some two-thirds or more – is impervious to such changes. Most services trade involves exporting and importing *knowledge*.

More and more merchandise trade is, however, also becoming impervious to short-term (and even to long-term) changes in the traditional *economic* factors. In *structural* trade the decision regarding where manufacturing will be done is being made when the product is first designed. For a new car model, such major parts as engines, transmissions, electronics, and body panels will be produced by plants – some owned by the car manufacturer, many more by suppliers – in a dozen different countries, such as the United States, Mexico, Canada, Belgium, Japan, and Germany. Final assembly will also be done in plants located in four or five countries. And until the model is redesigned in ten years, the plants and the countries specified in the original design are 'locked in'. There will be change only in the event of a major catastrophe, such as war or a fire which destroys a plant.

The big Irish plant of the Swiss pharmaceuticals company equally does not 'sell'. It ships chemical intermediates to the company's finished-product plants in nineteen countries on both sides of the Atlantic, charging a 'transfer price' that is pure accounting convention and has as much to do with taxes as with production costs. Markets and knowledge are very important in structural-trade decisions; labour costs, capital costs, and foreign-exchange rates are restraints rather than determinants.

But there is also 'institutional' trade. When a manufacturer builds a new plant or when a discounter opens a store, it will, nine times out of ten, use for it the machines, tools, equipment, and supplies it has been working with in its existing facilities, is familiar with, and knows it can rely on. It will buy them from the firms that supply its existing plants or stores. This holds true whether the new plant or the new store are in the firm's home country or abroad. It holds true whether the company is an American one building a plant in Spain, a German one building a superstore in the United States, or a Japanese one acquiring and re-equipping a plant in Shanghai. And as in structural trade the traditional 'factors of production' are largely irrelevant to it.

But that institutional trade, and structural trade as well, do not behave according to the accepted rules is far less important than that neither is 'foreign trade' – except legally – even when it is trade across national boundary lines. To the individual business, it makes absolutely no difference whether the stuff comes from its own home country or whether it comes from a plant or supplier in what is legally a foreign country. This is increasingly as true for shipments from outside suppliers as for intracompany shipments. For the individual business – the car manufacturer, the pharmaceuticals company, the discount retailer – these are transactions within its own 'system'.

Both structural and institutional trade have grown explosively these last thirty years as business after business has gone multinational. We have no reliable figures. Estimates range from one-third of total US merchandise trade (probably an understatement) to two-thirds (almost certainly too high). Whenever I have been able to get the figures, I have found structural and institutional trade to be 40–50 per cent of a company's total export and import volume – for big companies and mid-sized ones alike. Traditional transactional merchandise trade is still larger, I am sure. But the relationship trade is growing faster. Traditional transactional merchandise trade may be no more than a third of a developed country's trade by now. Two-thirds are either services trade or relationship-based merchandise trade – both behaving quite differently.

Similarly, 'investment' – the other area in the traditional model of the international economy – is now becoming something markedly different. Portfolio investment, as has been discussed, has mutated into money flows, which aren't investment at all. But now 'direct investment' – investment abroad to start a new business or to acquire an existing one – is also beginning to change, and fast. For a long time in the post-war years, direct investment seemed impervious to change. The multinational of 1970 – the carrier of direct investment – looked little different from the multinational of 1913 (and the multinationals of 1913 controlled as much of the world's manufacturing as multinationals now control and far more of its banking and insurance). Traditional direct investment is still growing; in fact, since the mid-1980s, direct investment in the United States – by Europeans, Japanese, Canadians, Mexicans – has grown explosively. But the action is rapidly shifting to 'alliances': joint ventures, partnerships, knowledge agreements, 'outsourcing'. And in alliances, investment is secondary, if there is any at all.

One example is the recent alliance between American-based Intel, the leading-edge microchip designer, and Sharp, a major Japanese electronics manufacturer. Intel will share with the Japanese the design of a very advanced microchip; the Japanese in turn will make the chip and share the product with Intel. One contributes technical competence, the other one production competence.

There are alliances between scores of university research labs and businesses – pharmaceuticals firms, electronics firms, engineering firms, computer firms, and food processors. There are alliances in which organizations outsource support activities: a great many American hospitals now let outside independent suppliers do their maintenance, housekeeping, billing, collections, and data processing and increasingly let them run the labs, physical therapy, and the diagnostic centres. And so, increasingly, do hospitals in the United Kingdom and in Japan. Computer makers now outsource the data processing for their own business to contractors like Electronic Data Systems, the company Ross Perot built and sold to General Motors. The same computer manufacturers are everywhere entering alliances with small, independent software designers. Commercial banks are entering alliances with producers and managers of mutual funds. And small and medium-sized colleges are entering alliances with one another to do the paperwork jointly.

In some of these alliances there is substantial capital investment, as was the case in the 1960s and 1970s joint ventures between Japanese and American companies entered into to produce in Japan and for the Japanese market American-designed goods. But even then the basis of the alliance was not capital but complementary knowledge: technical and manufacturing knowledge supplied by the Americans, marketing knowledge and management supplied by the Japanese. Increasingly, whatever investment there is is symbolical rather than substantial – a small minority share in each other's business to signify the bond between the partners. In more and more alliances there is no financial relationship at all between the partners – there is apparently none between Intel and Sharp. And there has never been any investment relationship in the oldest and most successful alliances around, the ones forged by the English retailer Marks & Spencer in the early 1930s with a host of manufacturers of textiles, clothing, and footwear (and later with manufacturers of speciality foods as well) – alliances that the Japanese copied after 1950 for their *keiretsu*. Marks & Spencer and the manufacturer in these alliances jointly develop the products, with Marks & Spencer committed to buying them from only that one manufacturer.

How many such alliances exist now nobody knows. In some cases they are not even embodied in a contract but are quite informal. Increasingly, however, alliances are becoming the dominant form of economic integration in the world economy. Some major companies – Toshiba, the Japanese electronics giant, or Corning Glass, the world's leading maker of high-engineered glass – may each have more than a hundred alliances all over the world. Integration in the European Union is proceeding far more through alliances than through mergers and acquisitions, especially among the middle-sized companies that dominate most European economies. As in structural and institutional trade, businesses make little distinction between domestic and foreign partners in their alliances. An alliance creates a systems relationship, a family relationship in which it does not matter that one partner speaks Japanese, another English, and the third German or Finnish. And while alliances increasingly generate both trade and investment, they are based on neither. They pool knowledge.

III

Economic theory and economic policy know that *developing* economies are greatly affected by their relationship to the world economy. Economists talk of 'export-led development' and 'foreign-investment-led development'. But for developed countries, and especially for middle-sized and large developed countries, economic theory and economic policy postulate that the domestic economy alone matters. The autonomy of the domestic economy and its position as the *locus* of policy making is an axiom for economists, policy makers, and the public at large.

But as the preceding discussion should have made clear, the distinction between domestic and international economy has ceased to be economic reality – however much it remains political, social, cultural, and psychological reality. *The one unambiguous lesson of the last forty years is that increased participation in the world economy has become the key to domestic economic growth and prosperity.* There is a one-to-one correlation between a country's domestic economic performance in the forty years since 1950 and its participation in the world economy. The two major countries that have grown the fastest in the world economy, Japan and South Korea, are also the two countries in which the domestic economy has grown the fastest. The same correlation applies to the two European countries that have done best in the world economy in the last forty years: West Germany and Sweden. The countries that have retreated in the world economy – notably the United Kingdom – are also the countries that have done consistently worst domestically. In the two major countries that have maintained their participation rate in the world economy within a fairly narrow range – the United States and France – the domestic economy has put in an average performance, neither doing exceptionally well nor suffering persistent malaise and crisis like the United Kingdom.

The same correlation holds true for major segments within a developed economy. In the United States, for instance, services have tremendously increased their world-economy participation in the last fifteen years – finance is one example, higher education and information are others. These are also the segments that have grown the most in the domestic economy. In manufacturing, the industries that have significantly increased their world-market participation – through exports, through investments abroad, through alliances – for example telecommunications, pharmaceuticals, software, films, are also the industries that have grown the most in the domestic market. American agriculture, which has consistently shrunk in terms of world-economy participation, has been in continual depression and crisis, masked only by ever-growing subsidies.

Conversely, there is no correlation at all between domestic economic performance and policies to stimulate the *domestic* economy. It is easy, the record shows, for a government to do harm to its domestic economy. All it has to do is to drive up the inflation rate – examples are the damage Lyndon Johnson's inflationary policies did to the US economy (which has not yet fully recovered twenty-five years later) and the damage which consistently pro-inflationary policies have done to the economy of Italy. But there is not the slightest evidence that any government policy to *stimulate* the economy has impact, whether that policy be Keynesian, monetarist, supply-side or neoclassic. Contrary to what economists confidently promised forty years ago, business cycles have not been abolished. They still operate pretty much the way they have been operating for the past 150 years. No country has so far been able to escape them. But whenever in a business downturn a government policy to stimulate the economy actually coincided with cyclical recovery (as has happened only very, very rarely), it was by pure coincidence. No one policy shows more such coincidences than any other. And no policy that worked in a given country in recession A showed any results whatever when tried again in the same country in recession B or recession C. The evidence not only suggests that government policies to stimulate the economy short term are ineffectual, it suggests something far more surprising: they are largely irrelevant. Government, the evidence shows clearly, cannot control the 'economic weather'.

But the one-to-one correlation between domestic economy and participation in the world economy – over long periods and over a wide range of different phenomena, including widely different economies with different structures, different fiscal and tax policies, and even different forms of participation in the world economy – shows convincingly that participation in the world economy has become the controlling factor in the domestic economy of a developed country. Two examples: that the US economy in 1990–92 did not slip into a deep recession (let alone a real depression), and that unemployment rates for adults, both men and women, never became as high as they had been in earlier post-Second World War recessions (and actually stayed low by any historical standard), resulted entirely from the increase in world-market participation on the part of both US manufacturing and US services, with a sharp increase, for instance, in manufacturing exports. And, similarly, that Japan has so far – as of the end of 1993 – not slid into a profound recession with unemployment figures at European levels, that is, around 8–10 per cent (hovering instead below 3 per cent), is clearly the result of Japan's manufacturing industry sharply increasing its exports, and especially institutional exports to mainland Asia.

The world economy has thus become the engine of growth, prosperity, and employment for every developed country. Every developed economy has become world-economy led.

IV

We can now address the question; What works and what does not work in the world economy? The debate today is largely between advocates of 'mandated trade', Japan-style, and conventional free traders. But both are wrong and the evidence is crystal-clear. Mandated trade means government picking 'winners' and pushing them. But not one industry picked by MITI (the Japanese Ministry of Trade and Industry) has turned out to be a real winner. MITI's efforts in the 1960s and 1970s were concentrated on aluminium, other non-ferrous metals, aircraft, and aerospace, and none has gone anywhere. In the late 1970s and 1980s MITI switched to high technology, sponsoring such industries as biomedicine, pharmaceuticals, mainframe computers, telecommunications – but also international brokerage and international commercial banking – again without great success in the world markets. The Japanese industries which have become the world-beaters either have been bitterly opposed by MITI, as were Sony in its early days and the car industry well into the 1970s, or have been ignored by MITI until after they had succeeded by their own efforts. The Japanese policy to create consortia in which major companies work together to produce new technology – for example, in supercomputers or biogenetics – has had only very limited results.

The reasons are clear, at least in hindsight. First, picking winners requires a fortune teller. MITI picked – and had to pick – what was successful at the time in the then more advanced countries, especially the United States. It did not pick – and could not have picked – what would be successful in an unknown future. Thus MITI pushed mainframe computers in the early 1970s, just before the totally unexpected debut of the PC, that is, just before the mainframe plateaued. Second, MITI picked what had been successful in other countries. But that means it picked industries that fit other countries' competencies. It did not pick – and could not have picked – what turned out to fit Japan's competencies, e.g. the extraordinary ability to miniaturize. One reason was that the existence of this competence was well hidden and unknown even to the Japanese. Another reason was that no one, inside Japan or outside, realized its importance before the advent of the microchip. Also, the Japanese ability to downsize the large American car and to make it small and fuel-efficient was not an asset on the US market until the 1973 and 1979 'oil shocks' made it into one. And no one could – or would – have predicted the inability of the industry's world leaders, the American giants, to respond to the Japanese invasion for all of twenty years. Finally, and most importantly, the world economy has become far too complex for anyone to be able to outguess it or to outanalyse it. The available data simply do not report such important developments as the growth of services trade, the growth of structural and institutional trade, the growth of alliances.

But as will be argued (and rightly), Japan has performed outstandingly. This surely cannot be explained as the free traders try to do – that is, it cannot be explained as really being a triumph of conventional free trade. And we do now know what underlies it, primarily because of a recent (1993) World Bank study entitled *The East Asian Miracle*.

The World Bank studied eight East Asian 'superstars': Japan, South Korea, Hong Kong, Taiwan, Singapore, Malaysia, Thailand, and Indonesia. The eight started at very different times, but once they got going, all have shown similar growth in both their domestic economy and in their international economy. Together they supplied 9 per cent of the world's manufactured goods exports thirty years ago. Now they supply 21 per cent (which means a loss of 12 percentage points primarily by the United Kingdom, The Netherlands and Belgium, the former Soviet Union, and some countries in Latin America). Thirty years ago, two-fifths of the population in the eight East Asian countries lived below the poverty line; the figure is less than 5 per cent today, despite rapid population growth in most of them. Several of them – Japan, Hong Kong, Singapore, and Taiwan – are now among the world's richest countries. Yet among the eight there are tremendous differences in culture, history, political systems and tax policies. They range from *laissez-faire* Hong Kong, through interventionist Singapore, to statist Indonesia.

What all eight have in common are two economic policies. First, they do not try to manage short-term fluctuations in the domestic economy. They do not try to control the 'economic weather'. In fact, in every case, the economic miracle did not begin until the country had given up the attempt to manage domestic short-term fluctuations. Each of the eight countries focuses instead on creating the right 'economic climate'. They keep inflation low. They invest heavily in education and training. They reward savings and investment and penalize consumption, thus encouraging a high savings rate.

The second economic policy that the eight East Asian Miracles have in common is that they put performance in the world economy ahead of the domestic economy. In their decisions the first question is always: how will this affect the competitiveness of our industry and its performance in the world economy? It is not: How will this affect domestic economy and domestic employment? – which is the question that most Western countries focus on, especially the United States and the United Kingdom. And then the eight actively foster, encourage, promote, their *successes* in the world economy. Though MITI did not anticipate Japan's successes, the whole Japanese system is geared to taking a world-market success and running with it – by offering substantial tax benefits to exporters; by making credit readily available for international trade and international investment (where it has been scarce and expensive for domestic business); by deliberately keeping high prices and profits on a protected domestic market to generate cash for investments abroad and for penetrating foreign markets (the popular belief in the 'low' profit margins of Japanese companies being pure myth); by reserving special recognition (e.g. the prestigious and highly coveted membership in the executive committee of Keidanren, Japan's top industrial organization) to the heads of companies that have done particularly well in the world economy; and so on. Each of the eight countries of the East Asian Miracle does things in its own and different way. But all of them follow the same two basic policies: first, provide the right economic climate at home through stressing the fundamentals of monetary stability, an educated and trained workforce, and a high savings rate; and second, make performance in the world economy the first priority of economic and business policy.

Exactly the same lessons are being taught by the examples of the two countries in the West that – until very recently – showed similar growth: West Germany and Sweden. These two countries also have very different domestic policies. But both first created and maintained an economic growth climate, and through the same measures: control of inflation; high investment in education and training; and a high savings rate obtained by high taxes on consumption and fairly low taxes on savings and investment. And they both have systematically given priority to the world economy in governmental and business decisions. In both countries, the first question asked is always: How will this affect our world-market standing, our world-market competitiveness, our world-market performance? And the moment these countries forgot this – when the trade unions a few years back subordinated Germany's competitive standing to their wage demands, and the Swedes subordinated their industry's competitive standing to ever-larger welfare spending – the domestic economy of both countries went into stagnation right away.

And one reason why creating the right climate is so important is that it stands as the one and only way to build into a domestic economy resistance to money flows and their shocks.

The last forty years of the world economy yield another lesson as to what works: investment abroad does not 'export jobs'. Instead, it creates jobs at home. We should have learned this from the US performance in the 1960s. When the American-based multinationals expanded investments rapidly, in Europe, in South America, in Japan, the domestic economy created jobs at a fast rate. And when in the 1980s American multinationals resumed heavy foreign investment – particularly in Europe – domestic employment again expanded fast. The same is true for

Japan, where, as has been said earlier, the jobs created by the rapidly expanding investment in East Asia – with very heavy investment in plants that produce goods for the Japanese home market – has not destroyed jobs but has saved them in large numbers. It was equally true for Sweden, which, of all industrialized countries, had gone the furthest in investing abroad in manufacturing plants.

The reason is, of course, the institutional trade generated by such investment. In manufacturing – and in a good many services, such as retailing – investment per worker in the machinery, the tools, and the equipment of a new facility is three to five times annual production. The employment generated by the institutional trade to get the new facility into production is thus substantially larger for several years to come than the annual output and the annual employment of the new facility. Most of this institutional trade comes from the home country of the investor; and most of it is produced by high-wage labour. 'Exporting jobs' will thus actually *create* – at least for the medium term – several jobs in the home country for every one it 'exports'. This explains why the Ford Motor Company, which has aggressively built in Mexico since that country opened itself to foreign investment five or six years ago, is the one US car company which has *added* jobs at home. It explains why the two Mexican manufacturers – a cement maker and a glass maker – that have aggressively built and bought plants in the United States are among the few major Mexican manufacturers who have *added* jobs in Mexico these last few years. So far, however, only the Japanese seem to understand this. Ten years ago they were panicky about 'hollowing out industry', that is, about exporting to mainland Asia labour-intensive work (for example, in consumer electronics) to supply the Japanese home market. Today the export of high-value machinery and tools to these Japanese-owned plants on the Asian mainland, that is, institutional trade, has become the biggest contributor to Japan's export surplus and the mainstay of Japan's engineering and high-tech employment.

The last forty years also teach that *protection rarely protects*. In fact the evidence shows quite clearly that *protection in a good many cases hastens the decline of the industry it is intended to protect.*

Every developed country massively protects agriculture. But in the United States some farm products, such as soy beans, fruits, beef, and poultry, are either not subsidized at all or are very much less subsidized than the 'traditional' crops, such as corn, cotton, and wheat. These less-protected products have done a good deal better on the world market – despite intense competition – than have the heavily protected ones. Farm population in all developed countries has declined steeply since the Second World War. But it has declined the most steeply in the two countries in which agriculture is most highly protected and/or subsidized: France and Japan. It is equally indicative that the decline in US market share of the American car industry dramatically speeded up as soon as it became highly protected in 1980, when the US government forced the Japanese into 'voluntary export restraints'. That protection breeds complacency, inefficiency, cartels has been known since well before Adam Smith. But the counterargument has always been that it protects jobs. The evidence of the last forty years strongly suggests that it does not even do that. At least it did not do so in agriculture in any developed country. It did not do so in the US car industry nor, as the last few years indicate, in the European car industry either. It equally did not protect jobs in the US steel industry or in the steel industries of Europe or Japan. Protection no longer protects jobs; it is more likely to hasten their demise.

Conclusion

What the last forty years teach is that *free trade is not enough*. We have to go beyond it.

The world economy has become too important for a country not to have a world-economy policy. Managed trade is delusion of grandeur. Protectionism can only do harm. But not to be protectionist is not enough. What is needed is a deliberate and active, indeed an aggressive, policy that gives the external economy, its demands, its opportunities, its dynamics, priority over domestic-policy demands and problems. For the United States (and for a country like France – as well as most of Latin America), this would mean a radical reversal of decades of traditional policy – it would mean abandoning, in large measure, economic policies that have governed American thinking and American economics ever since 1933, and certainly since 1945. We still see world-economy demands and world-economy opportunities as 'externalities'. We usually do not even ask: Will this domestic decision *hurt* American participation, American competitiveness, and American standing in the world economy? Yet what we *really* need to ask is: Will this domestic move advance, strengthen, promote American participation in the world economy and American competitiveness? The answer to this question then determines what are the right domestic economic policy decisions and domestic business decisions. This, the lessons of the last forty years teach us, is the only economic policy that can work. It is also – as the last forty years unambiguously teach – the only policy that can rapidly revive a domestic economy mired in turbulence and chronic recession.

1994

14
The US economy's power shift

Power in the economies of developed countries is rapidly shifting from manufacturers to distributors and retailers. The phenomenal success of Wal-Mart, which made the late Sam Walton one of the world's richest men in less than twenty years, was based squarely on the chain's controlling the operations of its main suppliers. Wal-Mart, rather than the manufacturer – a Procter & Gamble, for instance – controls what should be produced, in what product mix, in what quantities, when it should be delivered, and to which stores. Similarly, in Japan, Ito-Yokado Company controls the product mix, the manufacturing schedule, and the delivery of major supplies, such as Coca-Cola or beer, for its 4300 7-Eleven stores.

In hardware a few very large distributors – many of them owned by the independent retail stores they serve – actually design the products (or at least write the specifications for them), find a manufacturer, and lay down manufacturing schedules and delivery times. One example is Servistar, a company based in Butler, Ohio, which buys for 4500 stores across the United States and is owned by them.

The chains of hypermarkets that have come to dominate food retailing in France and Spain similarly control the product mix, manufacturing schedules, and delivery schedules of their main suppliers. And so do the discount chains that take a growing share of the US market in office products. In the United States, the free-standing community hospital is no longer the principal customer for health-care products. Buying is now done by chains: for-profit ones, such as Humana; voluntary ones; denominational ones, whether Catholic or Lutheran. They set the product specifications, find the manufacturer, negotiate price, and determine manufacturing schedules and delivery.

Distributing is increasingly becoming concentrated; manufacturing, by contrast, is increasingly splintering. Thirty years ago, three big car makers shared the US market. Today the market is split among ten – Detroit's Big Three, five Japanese, two Germans. But thirty years ago 85 per cent of all retail car sales were done in single-site dealerships; even three-dealership chains were quite uncommon. Today a fairly small number of large chain-dealers – no more than fifty or sixty – sell two-fifths of all cars in the United States. Yesterday's dealer handled only one make. Today's chains may sell GM cars in one dealership, Toyotas in the dealership across the street, and BMWs in a dealership in the next town. They have little commitment to any one maker but go by what their customers want.

In the mid-1960s Servistar (then called American Hardware) bought less than $20 million a year and had 600 member stores. Today it serves 4500 stores and has an annual volume of $1.5 billion. Twenty years ago, each of the current 7-Eleven outlets in Japan was an independent 'mom-and-pop' store. Mom and Pop still serve the customers, but they have become franchises: 7-Eleven runs the store, decides what merchandise it carries and in what quantity, buys it, stocks it, does the display, finances the store, does its accounting, and trains its people.

These large distributors are becoming less and less dependent on manufacturers' brands. Thirty years ago, only two very big American retailers successfully sold their own 'private labels': R. H. Macy and Sears, Roebuck. The largest American food retailer of that time, the Great Atlantic and Pacific Tea Company, tried to emulate these two. A&P's private labels were superior value. But the public refused to buy them, which all but destroyed A&P. Now private labels are flourishing.

The independent stationery store in my neighbourhood carries only national brands. But the only national brands carried by the recently opened local outlet of a stationery discount chain are goods that require service, such as computers and fax machines, and they account for less than half of the store's volume. Increasingly the retail chains use cable TV to promote their own brands; they no longer depend on the manufacturers' advertising on over-the-air networks.

What underlies this shift is information. Wal-Mart is built around information from the sales floor. Whenever a customer buys anything, the information goes directly – in 'real time' – to the manufacturer's plant. It is automatically converted into a manufacturing schedule and into delivery instructions: when to ship, how to ship, and where to ship. Traditionally, 20 per cent or 30 per cent of the retail price went toward getting merchandise from the manufacturer's loading dock to the retailer's store – most of this cost went to keep inventory in *three* warehouses: the manufacturer's, the wholesaler's and the retailer's. These costs are largely eliminated in the Wal-Mart system, which enables the company to undersell local competitors despite its generally higher labour costs.

The moment a 7-Eleven customer in Japan buys a soft drink or a can of beer, the information goes directly to bottler or brewery. It immediately becomes both production schedule and delivery schedule, actually specifying the hour when the new supply has to be delivered and to which of the 4300 stores.

We would not have needed the computer to do what Wal-Mart and 7-Eleven are doing. More than fifty years ago, Marks & Spencer, the British retail chain, integrated market information and the manufacturing schedules of its suppliers and created the first just-in-time system. In the mid-1960s, O. M. Scott of Marysville, Ohio, a producer of grass seeds, fertilizer, and pesticides, built real-time market information into its manufacturing system. Both almost immediately attained industry leadership. But once the computer is there and provides instant market information, the integration of this information with manufacturing production and delivery becomes inevitable.

Since I first said it in my 1954 book *The Practice of Management*, it has become commonplace to assert that results are only in the marketplace; where things are being made or moved, there are only costs. Everybody these days talks of the 'market-driven' or the 'customer-driven' company. But as long as we did not have market information, decisions (especially day-to-day operating decisions) had to be made as *manufacturing* decisions. They had to be controlled by what goes on in the plant, and they had to be based on the only information we had (or believed we had) – on manufacturing costs.

Now that we have real-time information on what goes on in the marketplace, decisions will increasingly be based on what goes on where the ultimate customers, whether housewives or hospitals, take *buying* action. These decisions will be controlled by the people who have the information – retailers and distributors. Increasingly, decision-making power will shift to them.

One implication of this is that producers will have to structure their plants for 'flexible manufacturing' – the buzzword for production organized around the flow of market information rather than around the flow of materials, as in traditional manufacturing. The more we automate, the more important this will be. General Motors largely wasted $30 billion on automating the traditional process, which only made its plants more expensive, more rigid, and less responsive. Toyota (and, to some extent, Ford) spent a fraction of what GM spent. But it spent the money restructuring production around market information – on 'flexible manufacturing'.

There is another important implication. When, during the past ten or fifteen years, companies began to organize themselves internally around the flow of information – we now call it 're-engineering' – they immediately found that they did not need a good many management levels. Some companies have since cut two-thirds of their management layers. Now that we are beginning to organize around *external* information, we are learning that the economy needs far fewer intermediaries. We are eliminating wholesalers.

In the US hardware industry, for example, the new distributors such as Servistar are doing what three levels of wholesalers used to do. In Japan, 7-Eleven has eliminated five or six wholesale levels. And this trend has only started.

Physical distribution is changing too. In many industries the warehouse is becoming redundant. In others it is changing function. One medium-sized supermarket chain now handles half its merchandise without any storage; it goes directly from manufacturer to store. The other half still goes through a warehouse. But it is not held there; it goes out within twelve hours, soon to be cut to three – in transportation parlance, the warehouse has become a 'switching yard' instead of a 'holding yard'.

This also means that the economy needs less and less of the financing that for two centuries provided banks with their safest and most lucrative business: short-term lending on inventory. The sharp drop in the demand for such money explains in large measure why banks in developed countries are seeing their commercial-loan business shrink, even in boom times, and why they have been trying to compensate by rushing into dubious real-estate deals, loans to Third World dictators and derivatives gambling.

But the biggest implication is that the *economy* is changing structure. From being organized around the flow of things and the flow of money, it is becoming organized around the flow of information.

1992

15
Where the new markets are

For forty years, since the the destruction of the Second World War was repaired in the 1950s, an unprecedented expansion of the world economy has been propelled by consumer demand, culminating in the developed countries' great shopping spree of the 1980s. But there is mounting evidence of a deep structural shift – namely, economic growth and expansion can no longer be based on consumer demand.

One symptom: Ever since the first TV set appeared on the market, each new consumer-electronics product has immediately set off a buying explosion, especially in Japan. Yet when several technically very exciting consumer-electronics products were introduced in the Japanese market last year, they produced little more than a yawn.

More important, the new markets are not consumer-goods markets. Nor are they traditional producer-goods markets, that is, markets for machinery and factories. (In fact, there is probably worldwide overcapacity in manufacturing plants, most acutely in Japan and in Western Europe.) Rather, three of the new markets are for various kinds of 'infrastructure', that is, for facilities that serve both producers and consumers. And the fourth new market is for things that are neither 'products' nor 'services' in any traditional meaning of those terms.

The most immediately accessible of the new markets involves communication and information. Demand for telephone service in Third World countries and the countries of the former Soviet bloc is practically insatiable. There is no greater impediment to economic development than poor telephone service, and no greater spur than good telephone service. A telephone system is highly capital-intensive. But technologies that replace the 'wiring' of traditional telephones with the 'beaming' of cellular phones are radically reducing the capital investment needed. And once a telephone service is installed, it begins to pay for itself fairly soon, especially if it is well maintained.

In the developed world, the information and communications market may be even larger. Both the office of tomorrow and the school of tomorrow are likely to be built around information and communication. We already know that the factory of tomorrow will be organized around information (rather than automation as we thought only ten years ago). The technology is already in use; it needs only to be properly packaged.

The second of the new markets – call it the 'environmental market' – may end up presenting an even greater opportunity than the first. It has three separate components, all rapidly developing:

1 *The market for equipment to purify water and air.* In the United States purification of water and of effluents is proceeding apace. Water use in US manufacturing is already down by one-third since 1977 and will be cut by as much again by the year 2000. Air pollution in US manufacturing has also been cut drastically. Japan may be even further ahead, whereas Europe is still way behind. But manufacturing is not the world's biggest polluter. When it comes to water pollution, for instance, municipal sewage is the worst offender. There the task has not been tackled in any country, though the technologies are available.

2 *The agrobiology market.* This market will replace chemical herbicides and pesticides with non-polluting, mainly biolo-

gical, products. The first of these products have just appeared on the market. By the year 2000, industry experts believe, practically all herbicides and pesticides used in commercial farming in developed countries will be biological rather than chemical.

3 *The energy market.* The biggest component of the environmental market – the energy market – will not become a major factor until after the year 2000. There is a growing need to cut down on high-polluting energy sources, such as petrol as used in car engines or coal as used in electricity-generating power plants. The first technologies to do so – solar power cells and non-polluting coal-burning furnaces – are no longer 'sci-fi'; within ten years they will be affordable.

The third new market is not really new at all. It is the growing need in developed and developing countries alike to repair, replenish, and upgrade physical infrastructure, especially transportation systems – roads, railways, bridges, harbours, and airports.

Little of the world's infrastructure is less than thirty years old, and in undeveloped countries, infrastructure has been neglected since 1929 or even since the First World War. Even the few Japanese superhighways date back to the 1960s: the US road system, once the wonder of the world, is older. No European rail system carries more than one-tenth of its country's freight, and all lose money. Likewise in Japan: although its railroads carry enormous numbers of passengers, they are unable to serve the economy by being freight carriers.

In contrast, America's railways are in reasonable shape – at least, they carry almost two-fifths of the country's freight and earn money doing so. But even in the United States, overloaded and undermaintained transportation systems cannot support much more activity. Ocean shipping – that part of transportation that in the developed countries of the non-Communist world has been left to private enterprise – is in good shape by and large.

But otherwise the world's transportation systems may require ten years or more of boom-time investment, comparable perhaps to the railway boom of the mid-nineteenth century.

And then there is the fourth of the new markets, the one created by demography. It is the market for the investment 'products' to finance survival into old age.

Life insurance, which should, of course, have been called 'death insurance', was a major investment product of the nineteenth century. It protected the family against economic catastrophe caused by the breadwinner's early death. The new growth industry in all developed countries is 'survival insurance' – the fund created by the income that wage earners put aside to provide for their retirement years. As everyone knows, pension funds have become the only true 'capitalists' in the American economy. They are rapidly becoming the true capitalists in the other developed countries as well – and for the same reason: the growing number of people who live well beyond retirement age. This development creates a demand for investment vehicles that goes way beyond anything seen earlier.

There is thus ample potential for economic growth, perhaps even for another forty years of it. The demand is there; so are the technological and capital resources. But this potential does not fit traditional assumptions – and proposals by America's Democrats and Britain's Labour Party – that increased government expenditures will stimulate consumption. In fact, this is likely to do little more than trigger inflation. What is needed is not more consumer spending but long-term investment and the jobs it creates.

The measures America's Republicans and Britain's Conservatives propose to encourage such investment are equally unlikely to do the trick. They assume that the investors are the 'rich', when actually today's investors are barely 'affluent'. The typical individual contribution to a pension fund is well below $10 000 a year; and the typical mutual-fund purchase (the preferred investment vehicle for individual savers) runs around $2500.

What is needed is something totally different: the privatization of infrastructure. The needs of communication, the environment, and transportation should be entrusted to investor-owned, profit-seeking enterprises, operating in competitive markets. There is a precedent for this: the concept of the 'public utility', invented in the United States in the second half of the nineteenth century. This enabled American railways, power companies, and telephone companies to remain private and to stay competitive, while such services everywhere else in the world were taken over by government.

We can already see some progress in the privatization of infrastructure markets. Germany long ago cleaned up its most polluted river, the Ruhr, by making it profitable for businesses not to pollute. And in California's Central Valley the water allotments of individual farmers have become tradable commodities, giving buyers incentives to conserve and to purify.

Privatization is the one way to make sure the needs for infrastructure will be fulfilled. No government in the world today is solvent enough to do so on its own, either through taxation or through borrowing. Yet the capital is there, and in abundance, and so are the opportunities for profitable investment.

1992

16
The Pacific Rim and the world economy

The next few years – the years between now and the year 2000 – will decide how Asia's Pacific Rim will integrate itself into a rapidly changing world economy. Will it be as a number of independent countries and economies fiercely competing with one another? Will it be through a number of regional trade blocs, as the prime minister of Malaysia has suggested? Or will it be as one – and by far the biggest – of the new superblocs such as those into which the West is now organizing itself, each free trade inside but heavily protectionist outside? Whichever way the decision goes, it will profoundly change Asia as well as world economy and world politics. And the decision is being forced on the Asian countries of the Pacific Rim both by developments outside, that is, in the West, and by their own economic growth.

The rapid reshaping of the West into regional superblocs was triggered by the completion of the European Economic Community – arguably the most important economic development of the 1980s. Now North America is in the process of turning itself into a similar superbloc. In fact, both Canada and Mexico are already so firmly integrated into the US economy that it is no longer too important that the North American Free Trade Agreement (that is, the agreement between the governments of the United States, Canada, and Mexico) became law. The only question now is whether other Latin American countries – Chile first, then perhaps Argentina, and eventually Brazil – will be pulled into the North American superbloc, the way all of Europe, beginning with Britain, was pulled into the European Community.

These superblocs into which the West is organizing its economy are creating the largest and richest free trade areas the world has ever seen. But at the same time, both the European Union and the North American economic bloc are being inexorably pushed away from free trade with the world outside and towards a new protectionism. They will aggressively push exports, while at the same time fiercely protecting their domestic industries. And the main reason is not economic. It is far more compelling: it is *social*. The social priority for both Western Europe and the United States will have to be manufacturing jobs in Eastern Europe and Mexico, respectively. The alternative is to be inundated by a mass immigration of unskilled or low-skilled people for whom there are no jobs at home. And as events in Germany (but also in Los Angeles) show only too clearly, such immigration already exceeds what is socially and politically manageable. But the only industries in which such people can possibly be employed in their home countries – whether Slovakia, the Ukraine, or Mexico – are traditional, labour-intensive industries: textiles, toys, footwear, cars, steel, shipbuilding, and consumer electronics. These, however, are the very industries on whose exports the growing Asian countries of the Pacific Rim would have to depend – the same industries on whose exports yesterday's Asian 'miracles' based their early growth: Japan in the 1960s and 1970s and the 'Four Tigers' later on. They are, of course, also the industries on which today's growth-economies – coastal China, Thailand, Indonesia – largely expect to base *their* growth.

But equally as important as what is happening in the West – in fact more important than the events there – is what is happening in Asia itself. China faces enormous problems during the next few years – beginning with the threat of disastrous inflation and reaching all the way to the threat of wrenching political instability. Yet the coastal areas of the country, with 300–400 million competent and ambitious people, should be one of the world's great economic powers by the year 2000. Per capita production and per capita income will still be those of a 'developing' rather than those of a 'developed' country. But total industrial production in coastal China might be so large within ten years as to make it a contender for the number two spot in world industry – the place now contested by Japan and Germany.

Like Japan and the Four Tigers, coastal China will be 'export-led' in its economic development. But the main *export* market for its products is a *domestic* market: the 800 million largely rural people in the country's vast interior, people who are after all quite distinct economically, socially, and culturally from the people of the coastal areas. Like Japan forty years ago, coastal China will not need large investments such as Western Europe needed for its reconstruction after the Second World War. Coastal China has one of the world's highest savings rates (if only because there was so little to buy until recently). And now that investment decisions are largely being made by individuals and in the market – rather than by bureaucrats indulging in central planning – capital productivity seems to be quite high (though still lower than it was in Japan in the 1960s and 1970s). Still, coastal China will need enormous amounts of foreign exchange. My guess is that within a few years, the exports coastal China needs to cover its foreign exchange requirements will be larger than the *combined* exports of all other Pacific Rim countries in Asia, excluding Japan.

But who will take these exports? Practically all of them will be in industries in which there is already substantial overcapacity in the developed world. The developed countries of Pacific Rim Asia, with Singapore in the lead, are rapidly moving out of traditional labour-intensive industries. By the year 2000 even Japan will have stopped exporting cars to the West's developed countries and will instead produce there. But developing countries – especially rapidly developing countries – have no choice. Thailand and Indonesia face pretty much the same problem. But coastal China, because of its huge population and its explosive growth, is the place where the problem will come to a head. Indeed, for the Clinton administration, eliminating the trade deficit with China is already a top priority. And the European Union has no intention at all of letting in Chinese goods that are in competition with the products of depressed European industries.

This calls for something totally new: *Asian* leadership in trade policy. So far, Asian countries have *reacted* to the trade policies of the developed countries. Even Japan's trade policy so far has been in large measure skilful exploitation of America's trade policy (or of the absence of any such thing). Now Asian *action* is needed. For only Asians can integrate a rapidly developing Asia into the world economy. But where will this leadership be coming from?

1993

17
China's growth markets

Coastal China, home to 400 million people of mercantile and urban culture, has been the world's fastest-growing economy over the past decade. But now it, and the rest of the country, face formidable problems.

To prevent runaway inflation, thousands of unproductive and unprofitable state enterprises that employ millions of workers and are a key power base for the Communist Party must be dismantled. Social tensions are mounting as peasants stream into overcrowded cities where there is no housing, no health care, and far too few jobs. And a nationwide power struggle has begun in anticipation of the octogenarian leadership's passing. Their successors may not be democrats.

Yet where the internal effects of China's growth are unsettling, the external effects are potentially destabilizing. It is hardly a harbinger of peace that the Chinese military – with no foreign enemy in sight – eagerly snaps up whatever high-tech weapons a cash-hungry Russia offers for sale. And the world is confounded by a Chinese trade dragon that exports like a capitalist but imports like a Communist. The world must find new ways to meet the challenge of this emerging power.

Trade is a good example. US trade policy towards China should be based on the assumption that by the early years of the next century, coastal China might become one of the largest economic powers in terms of total gross national product, industrial output, and industrial exports.

Yet a conventional approach to bilateral trade problems may fail to target the fundamentally different kind of commercial relationship a modern China will need to have with the world. This is because China is likely to be the first country where the balance of payments rather than the balance of trade is the key to economic relations. Indeed, China may be the first country to be integrated into the world economy through services rather than through trade in goods.

To be sure, the Chinese market has to open to foreign goods. In many ways it is far more tightly locked than Japan has ever been. But even if China's doors are fully opened, it is doubtful whether the country would become a major market for foreign-made goods. Despite the enormous size of its market – more than a billion people with rapidly rising incomes – and an insatiable appetite for foreign brands, China will not import Coca-Cola and Levis. Instead, such products will be manufactured in China – by joint ventures, by franchises such as soft-drink bottlers, by licences and by alliances of all kinds. (In 1993, Coca-Cola signed an agreement with the government in Beijing to invest $150 million in ten bottling plants in China over the next five years.)

The reason for this is compelling social necessity: manufacturing will be the primary vehicle to accommodate the Chinese peasant's transition from the feudal countryside to the modern era. Within the next ten years, as much as half of China's population might be employed in factories. Whatever can be made in China will be made there – and that means most manufactured products.

Bringing down barriers to the importation of goods into China has to be worked on, and hard. But far more important is creating a legal and administrative framework to enable a foreigner to do business in China as a partner. Laws today are often unenforced, sometimes even unpublished. There is nearly no protection for a licensor or minority partner and little respect for intellectual property rights. A trade policy with China must establish and safeguard access to partnership.

All that said, the biggest market opportunities for foreigners in a fast-growing China are not in manufacturing but in services.

Consider, for instance, education. Despite a literacy rate of 73 per cent, China's university system is one of the world's most backward and is unable to support sustained economic growth. There are barely 1.5 million college students in China, a proportion to population smaller than America's a hundred years ago. Even India, with a literacy rate about half that of China, has proportionately nearly four times as many university students. Worse still, most Chinese university education prepares students for bureaucratic careers that prove more useful for preventing others from doing than for getting things done.

Unless this changes, and changes fast, China's growth will be aborted by a shortage of engineers and chemists, statisticians and accountants, physicians and nurses, managers and teachers. In a similar fix forty years ago, South Korea sent thousands of its young people to US colleges for training; they then created the 'Korean miracle', which transformed a war-ravaged, rural country of profound poverty into one of the Four Tigers in less than thirty years.

But China's education problem will not be alleviated by despatching 40 000 students abroad every year, as it does now. What is needed is a massive and immediate overhaul of the country's educational system – a job that can be done only by large-scale outside service contractors who design, plan, and set up the needed educational institutions. Qualified suppliers of such services do exist – the English universities, for instance, are well trained in such endeavours, as are many American universities and colleges that generally provide educational contract services as a charitable activity.

Such generosity, however, ignores a potential market. If such ventures are organized and professionally run, there is money to be made. A number of American colleges already have branches in Japan, and it is not inconceivable that higher education will one day become America's biggest 'export' to China and the source of major export earnings.

Health care offers similar opportunities. Mao's flawed vision of a China cared for by 'barefoot doctors' is as much a travesty today as it was thirty years ago. What is needed are experienced (and that means foreign) contractors who plan, design, build, and manage health-care facilities and train medical staff. The needed hospitals could be built quite fast: the American military's field hospitals, developed over the past thirty years and tested in the Iraq war, provide a prototype.

Financial services, the circulatory system of a modern society, provide yet another major market opportunity. Chinese financial services are in worse shape than either higher education or health care. Simply put, China has a very high savings rate but no way to put the money to productive use. It lacks the legal structures for a financial industry: its financial institutions are primitive and its personnel poorly trained. An infusion of foreign commercial and investment banks, thrifts, insurance companies, mutual funds, and the reliable economic and business data they provide would help develop a system that the Chinese could not possibly develop by themselves, at least not to the extent they need to in the time they have.

What else does China need? It needs telecommunications and information services on a massive scale. The need is so great and China is so far behind that it will have to bypass a century of Western technology and leap directly into the more modern wireless forms of telecommunications – shortwave telephone transmission beamed directly into urban homes, microwave and satellite transmission to span the enormous distances in the countryside.

The same applies to China's last major development need: transportation. China is blessed with excellent natural harbours. But few are developed well enough to handle much traffic or cargo. And the few that are lack roads and railways to move goods to the interior. Almost seven decades have passed since new railway lines were built, and many of those are narrow-gauge and single-track, have obsolete switching yards, and still run on steam.

The measure of success in trade relations with China is thus selling services rather than selling goods. This is surely not 'free' trade. But no matter how desirable it might be, free trade is not a possible policy for China – at least not until the enormous surplus population from the farms has been absorbed into urban society and urban jobs.

A service-focused trade policy with China will be criticized, especially by trade unionists, for 'not creating jobs'. But this is yesterday's argument. In all developed countries the majority of jobs, especially of well-paid jobs, are precisely in those industries that would benefit the most from a successful service-focused trade policy: engineering, design, health care, education, management, training, and so on. What really matters is that these service areas are the ones where the emergence of China as a major economic power creates opportunities. They are where the markets are.

1993

18
The end of Japan, Inc?

Japan, Inc., is in disarray. Individual Japanese companies compete just as aggressively as before on the world market. But no distinctive Japanese policy exists any more, least of all in economics. Instead, short-term fixes and panicky reactions to the unexpected are the norm. As in the West, these are no substitutes for policy, and they are having little, if any, success. Part of the problem is that none of Japan's available choices looks attractive: none would produce consensus. They would instead cause division among the nation's major groups – bureaucrats, politicians, business leaders, academia, and labour. Japanese newspapers are full of plaints about 'weak leadership'. But that is only a symptom. The root problem is that the four pillars on which Japanese policy has been based for over thirty years have collapsed or are tottering.

The first pillar of Japanese policy was the belief that Japan was so important as a bulwark against Soviet Communism that the United States would subordinate economic interests to the maintenance of Tokyo's political stability and to the US–Japanese strategic alliance. During the 1970s and 1980s US ambassador Mike Mansfield repeatedly asserted the priority of the US–Japanese political relationship over all other considerations. The same priorities clearly existed in the Bush administration. The Japanese assumed, correctly, that no matter how loud the American bark, the bite would be only a nip and draw no blood.

Japan must now question this assumption. Will the Clinton administration subordinate US economic interests, real or perceived, to alliance politics? To be sure, America declares itself committed to the defence of Japan, were the country to be attacked by armed force. However, the Japanese are beginning to realize that the United States will increasingly exact a substantial economic price for this political support – and just at a time when China, Japan's big neighbour, has become the world's one major power that is increasing its military strength. The Europeans, who never subscribed to the Mansfield thesis, are less encumbered. In the next few years, Europe will be deciding not only how many Japanese-made goods to let in, but also whether goods made within Europe by Japanese companies can be sold freely and in large quantities on European markets.

The second pillar of Japan's economic policy was the belief that its businesses could dominate world markets by projecting Western trends and then doing better and faster what the West was doing slowly and halfheartedly. Such a strategy, first used in the early 1960s by Sony for transistor radios, followed a few years later by camera and copier-makers, has hit one bull's-eye after another. It can still be a winning strategy – witness the way the Japanese outflanked European luxury cars on the American market in the last few years, or speedily took over the fax-machine business from the Americans who invented it.

But these successes are no longer a sure thing. The strategy has failed in computers. Projecting where IBM was going and then attempting to outmanoeuvre it made the Japanese miss the growth industries of workstations and networking. In computer chips, the Japanese fumbled the shift to high-value, dedicated circuits and instead concentrated on low-value commodity products, in which they are now being hard pressed by producers from low-wage countries. In telecommunications, the Japanese missed the swing to over-the-air telephone transmission (cellular phones), where world market growth is likely to occur. In consumer electronics and high-definition television, where the final returns are not yet in, the Japanese are again on the defensive instead of delivering knockout blows.

Even though quantitatively Japan's export surplus with the United States rose again in 1992, qualitatively it is deteriorating. Almost three-quarters of it is now being earned by the products of one old industry with saturated markets in every developed country: cars. Even there the Japanese are no longer taking business away from US producers but rather from European imports. To be sure, General Motors is still losing market share, but now to Ford and Chrysler.

Japan's third traditional pillar of strength was the assumption that the country's domestic economy was largely immune to outside troubles. Underpinning this belief was the knowledge that the preponderance of imports are foodstuffs and raw materials and the preponderance of exports are manufactured goods. In a recession raw-materials prices slide faster and farther than manufactured-goods prices – that is, the prices of Japan's exports. Hence both Japan's terms of trade (its relative economic strength) and balance of trade (its absolute economic strength) tend to improve when the world economy goes down.

This equation still works. It largely explains the persistent Japanese trade surplus of the last few years. The depression in the world prices of foodstuffs and raw materials – now in its second decade – constitutes a massive subsidy to the Japanese economy. It gets its raw materials and its foodstuffs for about half of 1979 prices, in relation to the prices of manufactured goods. Yet at home Japan has now been mired in recession for more than two years. Employment, output, profits, and investments are still declining, and all four, it seems, are determined by trends in the world economy from which Japan should be immune.

The fourth pillar was the commitment to long-term policy, with the flexibility to make exceptions, to cater for special interests, and to seize opportunities. It was periodically reviewed and, if necessary, updated or revised. The strategy shunned short-term quick fixes whose ineffectualness would jeopardize national consensus.

Commitment to long-term policy was maintained for twenty-five years, from the 1960s until 1985, when floating the over-valued US dollar led to a 50 per cent drop against the yen in just a few months. The Japanese panicked at the threat to their exports, two-fifths of which went to the United States. To shore up lifetime employment and social stability by replacing the lost sales and profits of exports, the government rushed into a frenzied campaign to stimulate domestic consumption.

Whether Japan's manufacturers really needed such a heavy shot of economic adrenalin is debatable. Most adjusted quickly to the lower value of the dollar and to lower export earnings. Needed or not, stimulating domestic consumption could not have come at a worse time for the Japanese economy. It occurred just when purchasing power and lifestyles were shifting rapidly from a consumption-shy older generation, still scarred by wartime and post-war deprivations, to the 'yuppies' of the 'baby boom'. The government policy thus kicked off the biggest spending spree in economic history. It also ignited a speculative firestorm in real estate and stock prices. Three years ago, at the height of what the Japanese now call the 'bubble economy', shares on the Tokyo Stock Exchange were quoted at fifty or sixty times pretax earnings (that is, at an after-tax yield of less than 1 per cent). Real estate in Tokyo's better office districts was mortgaged for up to fifty times annual rental income.

The bubble burst in early 1990 with the stock market losing half its value in just a few months. If savings banks, commercial banks, and insurance companies had been forced to write down to realistic values their holdings of shares and real estate loans, there would have been massive financial collapse. Instead of organizing a managed and controlled retreat – akin to US management of Latin American loans and real estate loans by commercial banks and thrifts – Japan is pretending the losses never happened. Massive government purchase of stocks and bonds accounted for one-third of all purchases on the Tokyo Stock Exchange in the spring of 1993. The official line is that the markets 'must' go up as soon as the economy recovers, allowing the government to sell its equity holdings and even to make a profit. But that has never worked. The very existence of such holdings puts a lid on the market. And every day of postponement in facing financial reality makes the problem less tractable, more controversial, more divisive, and more politically corrosive.

The official line in Japan is still that the country will return to the traditional long-term policy once the situation becomes 'normal' again. It is doubtful that any informed Japanese, in or out of government, takes this profession seriously. The likelihood is that Japan will not, in the foreseeable future, return to having an economic policy. Rather, it will increasingly look like the major Western countries, whose economic irresolution and lack of direction the Japanese have been deriding for years. There will be no more 'Japan, Inc.', no consensus, and no one policy-setting group steering the economy through 'administrative guidance'. Individual companies, industries, and interest groups will go their own way, both domestically and internationally. Instead of 'policy' there will be *ad hoc*, short-term measures and perhaps also increasing immobility (probably accompanied, as in the West, by increasingly grandiose promises).

This policy discord will be universally deplored in Japan, as it is in the West, but it will not be universally unpopular. Leading manufacturers, especially those who are successful on the world markets, prefer a return to the days of a consistent economic policy in the hands of a powerful government bureaucracy. But many other Japanese business leaders are disenchanted with 'administrative guidance', which committed them in the last ten years to such strategic blunders as the emphasis on mainframe computers and supercomputers and the maintenance of the monopolies in telecommunications and telecommunications equipment.

If there is no consensus policy and no administrative guidance, individual Japanese companies should become tougher competitors on the world market. Their response to market opportunities and market challenges will be quicker. They are likely to work even harder on the three prongs of competition with which they attack Western competitors: control of the economics of the entire production and distribution process rather than accounting control of the costs of each step; zero-defects quality; and shortening development, production, and delivery cycles by spending money to save time.

Already, individual companies have shifted from the traditional strategy of outguessing and outflanking Western competitors to genuine research aimed at innovative breakthroughs. Just as some individual companies in the West have prospered by doing things entirely their own way, so some Japanese companies can be expected to prosper greatly by doing things their own way rather than the 'Japanese way'. But it remains questionable whether the Japanese economy as a whole will do any better without a consistent long-range policy and strong leadership than have the short-term-driven Western economies of the United States, the United Kingdom, France, or Germany.

The United States should, but probably will not, refrain from gloating and 'Japan bashing'. A financial crisis in Japan is the last thing the United States or anyone else in the developed world needs. Nor is it in America's interest for the world's second-largest economy to have a disorganized and drifting government or an increasingly disoriented society. Such circumstances could only mean that the Japanese would start hunting for a scapegoat and would find it in Americans.

Washington will rightfully press Tokyo much harder to eliminate the obstacles to the entry on fair terms of American goods, services, and investments. Japan is not nearly as protectionist as the American public believes – or else American manufactured-goods exports to Japan would not have almost doubled in the last ten years, particularly in high-technology products. In fact as a proportion of total US – Japanese trade, the deficit is now only a fraction of what it was ten years ago. And Japan is still the best customer by far for American foodstuffs and forest products, all of which the Japanese could easily buy from other suppliers at the same price and quality.

Still, there are real obstacles to foreign business in Japan. For better or worse, the disappearance of the Soviet threat means that there is now no reason the United States should not demand the same access for its products, service, and investments that the Japanese enjoy to the far less restricted US markets.

Washington needs a trade policy that focuses on those areas where removing Japanese barriers would actually make a difference. This means, for instance, forgetting about the Japanese ban on rice imports. US nagging on rice helps no one but the Japanese politicians who skilfully blame American pressure for whittling down increasingly onerous subsidies to Japan's politically powerful rice growers. If any foreign country gets to supply Japan with large quantities of rice, it will not be California; it will be lower-cost Thailand or Vietnam. Also, penalizing Japanese car imports, a move that Detroit's Big Three have been clamouring for, is nothing but pure emotion; the car workers' union would applaud, but it would not help Detroit at all. It would, however, greatly help the major Japanese car manufacturers' public relations. Such demands would give them the pretext they badly need to speed up their plans to move production for the US market entirely out of Japan and into their US plants, where costs are actually lower than they are at home. It would give them a perfect excuse for doing the politically unthinkable but economically inevitable – laying off Japanese workers who have lifetime employment.

Beyond using a little more intelligence and a good deal less rhetoric in relations with Japan, the only thing Washington can do is to understand the transition Japan is going through. It needs to take Japan seriously, for it is the only big customer left for US farm and forest products and one of America's biggest manufactured-goods customers. Japan is still the only fully developed and democratic non-Western country, with the world's second-largest economy. It is not a happy omen that there is, apparently, no one in a senior policy-making position in the present administration who seems to know or care much about Japan.

1993

19
A weak dollar strengthens Japan

For a decade now one US administration after another – Reagan, Bush, Clinton – has talked down the exchange value of the dollar against the yen. Every time the dollar declines – and it tumbled during these ten years from 250 yen to below 100 yen – we are told by the experts that 'this time' the trade deficit with Japan will surely go away. And every time the dollar declines, the Japanese howl that *endaka* – the high yen – will destroy their industries and drive them into bankruptcy.

US manufacturing exports to Japan have indeed nearly doubled in the past ten years. But they have increased even faster in countries – some in Europe, others in Latin America – where the dollar's value has actually *increased*. And despite *endaka*, Japanese manufactured exports to the United States have grown just as fast as US manufactured-goods exports to Japan. Therefore, the trade deficit has remained pretty much the same – even widening a bit since the dollar was first devalued.

In fact, neither US merchandise trade nor Japanese companies' sales and profits show the slightest correlation to the exchange rate. If they correlate to anything, it is to the relative levels of economic activity in the two countries. For example, while Japanese manufacturing-company profits have fallen sharply in the past three years, the main cause has not been fewer exports to the United States or lower export earnings. it has been the sharp drop in the *domestic* economy, aggravated by huge losses many of these companies incurred from gambling recklessly in the Tokyo stock market and in Japanese real estate.

According to all economic theory this simply could not have happened: the US trade deficit with Japan *must* have disappeared. At least it *must* have shrunk markedly. And the Washington experts still promise us that, indeed, this *will* happen the next time around, and 'inevitably' so. But if for a whole decade the inevitable does not happen, one should stop promising it. In fact, the cheap-dollar policy of US governments in the past ten years has rested in totally wrong assumptions regarding the Japanese economy. Japan, rather than the United States, is the beneficiary of a cheap dollar.

The key to this seeming paradox is that, on a flow-of-funds basis, Japan spends as many dollars on imports as it earns through exports. As far as US–Japanese merchandise trade is concerned, the exchange rate is irrelevant: the dollars are awash. Individual companies might, of course, be hurt by a lower dollar, but others benefit by it. And in its total trade accounts – that is, in merchandise and services trade combined – Japan actually spends more dollars abroad than it earns from exports. The weaker the dollar, the fewer yen Japan needs to spend to procure the dollars it requires for its foreign accounts.

Japan imports four-fifths of its fuel and energy, a little more than one-third of its food, and all its industrial raw materials. Together, these three categories constitute half of Japan's total imports. (By contrast, they account for no more than a quarter of US imports and for less than a third of Germany's imports.) Japan pays for all these commodity imports in US dollars, even if, as in the case of oil, they come from other countries. According to economic theory and economic history, commodity prices should have gone up in dollars by the same proportion by which the dollar went down. But they didn't.

On the contrary, during the past ten years the dollar prices of commodities – whether foods, industrial raw materials, or oil – have actually plummeted. In yen, Japan, the world's largest commodity importer, gets an incredible bargain. Feeding its population, running its factories, and heating its homes now costs Japan little more than a third of what it had cost it ten years ago. As an importer, Japan benefits heavily from *endaka* – and so does its standard of living.

Of Japan's exports, about two-fifths are paid in US dollars – everything that is sold to the United States (now around a fifth of the total), almost everything that goes to Latin America, and everything that goes to the three countries whose currencies have remained linked to the US dollar: Britain, Australia, and Canada. And these two-fifths of Japan's merchandise exports bring in almost exactly the number of dollars Japan needs to pay for its commodity imports.

In 1992 – the most typical of these ten years and almost exactly in the middle of the range – Japan's bill for commodity imports was $118 billion; its income from dollar-denominated exports was about $120 billion. Actually, Japan needs a few extra billion dollars to cover its deficit on service trade – almost all payable in dollars. It runs to some $10 billion a year. But this only means that a cheaper dollar hurts even less.

On top of this, however, Japan needs dollars – a lot of them – to invest abroad. During the past ten years Japan has become a major direct investor abroad, building plants and acquiring stakes in businesses all over the world. Until a year or two ago the bulk of this investment was in the United States. Now, to get access to the European Union, the Japanese are investing heavily in the United Kingdom. Since the British pound is the major European currency that has stayed most in sync with the US dollar during the past ten years, the pound also becomes cheaper for the Japanese as the dollar decreases in value.

All told, the Japanese in the peak year – 1991 – needed about $100 billion for overseas investment. This was financed out of their exports to countries other than the United States – mainly countries whose currencies were not linked to the dollar but were fairly stable in relation to the yen (e.g. the German mark). Thus Japan could get the dollars needed for investment in the United States at a steadily reduced price. This alone enabled the Japanese to build plants and to acquire companies in the United States (and in Britain, Canada, and Australia) at bargain-basement prices.

No one has yet been able to explain why world commodity prices failed to rise proportionately as the dollar fell against the yen (and against all other key currencies except the British pound). But whatever the answer is, it surely has nothing to do with US–Japanese trade. A very strong case can be made that a *more expensive* dollar would actually be the best way to shrink the US trade deficit with Japan – and within three to five years.

Increasingly, trade is not determined by the economist's traditional 'comparative advantage' factors, and thus it is less and less susceptible to exchange rates – the US experience with Japan is but one example. Increasingly trade follows investment.

A very large and growing part of Japan's exports to the United States – perhaps enough to account for the entire US trade deficit with Japan – comprises parts, supplies, and machinery for the plants Japan has built in the United States and the companies it has bought there. If Toyota, for instance, builds a plant in Kentucky, most of the machinery and tools it requires will be bought from the people who have supplied Toyota's plants in Japan for years. And the parts for the cars the plant builds will come from the people who supply Toyota in Nagoya.

US manufacturers act exactly the same way when they invest in plants or companies abroad. But the cheap dollar has made it prohibitively expensive for Americans to invest in Japan. In fact, it has forced a shrinking of the US investment base in Japan. Several companies – one example is Minneapolis-based Honywell – have sold their stakes in Japanese subsidiaries either because they could not afford the yen needed to modernize and expand a growing and profitable subsidiary or because they took advantage of the high yen rate to raise the dollars they needed at home.

A cheaper yen would, in all likelihood, unleash a flood of American investments in Japan – now the world's number two consumer market – and with it a flood of exports of high-value-added and high-quality-job goods. But it is also quite possible that a higher dollar would bring in substantially larger foreign-exchange earnings from our commodity exports to Japan – the world's largest commodity importer and by far the largest buyer of American food and raw materials exports, such as timber.

These, however, are conjectures. What is proven is that a cheaper dollar has not made the US trade deficit with Japan go away and will not make it go away. All it does is enable Japan to get dollars more cheaply.

1994

20
The new superpower the overseas Chinese

Newspapers and magazines in the United States, in Europe, and in Japan are full of stories about the new billionaires: the handful of overseas Chinese who have built huge multinationals, headquartered mostly in Hong Kong, Taipei, or Singapore, but also in Thailand, Malaysia, and Indonesia. Actually, these 'tycoons', though highly visible and individually super-rich, are only the small tip of an enormous iceberg. Largely invisible – and carefully shunning publicity – are a great many more multinationals owned by overseas Chinese. Most are mid-size; typically their sales worldwide run to several hundred million dollars. Collectively, however, they are far larger than all the tycoons together.

One example is the $400 million group built by an ethnic Chinese whose grandfather had come to the Philippines as a labourer during the First World War. The group comprises sixteen small manufacturing plants around the world. Each plant turns out only a few highly engineered products, usually for only one customer or two. Four plants, for instance – two in the United States, one each in Japan and the United Kingdom – make small but critical parts for workstations. Three plants – one each in Indonesia, the United States, and the United Kingdom – manufacture precision parts for the world's two leading sewing-machine makers, America's Singer and Germany's Pfaff, now both owned by another overseas Chinese group. And so on. Every plant is separately incorporated as a legally independent company with its ownership registered in the name of its local manager. Each manager is a citizen of his country, though all are of Chinese descent. But these ostensibly independent managers are kept on a very tight leash. Actual ownership is 100 per cent in the hands of the founder in Manila. And each plant reports in great detail and at least twice a week to the group's chief operating officer, who just moved himself and the group's top staff from Manila to Honolulu.

How many such groups there are, no one knows. They are privately owned, publish no figures or annual reports, and are secretive to a fault. In Taiwan, where many of them have their lawyers, the best estimate is that there are at least a thousand. How big the overseas Chinese economy is, is not known either. An often-heard guess – over $2 trillion in investments outside their own home territories – is wildly improbable. It would make the overseas Chinese foreign investments larger than those of the United States! But even $500 billion would mean foreign investments by the overseas Chinese roughly equal to those of the Japanese. The overseas Chinese are certainly the largest investors in mainland China. They have put in more money than either the Americans or the Japanese – more even than the Chinese government has invested this last decade in its own economy. They are thus the driving force behind the explosive economic growth of coastal China. And, with the sole exception of South Korea (which, by and large, is closed to them), they also lead the economies of the other fast-growing countries of Southeast Asia: not only the three islands with a solidly Chinese population – that is, Hong Kong, Taiwan, and Singapore – but also Malaysia (where ethnic Chinese are 30 per cent of the population), Thailand (10 per cent ethnic Chinese), Indonesia (2 per cent ethnic Chinese), and the Philippines (1 per cent ethnic Chinese). And they are branching out to wherever there are even small populations of ethnic Chinese, to the United States and Canada, to Australia and to Europe. The overseas Chinese have become the *new economic superpower*.

Outwardly, the new multinational groups of the overseas Chinese look exactly like other businesses. They are, for instance, incorporated as companies, with a board and with corporate officers. But they function in a drastically different way from anything else in the world economy. The best way to describe them is perhaps as a clan doing business together. Each plant manager in the Manila group is related to the founder – and to each other – by blood or marriage, if only distantly. 'We wouldn't dream of going into a new business,' said the COO to me, 'if we did not have a relative available to run it.' This COO is himself not an ethnic Chinese but a Dutchman – he used to run one of Phillips's big Asian plants. But he is married to the founder's niece. And, as he told me, when he joined the group, the founder said to him, 'I don't care how many concubines or mistresses you have. But on the day on which my niece and you separate or file for divorce, you can look for another job.' The word of the founder–CEO is law. But his authority far more resembles that of a Confucian head of the house (or that of a Scottish Highland chieftain of yore) than that of the head of a business. He is expected to base his decisions on the best interests of the clan and to manage so as to guarantee the clan's survival and prosperity. What holds together the multinationals of the overseas Chinese is neither ownership nor legal contract. It is mutual trust and the mutual obligations inherent in clan membership.

This structure has deep roots in Chinese culture and history, reaching back two millennia. It was the only way merchants could survive in a country that knew no civil law (it still doesn't) and in which there was (and still is) no appeal against a local mandarin who could be arbitrary, was often corrupt, and was usually contemptuous of 'trade'. Survival thus depended on the ability to shift one's money and one's business overnight to a distant cousin, without contract or anything in writing. The one sanction in this system – and an effective one – is then disgrace and ostracism by the entire business community for anyone who betrays this trust.

There is tremendous strength to this tradition. It explains in large measure why the groups of the overseas Chinese could grow so fast. If there is a qualified clan member available in a certain country or a certain industry, the group can often get him to join by appealing to his clan spirit. Thus, unlike the Japanese company, the group does not have to wait until it has grown its own managers from scratch in order to expand. And unlike the typical Western company, there is little internal resistance against bringing into a senior position someone from the outside; he is, after all, 'family'. 'Ten of our sixteen plant managers,' the COO of the Manila group told me, 'worked for Western companies but were willing to join the clan business.' And since it is accepted that the group has to be run to perpetuate the clan and its prosperity, the lazy or incompetent family member can usually be kept out of a top job and even out of the business altogether. The founder and CEO of the Manila-based group wanted his two sons to succeed him. But the clan members running the plants made it clear that they would not accept the sons. They persuaded the founder instead to make their choice, the Dutch COO, the heir-designate. 'My money,' I was told in Malaysia by the head of another overseas Chinese group, 'I can leave to whomever I pick; my power has to be left to whomever my associates trust.' The Japanese, it has often been said, owe their success to their ability to run the modern corporation as a family. The overseas Chinese owe their success to their ability to run their family as a modern corporation.

But with all its strengths, the overseas-Chinese multinational will have to change quite a bit in the next decade; indeed, wherever I went on a recent South-east Asian trip, the discussion centred on the need for drastic changes. For one, the founders who still run the groups are, in the majority of cases, getting old. The head of the Manila-based group, for instance, is seventy-three. The successors to the founders have grown up in a very different world; many are Western-educated, for example. 'Our next CEO,' the number-two man in a Taiwan-based (and fast-growing) multinational told me, 'cannot be a Confucian "head of house" or "elder brother"; he'll have to be a team builder and a team leader – that's what we learned as graduate students in the US.' But also for the overseas-Chinese multinational to grow, and especially for it to grow in mainland China, it will have to go into joint ventures of all kinds with foreigners – Westerners and Japanese – to whom the Chinese tradition is totally alien. Only foreigners – Americans, Japanese, Europeans – have the technology to build, for instance, the trains that China desperately needs. But Chinese-speaking businesses, that is, overseas Chinese, will be needed to maintain and service those trains. And joint ventures, as the younger overseas Chinese fully realize, mean written business plans and clear contractual arrangements – things the Chinese tradition abhors. It also means something even more abhorrent: sharing information. But above all, the overseas-Chinese multinational cannot grow unless it learns to bring in 'strangers', that is, Chinese from outside the clan. If you need a metallurgist or a computer specialist, what matters is the person's competence, not his membership in the clan. And that person will expect to be treated as an equal; if he's not treated so, he will leave. Wherever I went in South-east Asia, how to treat the stranger was the first topic raised and the one that provoked the most heated controversy. 'To maintain clan cohesion we cannot possibly treat as an equal a Chinese who is not a clan member,' everybody said. 'Yet to grow the business, we have to.'

And then there is, of course, the grave uncertainty of mainland China's future. Only a few, largely Hong Kong-based groups have all their eggs in the Chinese basket. There are even a few groups – in Singapore mostly, but also in Malaysia and Indonesia – that have kept out of mainland China altogether. But all overseas Chinese know that their future heavily depends on how

China does; and in countries in which they are a (greatly envied) minority, namely, in Thailand, Malaysia, Indonesia, and the Philippines, the Chinese also know that even their economic survival may depend on China's health and strength. And I did not meet a single overseas Chinese who expected anything but a decade of surprises and turbulence for mainland China.

Yet every single one of the younger overseas Chinese – the people who are now taking over the day-to-day management of their multinationals – was confident that his group could successfully solve its problems and yet maintain its basic Chinese character. 'They will change details, but they won't change the fundamentals any more than the Japanese changed theirs when they modernized,' said a Taipei lawyer who is the confidant of a large number of overseas-Chinese business leaders. '*And it will work!*'

Will *The Secrets of Chinese Management* be the title of the management best-seller of the year 2005?

1995

Part Four

The Society

21
A century of social transformations

Introduction

No century in human history has experienced so many social transformations and such radical ones as the twentieth century. They, I submit, will turn out to be the most significant events of this century, and its lasting legacy. In the developed free-market countries – only one-fifth of the earth's population, but the model for the rest – work and workforce, society and polity are all, in the last decade of this century, *qualitatively* and *quantitatively* different both from those of the first years of this century and from anything ever experienced before in human history: different in their configuration, in their processes, in their problems, and in their structures.

Far smaller and far slower social changes in earlier periods trigged violent intellectual and spiritual crises, rebellions, and civil wars. The extreme social transformations of this century have hardly caused any stir. They proceeded with a minimum of friction, with a minimum of upheavals, and indeed with altogether a minimum of attention from scholars, politicians, the press, and the public. To be sure, this century of ours may well have been the cruellest and most violent century in human history, with its world wars and civil wars, its mass tortures, ethnic cleansings, and genocides. But all these killings, all these horrors inflicted on the human race by this century's *Weltbeglücker*,* hindsight clearly shows, were just that: senseless killings, senseless horrors. Hitler, Stalin, and Mao, the three evil geniuses of this century, destroyed. But they created nothing.

Indeed, if this century proves anything, it is the futility of politics. Even the most dogmatic believer in historical determinism would have a hard time explaining the social transformations of this century as caused by the headline-making political events, or explaining the headline-making political events as caused by the social transformations. But it is the social transformations, running like ocean currents deep below the hurricane-tormented surface of the sea, that have had the lasting, indeed the permanent, effect. They – rather than all the violence of the political surface – have transformed the society and the economy, the community, the polity we live in.

The social structure and its transformations

Before the First World War the largest single group in every country were farmers. They were then no longer *the* population everywhere, as they had been since the dawn of history and as they had still been in every country at the end of the Napoleonic Wars, a hundred years earlier. But except in England and Belgium, farmers were still a near majority in every developed country – in Germany, in France, in Japan, in the United States – and, of course, in all developing and Third World countries too.

Eighty years ago, at the eve of the First World War, it was considered axiomatic that developed countries – North America being the only exception – would increasingly become unable to

---

*Weltbeglücker – those who establish paradise on earth by killing off nonconformists, dissidents, resisters, and innocent bystanders, whether Jews, the bourgeoisie, kulaks, or intellectuals – an untranslatable German term, alas.

feed themselves and would increasingly have to rely on food imports from non-industrial, non-developed areas. England and Belgium had already become massive food importers. Germany, Holland, and Switzerland were barely breaking even in their food accounts. And the fear of becoming dependent on food imports was emerging in Meiji Japan, after 1890, as a keynote of Japanese politics, as the justification for Japan's annexing food-surplus territories like Taiwan and Korea, and as the psychological force behind Japan's nascent imperialism.

Today, only Japan, among major, developed, free-market countries is a heavy importer of food. (Unnecessarily so – its weakness as a food producer is largely the result of an obsolete rice-subsidy policy that prevents the country from developing a modern, productive agriculture.) All other developed free-market countries have become surplus food producers despite burgeoning urban populations. In all these countries food production is today many times what it was eighty years ago – in the United States, eight to ten times as much.

But in all developed free-market countries – including Japan – farmers today are, at most, 5 per cent of population and workforce, that is, one-tenth of what they were eighty years ago. Actually, *productive* farmers are less than half of the total farm population, or no more than 2 per cent of the workforce. And these agricultural producers are not 'farmers' in any sense of the word; they are 'agribusinesses' and constitute arguably the most capital-intensive, most technology-intensive, and most information-intensive industry around. Traditional farmers are close to extinction, even in Japan. And those still around have become a protected species kept alive only by enormous subsidies.

The second-largest group in population and workforce in every developed country around 1900 were live-in servants. They were considered as much a 'law of nature' as farmers were. The British Census of 1910 defined 'lower middle class' as a household employing fewer than three servants. And while farmers as a proportion of population and workforce had been steadily shrinking throughout the nineteenth century, the numbers of domestic servants, both absolutely and as a percentage, were steadily growing right up to the First World War. (And nowhere faster than in the United States, with its enormous influx of immigrants. With free land largely gone by 1900, a job as domestic servant was, for many newcomers, the only work available.) Eighty years later, live-in domestic servants in developed countries have become practically extinct. Few people born since the Second World War, that is, few people under fifty, have even seen any except on the stage or in old films.

Farmers and domestic servants were not only the *largest* social groups, they were the oldest social groups, too. Together they were, through the ages, the foundation of economy and society, the foundation altogether of 'civilization'. Servants, whether slaves, indentured servants, or hired hands, actually antedate farmers by several millennia. The patriarchs of the Old Testament were still nomadic pastoralists, rather than settled farmers. But they had large numbers of servants of all kinds.

Big cities are nothing new. Nineveh and Babylon were very big cities, and so were the capital of the Han emperor in China two hundred years before Christ and the Rome of the Caesars. But these big cities were islets in a rural sea. This was still largely true for the social world of 1900, despite the visibility and glamour of a Paris, a London, a New York, a Boston, a Tokyo. It was then still generally accepted, as it had been in the Hellas of Hesiod's *Erga Kai Hemera* (*Days and Works*) written in the eighth century BC, or in the Rome of Virgil's *Georgica*, written in the first century BC, that cities are 'parasites' and farmers the 'real nation'. In its technology the society of 1900 was already much closer to that of the year 2000 than to that of 1800. It had steamships, railways, quite a few cars, and, by 1903, the airplane. It had electricity, telephone, wireless telegraphy, and the first films. But socially 1900 was still closer to 1800 and indeed to antiquity than to us, that is, to 1994. It was still organized around farmers and domestic servants, both still largely living the life their ancestors had lived at the time of Hesiod and Virgil, doing the same work and with very much the same tools.

In the developed society of 2000, farmers are little but nostalgia, and domestic servants are not even that.

Yet these enormous transformations in all free-market developed countries were accomplished without civil war, and, in fact, in almost total silence. Only now that their farm population has shrunk to near-zero do the totally urban French loudly assert that theirs should be a 'rural country' with a 'rural civilization'.

The rise and fall of the blue-collar worker

One reason, indeed the main reason, why the transformation caused so little stir was that by 1900 a new class, the blue-collar worker in manufacturing industry (Marx's 'proletarian'), had become socially dominant. Farmers – and not only in Kansas – were loudly adjured to 'raise more hell and less corn', but not even the farmers paid much attention. Domestic servants were clearly the most exploited class around. But when people before the First World War talked or wrote about the 'social question', they meant blue-collar industrial workers. These workers were still a fairly small minority of population and workforce – right up to the First World War, at most, an eighth or a sixth of the total – and still vastly outnumbered by the traditional 'lower' classes of farmers and domestic servants. But early twentieth-century society was obsessed with blue-collar workers, fixated on them, bewitched by them.

Farmers and domestic servants were everywhere. But as a 'class' they were invisible. Domestic servants lived and worked in small and isolated groups of two or three, inside individual homes or on individual farms. And farmers too were dispersed. Above all, these traditional lower classes were not organized. Indeed, they could not be organized. Slaves employed in mining or in producing goods had revolted frequently in the ancient world – though always unsuccessfully. But there is no record of a single demonstration or of a single protest march of domestic servants any place and at any time. There were peasant revolts galore – no place more frequently than in Tokugawa Japan from 1700 on, or in imperial China, also beginning in 1700. But except for two Chinese revolts in the nineteenth century – the Taiping Rebellion in mid-century and the Boxer Rebellion at the century's end, both of which lasted for years and came close to destroying the regime – all peasant rebellions in history have fizzled out after a few bloody weeks. Peasants, history shows, are very hard to organize and do not stay organized – which was the reason why they earned Marx's contempt.

The new class, the blue-collar worker in manufacturing industry, were extremely visible. This is what made them a 'class'. They lived perforce in dense population clusters and in cities – in St-Denis outside Paris, in Berlin's Wedding and Vienna's Ottakring, in the textile towns of Lancashire, the steel towns of America's Monongahela Valley, and in Japan's Kobe. And they soon proved eminently organizable, with the first strikes occurring almost as soon as there were factory workers. Charles Dickens's harrowing tale of a murderous labour conflict at a cotton textile mill, *Hard Times*, was published in 1854, only six years after Marx and Engels wrote *The Communist Manifesto*.

By 1900 it had become quite clear that industrial blue-collar workers would not become the majority as Marx had predicted only a few decades earlier. They therefore would not overwhelm the capitalists by their sheer numbers. Yet the most influential radical writer of the period before the First World War, the French former Marxist and revolutionary syndicalist Georges Sorel, found widespread acceptance for his 1906 thesis that the proletarians would overturn the existing order and take power by their organization and in and through the violence of the general strike. It was not only Lenin who made Sorel's thesis the foundation of his revision of Marxism and built around it his strategy in 1917 and 1918; both Mussolini and Hitler – and Mao, ten years later – equally built their strategies on Sorel's thesis.

Mao's 'power grows out of the barrel of a gun' is almost a straight quote from Sorel. The blue-collar worker became the 'social question' of 1900 because he was the first 'lower class' in history that could be organized and stay organized.

No class in history has ever risen faster than the blue-collar worker. And no class in history has ever fallen faster.

In 1883, the year of Marx's death, 'proletarians' were still a minority of industrial workers. The majority were then skilled workers employed in small craft shops each containing twenty or thirty workers at most. Of the anti-heroes of the nineteenth century's best 'proletarian' novel, *The Princess Casamassima* by Henry James – published in 1886, only three years after Marx's death (and surely only Henry James could have given such a title to a story of working-class terrorists!) – one is a highly skilled bookbinder, the other one an equally skilled pharmacist. Similarly, the protagonists of Gerhart Hauptmann's *Die Weber* (*The Weavers*) – written in 1892 and the only successful 'proletarian' play (its author eventually received the Nobel Prize for Literature for it) – are skilled men still working in their homes rather than in a factory.

By 1900, *industrial worker* had become synonymous with *machine operator* in a factory employing hundreds, if not thousands, of people. These factory workers were indeed Marx's proletarians, without social position, without political power, without economic or purchasing power.

Popular myth has it that Henry Ford's 1907 Model T was so cheap that workers could afford it. But at $750 its price was equal to more than three times the entire *annual* income of an American machine operator – 70 or 80 cents was a good daily wage. Yet American machine operators were then already the world's most highly paid industrial workers.

The workers of 1900 – and even of 1913 – had no pension; no paid vacation; no overtime pay; no extra pay for Sunday or night work; no health insurance (except in Germany); no unemployment compensation; no job security whatever. One of the earliest laws to limit working hours for adult males – enacted in Austria in 1884 – set the working day at *eleven* hours, six days a week. Industrial workers, in 1913, everywhere worked a minimum of 3000 hours a year. Their unions were still officially proscribed or, at best, barely tolerated. But the workers had shown their capacity to be organized. They had shown their capacity to act as a 'class'.

In the 1950s, industrial blue-collar workers had become the largest single group in every developed country, including the Communist ones, though they were an actual majority only during wartime. They had become eminently respectable. In all developed free-market countries they had economically become 'middle class'. In the United States, in fact – and soon in non-Communist Europe, too – unionized industrial workers in mass-production industry (which then was dominant everywhere) had attained and sometimes even exceeded near upper-class income levels, with annual incomes including benefits reaching $50 000 – and in the US car industry (e.g. at Ford) exceeding $100 000. They had extensive job security; pensions; long, paid vacations; comprehensive unemployment insurance or 'lifetime employment'. Above all, they had achieved political power. It was not only in Britain that the labour unions were considered to be the 'real government', with greater power than prime minister and Parliament. In the United States, too, and equally in Germany, France and Italy, the labour unions had emerged as the country's most powerful and best-organized *political* forces. And in Japan they had come very close, in the 1948 Toyota and the 1954 Nissan strikes, to overturning the 'system' and to taking over power themselves.

In 1990, however, both the blue-collar worker and his union were in total and irreversible retreat. They had become marginal in numbers. Whereas blue-collar workers who made or moved things had accounted for two-fifths of the American workforce in the 1950s, they accounted for less than one-fifth of the workforce in the early 1990s – that is, for no more than they had accounted for in 1900, when their meteoric rise had begun. In the other developed free-market countries the decline was slower at first; but after 1980 it began to accelerate everywhere. By the year 2000 or 2010, in every developed free-market country, blue-collar industrial workers will account for no more than one-tenth or, at most, one-eighth of the workforce. Union power has been going down equally fast. Where in the 1950s and 1960s the National Union of Mineworkers in the United Kingdom broke prime ministers as if they were matchwood, Margaret Thatcher in the 1980s won election after election by being openly contemptuous of organized labour and by whittling down its political power and its privileges. The blue-collar worker in manufacturing industry and his union are going the way of the farmer.

Unlike domestic servants, blue-collar workers will not disappear – no more than producers on the land have disappeared or will disappear. But just as the traditional 'farmer' has become a recipient of subsidies rather than a 'producer', so will the traditional blue-collar worker largely become an auxiliary force. His place is already being taken by a 'technologist', that is, by people who work both with their hands and their theoretical knowledge. (Examples are computer technicians or paramedical technicians such as X-ray technicians, physical therapists, medical-lab technicians, pulmonary technicians, and so on, who have been the fastest-growing group in the United States workforce since 1980.)

And instead of a 'class', that is, a coherent, recognizable, defined, and self-conscious group, the blue-collar worker in manufacturing industry may soon be just another 'pressure group'.

Chroniclers of the rise of the industrial worker tend to highlight the violent episodes – the clashes between strikers and police especially, such as America's Pullman strike. The reason is probably that the theoreticians and propagandists of socialism, anarchism, and Communism – beginning with Marx and down to

Herbert Marcuse in the 1960s – incessantly wrote and talked of 'revolution' and 'violence'. Actually, the rise of the industrial worker was remarkably *non-violent*. The enormous violences of this century – the world wars, civil wars, genocides, ethnic cleansings, and so on – were all violences from above rather than violences from below; and they were unconnected with the transformations of society, whether the shrinking of the number of farmers, the disappearance of the domestic servant, or the rise of the industrial worker. In fact, no one any longer even tries to explain these great convulsions with 'the crisis of capitalism', as was standard Marxist rhetoric only thirty years ago.

In contrast to Marxist and syndicalist predictions, the rise of the industrial worker did not destabilize society. On the contrary, it emerged as the century's most *stabilizing social development*. It explains why the disappearance of farmer and domestic servant produced no social crises.

The 'enclosures' in seventeenth- and eighteenth-century England, which drove farmers off the land, were quite limited locally; but they produced serious and often very violent reactions. They also were widely noticed and hotly discussed – by writers, poets, politicians, and the public, one example being Oliver Goldsmith's great 1770 poem 'The Deserted Village', perhaps the best-known and most-quoted poem in the England of 1800. Similarly, the early-nineteenth-century *Bauernlegen* in East Prussia, in which tenant farmers were pushed off the land to make way for large-scale agriculture, had profound political and cultural reverberations. But the far more massive 'flight from the land' that began in the closing decades of the nineteenth century and has continued unabated has gone almost unnoticed except by statisticians. The equally massive 'flight from service' that began after the First World War, even the statisticians have barely noticed.

Both the flight from the land and the flight from service were voluntary. Farmers and maids were not 'pushed off' or 'displaced'. They went into industrial employment as fast as they could. Industrial jobs required no skills they did not already possess, and no additional knowledge. On the contrary, farmers on the whole had a good deal more skill than was required to be a machine operator in the mass-production plant – and so had many domestic servants. To be sure, industrial work paid poorly until the First World War. But it paid better than farming or household work. Industrial workers, until 1913 – and until the Second World War in some countries, such as Japan – worked long hours. But they worked shorter hours than farmers and domestic servants. What's more, they worked *specified* hours; the rest of the day was their own, which was true of neither work on the farm nor of work as a servant in a household.

The history books record the squalor of early industry, the poverty of the industrial workers, and their exploitation. They did indeed work in squalor and live in poverty, and they were indeed exploited. But they lived better than they would either on a farm or in an employer's household, and they were treated better.

Proof of this is that infant mortality dropped as soon as farmers and domestic servants moved into industrial work in the factory. Historically, cities never reproduced themselves. They depended for their perpetuation on a constant influx of people from the countryside. This was still true in the mid-nineteenth century. But with the spread of factory employment, the city became the centre of population growth. In part this was the result of the new public health measures: provision of clean water; collection and treatment of wastes; quarantine and inoculation against epidemics. These measures – and they were effective mostly in the city – counteracted, or at least contained, the hazards of crowding that had made the traditional city the breeding ground for pestilence. But the largest single factor in the exponential drop in infant mortality as industrialization spread was surely the improvement in living conditions brought about by the advent of the factory – better housing, better nutrition, lighter workloads, and fewer accidents. The drop in infant mortality – and with it the explosive growth in population – correlates with only one development: industrialization. The early factory was indeed the 'satanic mill' of William Blake's great poem. But the countryside was not the 'green and pleasant land' of which Blake sang; it was (I have said so before) a picturesque but even more satanic slum.

For farmer and domestic servant, industrial work was an opportunity. It was in fact the first opportunity in social history to better oneself substantially without having to emigrate. In the developed, free-market countries, every generation in the last 100 or 150 years could expect to do substantially better than the generation preceding it. The main reason was that farmers and domestic servants could and did become industrial workers.

Because industrial workers were concentrated in groups, that is, because they worked in a large factory rather than in a small shop or in their homes, there could be systematic work on their *productivity*. Beginning in 1881 – two years before Marx's death – the systematic study of work, tasks, and tools has raised the productivity of manual work making and moving of things by 3–4 per cent, compounded each year, for a total fiftyfold increase in output per worker over a hundred years. On this rest all the economic and social gains during that time. And contrary to what 'everybody knew' in the nineteenth century – not only Marx but all the 'conservatives' as well, such as J. P. Morgan, Bismarck, and Disraeli – practically all these gains have accrued to the blue-collar worker, half of the gains in the form of sharply reduced working hours (with the cuts ranging from 40 per cent in Japan to 50 per cent in Germany), half of them in the form of a twenty-fivefold increase in the real wages of blue-collar workers making or moving things.

There were thus very good reasons why the *rise* of blue-collar workers was peaceful rather than violent, let alone 'revolutionary'. But what explains that the *fall* of the blue-collar worker has been equally peaceful and almost entirely free of social protest, of upheaval, of serious dislocation, at least in the United States?

The rise of the knowledge worker

The rise of the 'class' succeeding the industrial blue-collar worker is not an opportunity to him. It is a challenge. The newly emerging dominant group are 'knowledge workers'. The very term was unknown forty years ago – I first coined it in a 1959 book (*The Landmarks of Tomorrow*). By the end of this century, knowledge workers will amount to a third or more of the workforce in the United States, that is, to as large a proportion as industrial blue-collar workers ever were, except in wartime. The majority of knowledge workers are paid at least as well as blue-collar workers ever were, or better. And the new jobs offer much greater opportunities to the individual.

But – and it is a big but – the new jobs require, in the great majority, qualifications the blue-collar worker does not possess and is poorly equipped to acquire. The new jobs require a good deal of formal education and the ability to acquire and to apply theoretical and analytical knowledge. They require a different approach to work and a different mindset. Above all, they require a habit of continuous learning.

Farmers, domestic servants, machine operators have learned everything they need for their life's work and jobs after a fairly short apprenticeship – a year or two for farmers and domestic servants, a few weeks for machine operators. But knowledge work – and a good deal of service work, such as direct selling – is not *experience*-based, as all manual work has always been. It is *learning*-based. Access to it requires formal education, or at least formal training. Industrial work as a machine operator was, in its work characteristics, still traditional work. Knowledge work and most of services work, in *their* work characteristics, are non-traditional. Displaced industrial workers thus cannot simply move into knowledge work or services work the way displaced farmers and displaced domestic workers moved into industrial work. At the very least they have to make a major change in their basic attitudes, values, and beliefs.

In the United States the industrial workforce has shrunk faster and further in the closing decades of this century than in any other developed country. At the same time, industrial production has grown faster than in any other developed country, except only Japan.

The shift aggravated America's oldest and least tractable problem: the position of the Blacks. In the forty years since the Second World War the economic position of the Negro in America improved faster than that of any group in American social history – or in the social history of any country. Three-fifths of America's Blacks rose into middle-class incomes – before the Second World War the figure was one-twentieth. But half of that group rose into middle-class *incomes* and not into middle-class *jobs*. Since the Second World War more and more Blacks have moved into blue-collar, unionized, mass-production industry, that is, into jobs paying middle-class and upper-middle-class wages while requiring neither education nor skill. These are precisely the jobs, however, that are disappearing the fastest. What is amazing is not that so many Blacks did not acquire an education but that so many did. For the economically rational thing to do for a young Black in America from 1945 to 1980 was *not* to stay in school and to learn. It was to leave school as early as possible and to take one of the plentiful mass-production jobs. As a result, the fall of the industrial worker hits America's Blacks disproportionately hard – quantitatively, but qualitatively even more. It denigrates what has been the most potent role model in the Black community in America: the well-paid industrial worker with high job security, full health insurance, and a guaranteed retirement pension – yet possessing neither skill nor much education.

That half of that group of newly middle-class Blacks advanced because they used the opportunities education offers and successfully moved into knowledge work, does not, it seems, compensate for the loss of the opportunity blue-collar industrial work offered uneducated Blacks. Black youngsters aged ten or eleven in the inner city could and did identify with the cousin who, only seven or eight years older, had a well-paying job in the car plant. They could not easily identify with cousins who were dentists, accountants, lawyers – which meant that they were twenty years older and had sat in schools for at least sixteen years. And thus the fall of the industrial blue-collar worker has been a traumatic shock for the Black community in America. It explains in large measure not only the growing defeatism, despair, and rage of inner-city Blacks. It explains their growing alienation from, and rage against, their achieving brothers and sisters, that is, the large and growing number of Blacks who are moving into the new 'middle class', as knowledge workers.

But, of course, the Blacks are a small minority of population and workforce in the United States. For the rest – Whites and also Latinos and Asians – the fall of the industrial blue-collar worker has caused amazingly little disruption and nothing that could be called an upheaval. Even in communities that were totally dependent on one or two mass-production plants that have gone out of business or have cut employment by two thirds – steel cities in western Pennsylvania or eastern Ohio, for instance, or car cities like Flint, Michigan – unemployment rates for adult, non-Black men and women fell within a few short years to levels barely higher than the US average. And that means to levels barely higher than the US 'full-employment' rate. And there has been no radicalization of America's blue-collar workers.

The only explanation is that for the non-Black, blue-collar community the development came as no surprise, however unwelcome, painful, and threatening to individual worker and individual family. Psychologically – in terms of values perhaps, rather than in terms of emotions – America's industrial blue-collar workers must have been prepared to accept as right and proper the shift to jobs that require formal education and that pay for knowledge rather than for manual work, whether skilled or unskilled.

One possible factor may have been the GI Bill of Rights after the Second World War, which by offering a college education to every returning American veteran established advanced education as the 'norm' and everything less as 'substandard'. Another factor may have been the draft the United States introduced in the Second World War and maintained for thirty-five years afterwards, as a result of which the great majority of American male adults born between 1920 and 1950 – and that means the majority of American adults alive today – served in the military for several years where they were *forced* to acquire a high-school education if they did not already have one. But whatever the explanation, in the United States the shift *to* knowledge work *from* blue-collar manual work making and moving things has largely been accepted (except in the Black community) as appropriate or, at least, as inevitable.

In the United States the shift, by 1990 or so, had largely been accomplished. But so far only in the United States. In the other developed free-market countries, in western and northern Europe and in Japan, it is just beginning in the 1990s. It is, however, certain to proceed rapidly in these countries from now on, and perhaps to proceed there faster than it originally did in the United States. Will it then also proceed, as it did by and large in the United States, with a minimum of social upheaval, of social dislocation, of social unrest? Or will the American development turn out to be another example of 'American exceptionalism' (as has so much of American social history and especially of American labour history)? In Japan, the superiority of formal education and of the formally educated person is generally accepted so that the fall of the industrial worker – still a fairly recent class in Japan and outnumbering farmers and domestic servants only since well after the Second World War – may well be accepted as appropriate as it has been in the United States, and perhaps even more so. But what about industrialized Europe – the United Kingdom, Germany, France, Belgium, northern Italy, and so on – where there has been a 'working-class culture' and a 'self-respecting working class' for well over a century, and where, despite all evidence to the contrary, the belief is still deeply ingrained that industrial, blue-collar work, rather than knowledge, is the creator of all wealth? Will Europe react the way the American Black has reacted? This surely is a key question, the answer to which will largely determine the social as well as the economic future of the developed free-market countries of Europe. And the answer will be given within the next decade or so.

The fall of the industrial blue-collar worker in the developed, free-market countries will also have major impacts outside of the developed world. It means that developing countries can no longer expect to base their development on their comparative labour advantage, that is, on cheap industrial labour.

It is widely believed, especially, of course, by labour-union officials, that the fall of the blue-collar industrial worker in the developed countries was largely, if not entirely, caused by moving production 'offshore' to countries of abundant supply of unskilled labour and low wages. But this is not true.

There *was* something to the belief thirty years ago, this is, before 1965 or 1970. Japan, Taiwan, and, later on, South Korea did indeed (as explained in some detail in my 1993 book *Post-Capitalist Society*) gain their *initial* advantage in the world market by combining America's invention of training for full productivity almost overnight with wage costs that were still those of a pre-industrial country. They thereby created a workforce that had the productivity and quality of a developed country and the labour costs of a developing one. But this worked only for some twenty or thirty years. It has not worked at all since 1970 or 1975.

In the 1900s, only an insignificant percentage of manufactured goods imported into the United States is based on low labour costs. While total imports in 1990 accounted for about 12 per cent of American gross national product, imports into the United States from countries with wage costs that are significantly

lower than US wage costs accounted for less than 3 per cent –
and only half of those, that is, only 1 per cent or $1\frac{1}{2}$ per cent of
the gross domestic product, were imports of *manufactured* products.* Of the decline in American blue-collar, industrial employment from some 30 per cent or 35 per cent to 15–18 per
cent of the workforce, practically nothing can therefore be
blamed on moving work to low-wage countries. The *main* competition for American manufacturing industry – in cars for instance, in steel, in machine tools – has come from countries such
as Japan or Germany where wage costs have long been equal to
US wage costs, if not higher. The comparative advantage which
now counts is in the application of knowledge, e.g. in Japan's
Total Quality Management, Lean Manufacturing, Just-in-Time
Delivery and Price-based Costing, or in the customer service of
the medium-sized German or Swiss engineering company. This
means, however, that *developing* countries can no longer expect
to base their development on low wages. They, too, must learn
to base it on applying knowledge – just at the time when most of
them (e.g. most of Latin America and China) will have to find
jobs for millions of uneducated and unskilled young people
qualified for little except yesterday's blue-collar industrial jobs.

But for the developed countries, too, the shift poses major
social challenge. Blue-collar workers are *manual* workers as
were farmers and domestic servants. They still 'earn their bread
by the sweat of their brow'. Marx proclaimed that blue-collar,
industrial workers were something totally new and totally different. Yes, they worked in a factory. But otherwise they were
traditional workers. Most earlier workers were similarly not
independent but dependent – as hired hands and landless
labourers on the land; as domestic servants whether free or
unfree; as apprentices and journeymen in the craftsman's shop.

---

* See Robert Lawrence and Mark Slaughter, *International Trade and
American Wages in the 1980s* (Brookings Institute paper on economic activity, 1993).

That the blue-collar, industrial worker did not own 'the tools of production' was also not new, as Marx asserted. Even tenant farmers did not, let alone the far more numerous hired hands. Nor did domestic servants or the craftsmen's apprentices and journeymen. Despite the factory, industrial society was still, essentially, a traditional society in its basic social relationships of production.

But the emerging society, the one based on knowledge and knowledge worker, is not. It is the first society in which 'honest work' does not mean a calloused hand. It is also the first society in which everybody does not do the same work, as was the case when the huge majority were farmers or were, as seemed likely only forty or thirty years ago, going to be machine operators.

This is far more than a social change. It is a change in the *human condition*. What it means – what the values are of this society, what its commitments are, what its problems are – we do not know. But we do know that they will be different. We do know that the twenty-first century will be different – as regards politics and society, but above all, as regards humans.

The emerging knowledge society

Knowledge workers will not be the majority in the knowledge society. But in many countries, if not most developed countries, they will be the largest single group in the population and the workforce. And even if outnumbered by other groups, know-ledge workers will be the group that gives the emerging knowledge society its character, its leadership, its social profile. They may not be the *ruling* class of the knowledge society, but they already are its *leading* class. And in their characteristics, their social position, their values, and their expectations, they differ fundamentally from any group in history that has ever occupied the leading, let alone the dominant, position.

In the first place, the knowledge worker gains access to work, job, and social position through *formal education*.

A great deal of knowledge work will require high manual skill and substantial work with one's hands. An extreme example is neurosurgery. The neurosurgeon's performance capacity rests on formal education and theoretical knowledge. Absence of manual skill disqualifies for work as a neurosurgeon, but manual skill alone, no matter how advanced, will never enable anyone to be a neurosurgeon. The formal education that is required for knowledge work is education that can only be acquired in and through formal schooling. It cannot be acquired through apprenticeship.

In the amount and kind of formal knowledge required, knowledge work will vary tremendously from one occupation to the next. Some will have fairly low requirements, others will require the kind of knowledge the neurosurgeon has to possess. But even if the knowledge itself is quite primitive, it is knowledge that only formal education can provide. Filing is hardly advanced knowledge work. But it is based on a knowledge of the alphabet – or in Japan on a knowledge of Chinese ideographs – which can be acquired only in and through systematic learning, that is, in and through formal schooling.

The first implication of this is that education will become the centre of the knowledge society, and schooling its key institution. What knowledge is required for everybody? What mix of knowledges is required for everybody? What is 'quality' in learning and teaching? All these will, of necessity, become central concerns of the knowledge society, and central political issues. In fact, it may not be too fanciful to anticipate that the acquisition and distribution of formal knowledge will come to occupy the place in the politics of the knowledge society that acquisition and distribution of property and income have occupied in the two or three centuries that we have come to call the Age of Capitalism.

Paradoxically, this may not necessarily mean that the school as we know it will become more important. For in the knowledge society clearly more and more knowledge, and especially advanced knowledge, will be acquired well past the age of formal schooling, and increasingly, perhaps, in and through educational processes that do not centre on the traditional school – for example, systematic continuing education offered at the place of employment. But at the same time, there is very little doubt that the performance of the schools and the basic values of the schools will increasingly become of concern to society as a whole, rather than be considered 'professional' matters that can safely be left to the 'educator'.

We can also predict with high probability that we will redefine what it means to be an 'educated person'. Traditionally, and especially during the last 200 or 300 years, at least in the West (and since about that time in Japan, as well), an educated person was somebody who shared a common stock of formal knowledge – someone who had what the Germans called *Allgemeine Bildung* (a general education) and the English (and following them, the nineteenth-century Americans) called a *'Liberal education'*. Increasingly, an 'educated person' will be somebody who has learned how to learn and who throughout his or her lifetime continues learning, and especially learning in and through formal education.

There are obvious dangers to this. Such a society can easily degenerate into one in which the emphasis is on formal degrees rather than on performance capacity. It can easily degenerate into one of totally sterile, Confucian-type mandarins – a danger to which the American university, particularly, is singularly susceptible. It can, on the other hand, also fall prey to overvaluing immediately usable, 'practical' knowledge, and underrate the importance of fundamentals, and of wisdom altogether.

This society in which knowledge workers dominate is in danger of a new 'class conflict': the conflict between the large minority of knowledge workers and the majority of people who will make their living through traditional ways, either by manual work, whether skilled or unskilled, or by services work, whether skilled or unskilled. The productivity of knowledge work – still abysmally low – will predictably become the *economic* challenge of the knowledge society. On it will depend the competitive position of every single country, every single industry, every single institution within society. The productivity of the non-knowledge-services worker will increasingly become the *social* challenge of the knowledge society. On it will depend the ability of the knowledge society to give decent incomes, and with them dignity and status, to non-knowledge people.

No society in history has faced these challenges. But equally new are the opportunities of the knowledge society. In the knowledge society, for the first time in history, access to leadership is open to all. Equally, access to the acquisition of knowledge will no longer be dependent on obtaining a prescribed education at any given age. Learning will become the tool of the individual – available to him or her at any point in life – if only because so much of skill and knowledge can be acquired by means of the new learning technologies.

Another implication is that the productivity of an individual, an organization, an industry, a country, in acquiring and applying knowledge will increasingly become the key competitive factor – for career and earnings opportunities of the individual; for the performance, perhaps even the survival, of the individual organization; for an industry; and for a country. The knowledge society will inevitably become *far more competitive* than any society we have yet known – for the simple reason that with knowledge being universally accessible, there are no excuses for non-performance. There will be no 'poor' countries. There will only be ignorant countries. And the same will be true for individual companies, individual industries, and individual organizations of any kind. It will be true for the individual, too. In fact, developed societies have already become infinitely more competitive for the individual than were the societies of the early twentieth century – let alone earlier societies, those of the nineteenth or eighteenth centuries. Then, most people had no opportunity to rise out of the 'class' into which they were born, with most individuals following their fathers in their work and in their station in life.

I have been speaking of knowledge. But the proper term is knowledges. For the knowledge of the knowledge society is fundamentally different from what was considered knowledge in earlier societies, and in fact, from what is still widely considered knowledge. The knowledge of the German *Allgemeine Bildung* or of the Anglo-American Liberal education had little to do with one's life's work. It focused on the person and the person's development rather than on any application – and often even prided itself on having no utility whatever. In the knowledge society, however, knowledge basically exists only in application.

Knowledge in application is, by definition, highly specialized – which was the reason why Plato's Socrates, 2500 years ago, refused to accept it as knowledge and considered it mere *techne*, that is, mere skill.

Some knowledge work requires a fairly limited amount of knowledge – examples are some paramedical technologists, such as the X-ray technologist, the technologist in the clinical laboratory, or the pulmonary technologist. Other knowledge work requires far more advanced theoretical knowledge: for example, most of the knowledge work required in business, whether in market research; in product planning; in designing manufacturing systems; in advertising and promotion; in purchasing. In some areas the knowledge base is vast indeed, as in neurosurgery and in a good many areas of management, such as managing a major hospital, a big and complex university, or a multinational enterprise.

Whatever the base, knowledge in application is specialized. It is always specific, and therefore not applicable to anything else. Nothing the X-ray technician needs to know can be applied to market research, for instance, or to teaching medieval history.

The central workforce in the knowledge society will, therefore, consist of highly specialized people. In fact, it is a mistake to speak of 'generalists'. Those whom we refer to by that term will increasingly be those who have learned how to acquire additional specialities and especially to acquire rapidly the specialized knowledge needed for them to move from one kind of work or job to another, such as from being a market researcher to being in general management, or from being a nurse in the hospital to being a hospital administrator. But 'generalists' in the sense in which we used to talk of them are becoming dilettantes rather than educated people.

This too is new. Historically, workers were generalists. They did whatever had to be done – on the farm, in the household, in the craftsman's shop. This was also true of the industrial worker. Manufacturing industry only expanded and became dominant when it learned to take the specialized skill out of the work, that is, when it converted the skilled craftsmen of pre-industrial times into the semi-skilled or unskilled machine operator of the nineteenth and twentieth centuries.

But knowledge workers, whether their knowledge is primitive or advanced, whether they possess a little of it or a great deal, will, by definition, be specialized. Knowledge in application is effective only when it is specialized. Indeed, it is more effective, the more highly specialized it is. This goes for the technician, such as the person who services a computer, an X-ray machine, or the engine of a fighter plane.* But it equally applies to work that requires the most advanced knowledge, whether research into genetics or astrophysics or putting on the first performance of a new opera.

As said earlier, the shift from knowledge to knowledges offers tremendous opportunities to the individual. It makes possible a 'career' as a knowledge worker. But it equally presents a great many new problems and challenges. It demands for the first

---

*See *The Five Pillars of TQM: How to Make Total Quality Management Work for You*, by General Bill Creech, former commanding general of the US Tactical Air Force (New York: Truman Talley Books Dutton, 1994), which brilliantly recounts the conversion of a skill-based organization, that is, the US Tactical Air Force, into a knowledge-based organization.

time in history that people with knowledge take responsibility for making themselves understood by people who do not have the same knowledge base. It requires that people learn – and preferably early – how to assimilate into their own work specialized knowledges from other areas and other disciplines.

This is particularly important, as innovation in any one knowledge area tends to originate outside the area itself. This is true in respect to products and processes – where, in sharp contrast to the way it was in the nineteenth and twentieth centuries, innovations now tend to arise outside the industry or process itself. It is true just as much in scientific knowledge and in scholarship. The new approaches to the study of history have, for instance, come out of economics, psychology, and archaeology – all disciplines which historians never considered relevant to their field and to which historical research had rarely before been exposed.

How knowledges work

That knowledge in the knowledge society has to be highly specialized to be productive implies two new requirements:

1 Knowledge workers work in *teams*.
2 Knowledge workers have to have access to an *organization*. If not employees they, at least, have to be affiliated with an organization.

There is a great deal of talk these days about 'teams' and 'teamwork'. Most of it starts out with the wrong assumption, namely, that we never before worked in teams. Actually, people have always worked in teams – very few people ever could work effectively by themselves. The farmer had to have a wife, and the farmwife had to have a husband. The two worked as a team. And both worked as a team with their employees, the hired hands. The craftsman also had to have a wife, with whom he worked as a team – he took care of the craft work, she took care of the customers, the apprentices, and the business altogether. And both worked as a team with journeymen and apprentices. The present discussion also assumes as self-evident that there is only one kind of team. Actually there are quite a few.* But until now the emphasis has been on the individual worker and not on the team. With knowledge work being the more effective, the more specialized it is, teams become the actual work unit rather than the individual.

But the team that is being touted now as the team – I call it the 'jazz-combo' team – is only one kind of team. Jazz-combo teamwork is actually the most difficult kind to master: it is the team that requires the longest time to gain performance capacity.

We will have to learn to use different kinds of teams for different purposes. We will have to learn to *understand* teams – and this is something to which, so far, very little attention has been paid. The understanding of the performance capacities of different kinds of teams, their strengths, their limitations, the trade-offs between various kinds of teams – those considerations will increasingly become central concerns in the management of people.

The individual knowledge worker will also have to learn something that today practically no one has learned: how to switch from one kind of team to another; how to integrate himself or herself into teams: what to expect of a team; and, in turn, what to contribute to a team.

The ability to diagnose what kind of team a certain kind of knowledge work requires for full effectiveness, and the ability, then, to organize such a team and integrate oneself into it, will increasingly become a requirement for effectiveness as a knowledge worker. So far, it is not taught or learned anywhere (except in a few research labs). So far, very few executives in any kind of

---

*On this see Chapter 8 above.

organization even realize that it is their job, to a large extent, to decide what kind of team is needed for a given situation, how to organize it, and how to make it effective. We are not even in the very early stages of work on teams, their characteristics, their specifications, their performance characteristics, and their appraisal.

Equally important is the second implication of the fact that knowledge workers are, of necessity, specialists: the need for them to work as members of an organization. It is only the organization that can provide the basic continuity that knowledge workers need to be effective. It is only the organization that can convert the specialized knowledge of the knowledge worker into performance.

By itself, specialized knowledge yields no performance. The surgeon is not effective unless there is a diagnosis, which, by and large, is not the surgeon's task and not even within the surgeon's competence. Market researchers, by themselves, produce only data. To convert the data into information, let alone to make them effective in knowledge action, requires marketing people, production people, service people. As a loner in his or her own research and writing, the historian can be very effective. But to produce the education of students, a great many other specialists have to contribute – people whose speciality may be literature, or mathematics, or other areas of history. And this requires that the specialist have access to an organization.

This access may be as a consultant. It may be as a provider of specialized services. But for a large number of knowledge workers it will be as employees of an organization – full-time or part-time – whether a government agency; a hospital; a university; a business; a labour union, any of hundreds of others. In the knowledge society, it is not the individual who performs. The individual is a cost centre rather than a performance centre. It is the organization that performs. The individual physician may have a great deal of knowledge. But the physician is impotent without the knowledge provided by a host of scientific disciplines, including physics, chemistry, genetics, and so on. The physician is impotent without the test results produced by a host of diagnosticians, running imaging machines, whether X-ray or ultrasound; making and interpreting blood tests; administering brain scans; and so on. And the physician is impotent without the services of the hospital, which administers intravenous solutions and cares for the critically ill patients, and which also provides the physical and/or psychiatric rehabilitation without which there is no full recovery. To provide any of these services, whether the electrocardiogram, the analysis of the blood samples, the magnetic resonance imaging, or the exercises of the physical therapist, physicians need access to the organization of the hospital, that is, to a highly structured enterprise, organized to operate in perpetuity.

The employee society

The knowledge society is an *employee society*. Traditional society, that is, society before the rise of the manufacturing enterprise and the blue-collar manufacturing worker, was not a society of independents. Thomas Jefferson's society of independent small farmers, each being the owner of his own family farm and farming it without any help except for that of his wife and his children, was never much more than fantasy. Most people in history were dependants. But they did not work for an organization. They were working for an owner, as slaves, as serfs, as hired hands on the farm; as journeymen and apprentices in the craftsman's shops; as shop assistants and salespeople for a merchant; as domestic servants, free or unfree; and so on. They worked for a 'master'. When blue-collar work in manufacturing first arose, they still worked for a 'master'.

In Dickens's great 1854 novel *Hard Times*, the workers work for an 'owner'. They do not work for the 'factory'. Only late in the nineteenth century did the factory rather than the owner become the employer. And only in the twentieth century did the corporation, rather than the factory, then become the employer. Only in this century has the 'master' been replaced by a 'boss', who, himself, ninety-nine times out of a hundred, is an employee and has a boss himself.

Knowledge workers will be both 'employees' who have a 'boss' and 'bosses' who have 'employees'.

Organizations were not known to yesterday's social science, and are, by and large, not yet known to today's social science. The great German sociologist Ferdinand Tönnies (1855–1936), in his 1888 book *Gemeinschaft und Gesellschaft* (*Community and Society*), classified the known forms of human organization as being either 'community', which is 'organic', and 'fate', or 'society', which is a 'structure' and very largely under social control. He never talked of 'organization'. Nor did any of the other sociologists of the nineteenth or early twentieth centuries. But organization is neither community nor society, although it partakes of some characteristics of each. Membership in an organization is not 'fate'. It is always freely chosen. One joins a company or a government agency or the teaching staff of a university. One is not born into it. And one can always leave – in traditional communities one could only emigrate. It is not society, either, especially as it does not embrace the totality of its members. The director of market research in a company is also a member of half a dozen other organizations. She may belong to a church, to a tennis club, and may well spend – especially if an American – five hours a week as a volunteer for a local non-profit organization, for example as a leader of a Girl Guide troop. Organizations, in other words, are not true collectives. They are tools, that is, means to an end.

There have been earlier organizations. The professional military as it arose after the seventeenth century was an 'organization'; it was neither a society nor a community. The modern university, as it emerged after the foundation of the University of Berlin in 1809, was an organization. Faculty members freely joined and could always leave. The same can be said for the civil service as it arose in the eighteenth century, first in France, then in the rest of the Continent, and finally in the late nineteenth century in Britain and Meiji Japan (though in the United States not until 1933 or the Second World War). But these earlier organizations were still seen as exceptions. The first 'organization' in the modern sense, the first that was seen as being protypical rather than exceptional, was surely the modern business enterprise as it emerged after 1870 – which is the reason why, to this day, most people think of 'management', that is, of the organization's specific organ, as being 'business management'.

With the emergence of the knowledge society, society has become a society of organizations. Most of us work in and for an organization, are dependent for our effectiveness and equally for our living on access to an organization, whether as an organization's employee or as a provider of services to an organization – as a lawyer, for instance, or a freight forwarder. And more and more of these supporting services to organizations are, themselves, organized as organizations. The first law firm was organized in the United States a little over a century ago – until then lawyers practised as individuals. In Europe there were no law firms to speak of until after the Second World War. Today, the practice of law is increasingly done in larger and larger partnerships. But that is also true, especially in the United States, of the practice of medicine. The knowledge society is a society of organizations in which practically every single social task is being performed in and through an organization.

What is an employee?

Most knowledge workers will spend most if not all of their working life as 'employees'. But the meaning of the term is different from what it has been traditionally – and not only in English but in German, Spanish and Japanese as well.

Individually, knowledge workers are dependent on the job. They receive a wage or salary. They are being hired and can be fired. Legally, each is an 'employee'. But collectively, they are the only 'capitalists'; increasingly, through their pension funds and through their other savings (e.g. in the United States through mutual funds), the employees own the means of production. In traditional economics (and by no means only in Marxist economics) there is a sharp distinction between the 'wage fund' – all of which went into consumption – and the 'capital fund'. And most social theory of industrial society is based, one way or another, on the relationship between the two, whether in conflict or in necessary and beneficial cooperation and balance. In the knowledge society, the two merge. The pension fund is 'deferred wage' and, as such, a wage fund. But it is also increasingly the main source of capital, if not the only source of capital, for the knowledge society.

Equally important, and perhaps more important, is that in the knowledge society the employees, that is, knowledge workers, again own the tools of production. Marx's great insight was the realization that the factory worker does not and cannot own the tools of production and, therefore, has to be 'alienated'. There was no way, Marx pointed out, for workers to own the steam engine and to be able to take the steam engine with them when moving from one job to another. The capitalist has to own the steam engine and had to control it. Increasingly, the true investment in the knowledge society is not in machines and tools. It is in the knowledge worker. Without it, the machines, no matter how advanced and sophisticated, are unproductive.

The market researcher needs a computer. But increasingly this is the researcher's own personal computer, and a cheap tool the market researcher takes along wherever he or she goes. And the true 'capital equipment' of market research is the knowledge of markets, of statistics, and of the application of market research to business strategy, which is lodged between the researchers' ears and is their exclusive and inalienable property. The surgeon needs the operating room of the hospital and all its expensive capital equipment. But the surgeon's true capital investment are the twelve or fifteen years of training and the resulting knowledge which the surgeon takes from one hospital to the next. Without that knowledge, the hospital's expensive operating rooms are so much waste and scrap.

This is true whether the knowledge worker commands advanced knowledge, like the surgeon, or simple and fairly elementary knowledge, like the junior accountant. In either case, it is the knowledge investment that determines whether the employee is productive or not, rather than the tools, machines, and capital the organization furnishes. The industrial worker needed the capitalist infinitely more than the capitalist needed the industrial worker – the basis for Marx's assertion that there would always be a surplus of industrial workers, and an 'industrial reserve army' that would make sure that wages could not possibly rise above the subsistence level (probably Marx's most egregious error). In the knowledge society the most probable assumption – and certainly the assumption on which all organizations have to conduct their affairs – is that they need the knowledge worker far more than the knowledge worker needs them. It is up to the organization to market its knowledge jobs so as to obtain knowledge workers in adequate quantity and superior quality. The relationship increasingly is one of interdependence with the knowledge worker having to learn what the organization needs, but with the organization also having to learn what the knowledge worker needs, requires, and expects.

Because its work is based on knowledge, the knowledge organization it altogether not one of superiors and subordinates.* The prototype is the symphony orchestra. The first violin may be the most important instrument in the orchestra. But the first violin-

---

*On this see again the book by General Bill Creech cited above, which makes it clear that even a military organization like the Tactical Air Force becomes a collegial organization when it becomes a knowledge organization despite all military rank and protocol. The colonel commanding a maintenance unit is a colleague of the sergeant doing the maintenance work. He is accountable for the sergeant's work, but is not the sergeant's superior.

ist is not the 'superior' of the harp player. He is a colleague. And
the harp part is the harp player's part and not delegated to her
by either the conductor or the first violinist.

There was endless debate in the Middle Ages about the hier-
archy of knowledges, with philosophy claiming to be the 'queen'
of the knowledges. We long ago gave up that moot argument.
There is no higher knowledge and no lower knowledge. When
the patient's complaint is an ingrown toenail, the chiropodist's
knowledge controls, and not that of the brain surgeon – even
though the brain surgeon represents many more years of training and gets a much larger fee. Conversely, if an executive is
posted to a foreign country, the knowledge he or she needs, and
in a hurry, is the fairly low skill of acquiring fluency in a foreign
language – a language that every native of that country has
mastered by age two and without any great investment. The
knowledge of the knowledge society, precisely because it is
knowledge only when applied in action, derives its rank and
standing from the situation and not from its knowledge content.
What is knowledge, in other words, in one situation, such as the
knowledge of Korean for the American executive posted to
Seoul, is only information, and not very relevant information at
that, when the same executive a few years later has to think
through his company's market strategy for Korea. This, too, is
new. Knowledges were always seen as fixed stars, so to speak,
each occupying its own position in the universe of knowledge. In
the knowledge society, knowledges are tools and, as such, dependent for their importance and position on the task to be
performed.

One additional conclusion: because the knowledge society
perforce has to be a society or organizations, its central and
distinctive organ is *management*.

When we first began to talk of management, the term meant
'business management' – since large-scale business was the first
of the new organizations to become visible. But we have learned
this last half-century that management is the distinctive organ of

all organizations. All of them require management – whether they use the term or not. All managers do the same things whatever the business of their organization. All of them have to bring people – each of them possessing a different knowledge – together for joint performance. All of them have to make human strengths productive in performance and human weaknesses irrelevant. All of them have to think through what are 'results' in the organization – and have then to define objectives. All of them are responsible to think through what I call the 'theory of the business', that is, the assumptions on which the organization bases its performance and actions, and equally, the assumptions which organizations make to decide what things not to do. All of them require an organ that thinks through strategies, that is, the means through which the goals of the organization become performance. All of them have to define the values of the organization, its system of rewards and punishments, and with it its spirit and its culture. In all of them, managers need both the knowledge of management as work and discipline and the knowledge and understanding of the organization itself, its purposes, its values, its environment and markets, its core competencies.

Management as a *practice* is very old. The most successful executive in all history was surely that Egyptian who, 4700 years or more ago, first conceived the pyramid – without any precedent – and designed and built it, and did so in record time. With a durability unlike that of any other human work that first pyramid still stands. But as a *discipline*, management is barely fifty years old. It was first dimly perceived around the time of the First World War. It did not emerge until the Second World War and then primarily in the United States. Since then, it has been the fastest-growing new function, and its study the fastest-growing new discipline. No function in history has emerged as fast as management and managers have in the last fifty to sixty years, and surely none has had such worldwide sweep in such a short period.

Management, in most business schools, is still taught as a bundle of techniques, such as the technique of budgeting. To be sure, management, like any other work, has its own tools and its own techniques. But just as the essence of medicine is not the urinalysis, important though it is, the essence of management is not techniques and procedures. The essence of management is to make knowledge productive. Management, in other words, is a social function. And in its practice, management is truly a 'liberal art'.

The social sector

The old communities – family, village, parish, and so on – have all but disappeared in the knowledge society. Their place has largely been taken by the new unit of social integration: the organization. Where community membership was seen as fate, organization membership is voluntary. Where community claimed the entire person, organization is a means to a person's end, a tool. For 200 years a hot debate has been raging, especially in the West: are communities 'organic' or are they simply extensions of the person? Nobody would claim that the new organization is 'organic'. It is clearly an artifact, a human creation, a social technology.

But who, then, does the social tasks? Two hundred years ago, social tasks were being done in all societies by the local community – primarily, of course, by the family. Very few, if any, of these tasks are now being done by the old communities. Nor would they be capable of doing them. People no longer stay where they were born, neither in terms of geography nor in terms of social position and status. By definition, a knowledge society is a society of mobility. And all the social functions of the old communities, whether performed well or poorly (and most were performed very poorly, indeed), presupposed that the individual and the family would stay put. 'Family is where they have to take you in,' said a nineteenth-century adage; and community, to repeat, was fate. To leave the community meant becoming an outcast, perhaps even an outlaw. But the essence of a knowledge society is mobility in terms of where one lives, mobility in terms of what one does, mobility in terms of one's affiliation.

This very mobility means that in the knowledge society, social challenges and social tasks multiply. People no longer have 'roots'. People no longer have a 'neighbourhood' that controls where they live, what they do, and indeed, what their 'problems' are allowed to be. The knowledge society, by definition, is a competitive society; with knowledge accessible to everyone, everyone is expected to place himself or herself, to improve himself or herself, and to have aspirations. It is a society in which many more people than ever before can be successful. But it is therefore, by definition, also a society in which many more people than ever before can fail, or at least can come second. And if only because the application of knowledge to work has made developed societies so much richer than any earlier society could even dream of becoming, the failures, whether poverty or alcoholism, battered women or juvenile delinquents, are seen as failures of society. In traditional society they were taken for granted. In the knowledge society they are an affront, not just to the sense of justice but equally to the competence of society and its self-respect.

Who then, in the knowledge society, takes care of the social tasks? We can no longer ignore them. But traditional community is incapable of tackling them.

Two answers have emerged in this century – a majority answer and a dissenting opinion. Both have been proven to be the wrong answers.

The majority answer goes back more than a hundred years, to the 1880s, when Bismarck's Germany took the first faltering steps towards the welfare state. The answer: the problems of the social sector can, should, and must be solved by government. It is still probably the answer which most people accept, especially in the developed countries of the West – even though most people probably no longer fully believe it. But it has been totally disproven. Modern government, especially since the Second World War, has become a huge welfare bureaucracy everywhere. And the bulk of the budget in every developed country today is devoted to 'entitlements', that is, to payment for all kinds of social services. And yet, in every developed country, society is becoming sicker rather than healthier, and social problems are multiplying. Government has a big role to play in social tasks – the role of policy maker, of standard setter, and, to a substantial extent, the role of paymaster. But as the agency to *run* social services, it has proven itself almost totally incompetent – and we now know why.

The second dissenting opinion was first formulated by me in my 1942 book *The Future of Industrial Man*. I argued then that the new organization – and fifty years ago that meant the large business enterprise – would have to be the community in which the individual would find status and function, with the plant community, I argued, becoming the place in and through which the social tasks would be organized. In Japan (though quite independently and without any debt to me) the large employer – government agency or business – has indeed increasingly attempted to become a 'community' for its employees. 'Lifetime employment' is only one affirmation of this. Company housing, company health plans, company vacations, and so on, all emphasize for the Japanese employee that the employer, and especially the big corporation, is the community and the successor to yesterday's village and to yesterday's family. But this, too, has not worked.

There is a need indeed, especially in the West, to bring the employee increasingly into the government of the plan community. What is now called 'empowerment' is very similar to the things I talked about more than fifty years ago. But is does not create a community. And it does not create the structure through which the social tasks of the knowledge society can be tackled. In fact, practically all these tasks, whether providing education or health care; addressing the anomalies and diseases of a developed and, especially, of a rich society, such as alcohol and drug abuse; or tackling the problems of incompetence and irresponsibility such as those of the 'underclass' in the American city – all lie outside the employing institution.

The employing institution is, and will remain, an 'organization'. The relationship between it and the individual is not that of 'membership' in a 'community', that is, an unbreakable, two-way bond. Even in Japan, lifetime employment has proven not to be tenable except, perhaps, for government employees (as it is in the West, as well).

We may need more employment security than the United States traditionally offers. But in no society, in an increasingly competitive world economy, can the employing institution, whether a business, a university, or a hospital, become a cocoon of security. To survive, it needs employment flexibility. But increasingly also, knowledge workers, and especially people of advanced knowledge, see the organization as the tool for the accomplishment of their own purposes and, therefore, resent – increasingly even in Japan – any attempt to subject them to the organization as a community, that is, to the control of the organization; to the demand of the organization that they commit themselves to lifetime membership; and to the demand that they subordinate their own aspirations to the goals and values of the organization. The young knowledge people in Japan still sing the company song. They still expect the company to provide them with job security. However, not only do they refuse, increasingly, to sacrifice their family life to the company. But they increasingly are as ready as their Western counterparts to change jobs if there is a better one available. For blue-collar workers in Japan who are employed by a major business corporation, a change in jobs is still exceedingly painful. If possible at all, it imposes a huge penalty in terms of income and social standing. But the turnover rate among young engineers in the 1990s in big

Japanese corporations is rapidly approaching the turnover rate of Western companies and in some areas actually exceeds it. This is inevitable because the possessor of knowledge, as said earlier, owns his or her 'tools of production' and has the freedom to move to wherever opportunities for effectiveness, for accomplishment, and for advancement seem greatest.

The right answer to the question 'Who takes care of the social challenges of the knowledge society?' is thus neither 'the government' nor 'the employing organization'. It is a separate and new *social sector*.

It is less than fifty years, I believe, since we first talked in the United States of the 'two sectors' of a modern society: the 'public sector', that is, government, and the 'private sector', that is, business. In the last twenty years the United States has begun to talk of a 'third sector', the 'non-profit sector', the organizations that take care of the social challenges of a modern society.

In the United States, with its tradition of independent and competitive churches, such a sector has always existed. Even now, churches are the largest single part of the social sector in the United States, accounting for almost half of the money given to non-profit, charitable institutions, and for somewhat less than half of the time given to non-profit volunteer work by individuals. But the non-church part of the social sector has been the growth sector in the United States. In the 1990s, about one million organizations were registered in the United States as non-profit or charitable organizations doing social sector work. The overwhelming majority of these, some 70 per cent, have come into existence in the last thirty years. And most are community services concerned with this earth rather than with the Kingdom of Heaven. Quite a few of the new organizations are, of course, religious in their orientation. But even of these, few are 'churches'. They are 'parachurches' engaged in a specific social task, for example, rehabilitation of alcohol and drug addicts, the rehabilitation of criminals, or the education of young children. Even within the church segment of the social sector, the organizations that have shown the capacity to grow are radically new. They are the fast-growing 'pastoral' churches, which focus on the spiritual needs of individuals, and especially of educated knowledge workers, and which then put the spiritual energies of their members to work on the social challenges and social problems of the community and especially, of course, of the urban community.

We still talk of these organizations as 'non-profits'. But this is a legal term. It means nothing except that under American law these organizations do not pay taxes.

Whether they are organized as 'non-profit' or not is actually irrelevant to their function and behaviour. Many American hospitals since 1960 or 1970 have become 'for-profits' and are organized in what legally are business corporations. They function exactly the same way as traditional 'non-profit' hospitals. What matters is thus not the legal basis. What matters is that the social sector institutions have a different purpose. Government demands compliance. It makes rules and enforces them. Business expects to be paid; it supplies. The social sector institutions aim at *changing the human being*. The 'product' of the school is the student who has learned something. The 'product' of the hospital is a cured patient. The 'product' of the church is a church-goer whose life is being changed. *The task of the social sector organizations is to create human health.*

Increasingly, these organizations of the social sector serve a second and equally important purpose. *They create citizenship*. Modern society and modern polity have become so big and complex that citizenship, that is, responsible participation, is no longer possible. All we can do as citizens is to vote once every few years and to pay taxes all the time.

As a volunteer in the social sector institution, the individual can again make a difference. In the United States, where there has been a volunteer tradition all along because of the old independence of the churches, almost every other adult in the 1990s worked at least three – and often five – hours a week as a volunteer in a social organization. Only in Britain is there something like this tradition, although on a very much lower scale (in part because the welfare state is far more embracing, but in much larger part because of the tradition of an Established Church that is paid for by the state and run as a civil service). Outside of the English-speaking countries, there is not much volunteer tradition. In fact, the modern state in Europe and Japan has been openly hostile to anything that smacks of volunteerism – most so in France and Japan. It is *ancien régime* and fundamentally suspected of being subversive.

But even in these countries – Japan is perhaps the main example – things are changing. For the knowledge society needs the social sector, and the social sector needs the volunteer. But knowledge workers also need a sphere in which they can act as citizens, that is, a sphere in which they create a community. Organization does not give it to them.

Nothing has been disproved faster than the concept of the 'organization man', which was almost generally accepted forty years ago. In fact, the more satisfying one's knowledge work is, the more one needs a separate sphere of community activity. The volunteer who works in an American church as a counsellor to young marrieds; who works in a local school with learning-impeded children as a tutor; who works with normal children as a scout leader – and there are thousands of such volunteer activities – creates a sphere of personal achievement but also a community in which people sharing their values work together for a common good.

Many social sector organizations will become partners with government – as is the case in a great many 'privatizations', where, for instance, a city pays for street cleaning and an outside contractor then does the work. In American education, predictably, within the next twenty years there will be more and more government-paid 'vouchers,' which enable parents to put their children into a variety of different schools, some public and tax-supported, some private and largely dependent on the income from the parents' vouchers. These social sector organiz-ations, while partners with government, also clearly compete with government. The relationship between the two has yet to be worked out – and there is practically no precedent for it. (Or, rather, the one precedent we have, the relationship between a government agency, for example the Department of Defense of the United States, and independent defence contractors, shows that the relationship is complicated and requires both interde-pendence and mutual trust, and profound mutual distrust and constant guerrilla warfare.)

But one thing is already clear. The knowledge society has to have *three sectors*: a public sector, that is, government; a private sector, that is, business; and a social sector. And it is also, I submit, becoming increasingly clear that it is in and through the social sector that a modern developed society can again create responsible and achieving citizenship, can again give individuals – and especially knowledge people – a sphere in which they can make a difference in society, and a sphere in which they re-create community.

Knowledge economy and knowledge polity

The emergence of knowledge society and of the society of organizations has profound *political* implications:

- It creates a new centre of policy
- It totally changes economic policy
- It challenges the capacity of government to function

School and education as society's centre

Knowledge has become the key resource – for a nation's military strength as well as for a nation's economic strength. And it is knowledge that can be acquired only in a formal process, that is, through schooling.

Knowledge as the key resource is fundamentally different from any of the traditional key resources, that is, from land and labour, and even from capital. It is not tied to any country. It is transnational. It is portable. It can be created everywhere, fast, and cheaply. Finally, it is, by definition, changing. Knowledge always makes itself obsolete within a short period of time. The one thing that is predictable about a competitive advantage based on knowledge – whether the advantage be that of a country, of an industry, of an institution (whether a business or a university), or of an individual – is that the advantage will soon be challenged, and probably by a total newcomer.

For that reason alone the acquisition of knowledge, that is, *learning*, can no longer stop at any age. 'Life-long learning' – the now-fashionable term – may be hyperbole; a good many people stop learning when they stop working and retire. But continuous learning during one's working life will increasingly be a requirement for any knowledge worker.

The school can no longer be content to be a place that takes care of juveniles not old enough to work. It will increasingly be the *partner* of adults as well as the partner of their employing organizations. And organizations, in turn – businesses and government agencies – social sector non-profits in respect to their volunteers – will increasingly have to become both partners with the schools and themselves teaching and learning institutions.

But also schools and education are bound to become central political issues. Of course, every existing educational system expresses basic political and social values (on this see the discussion 'Education as Social Purpose' in my 1989 book *The New Realities*). But neither the content nor the quality nor the productivity and yield of schools and schooling were major *public* issues in earlier times. They were concerns primarily of the educator. Now, increasingly, they will become political issues – in the United States we are already moving there, and quite fast.

The competitive knowledge economy

That knowledge has become the key resource means that there is a world economy. It means that the world economy, rather than the national economy, controls. Every country, every industry, and every business will, in its decisions, have to take into serious consideration its competitive standing in the world economy and the competitiveness of its knowledge competencies.

That knowledge creates a world economy, and a highly competitive one, already underlay the transformation of the world economy after the Second World War. The rise of Japan was based on applying knowledge, primarily management and training as it had been developed by the Americans during the war. The process began no earlier than 1950 or 1952. But by 1960 it had created a Japanese economy capable of attacking the world's leading manufacturing companies on their own ground. And South Korea, a few years later, trod the same path.

It is no longer possible to do what the Japanese and the South Koreans did. Low manufacturing wages, even combined with high productivity, no longer give enough of a competitive advantage to build a major economy. But the same process applied to advanced knowledge – whether in engineering, in marketing, or in research – can lead to very much the same results, and in a fairly short time.

At least this is what Singapore's experience indicates. In 1965, when the city seceded from Malaysia and became independent, it was still dependent on the unskilled manual labour of dockworkers. A dozen years later it had pushed itself into the world economy as an exporter of low-skilled manufactured goods made with cheap but well-trained labour. But Singapore at the same time heavily promoted and financed education. The Singapore of 1994 is no longer a low-wage producer. It has become producer and exporter of high-value-added and highly engineered products – pharmaceuticals, electronics, computers, telecommunication equipment, optics – turned out by well-educated, young knowledge people. In fact, within less than fifteen years Singapore has even acquired the capacity to *design* such knowledge-intensive products.

And now the Singaporeans are using this recently acquired knowledge competence to become leaders in mainland China's new 'capitalism' – as bankers, industrialists, and mass merchants.

Politics and policies still centre on domestic issues in every single country. Few, if any, politicians, journalists, or civil servants look beyond the boundaries of their own country when a new measure is being discussed, whether taxes, regulations of business, or social spending. Even in West Germany – Europe's most export-conscious and export-dependent major country – almost no one even asked in 1990 what the government's unbridled spending in the East would do to the country's competitiveness.

This will no longer do. Every country and every industry will have to learn that the first question is not 'Is this desirable?' The first question is 'What will be the impact on the country's (or the industry's) competitive position in the world economy?' We need to develop in politics something similar to the environmental impact statement, which, in the United States, is now required for any political action: we need a 'competitive impact statement'. The impact on one's competitive position in the world economy should not be the main, let alone the only, factor in a decision. But to make a decision without considering it has become irresponsible.

Altogether, the fact that knowledge has become the key resource means that the standing of a country in the world economy will increasingly determine its domestic prosperity.* Since 1950 the ability to improve a country's position in the world economy has been the main, and indeed perhaps the sole, determinant of economic performance in the *domestic* economy.

---

* On this see Chapter 13 above.

Domestic economic policies have been practically irrelevant, both for better and, very largely, even for worse (with the single exception of governmental policies creating inflation, which very rapidly undermine both a country's competitive standing in the world economy and its domestic stability and ability to grow).

The 'primacy of foreign affairs' is an old political precept going back in European politics to the seventeenth century. Since the Second World War it has also been accepted in American politics – though only grudgingly, and as a 'temporary emergency' only. It always meant that military security had to be given priority over domestic policies – and in all likelihood this will continue, cold war or no cold war. But the 'primacy of foreign affairs' is now acquiring a different dimension. It asserts that a country's competitive position in the world economy – and equally that of an industry or an organization – has to be the first consideration in its domestic policies and its strategies. This is just as true for a country that is only marginally involved in the world economy (should there still be such a one) as it is for a business that is only marginally involved in the world economy, or for a university that sees itself as totally domestic. Knowledge knows no boundaries. There is no 'domestic knowledge' and no 'international knowledge'. There is only knowledge. And with knowledge becoming the key resource, there is only a world economy, even though the individual organization in its daily activities operates within a national, regional, or even a local setting.

How can government function?

The emergence of the society of organizations challenges the function of government. All social tasks in the society of organizations are increasingly being done by individual organizations, each created for one, and only one, social task, whether education, health care, or street cleaning. Society, therefore, is rapidly becoming pluralist. Yet our social and political theories still assume a society in which there are no power centres except government. To destroy or at least to render impotent all other power centres was, in fact, the thrust of Western history and Western politics for 500 years, from the fourteenth century on. It culminated in the eighteenth and nineteenth centuries when (except in the United States) such original institutions as still survived – for example, the universities or the established churches – all became organs of the state, with their functionaries becoming civil servants. But then, immediately beginning in the mid-nineteenth century, new centres arose – the first one, the modern business enterprise, emerged around 1870. And since then one new organization after another has come into being.

This is not a new 'feudalism'. Feudalism meant 'public power in private hands'.* Whether land-owning aristocracy or abbeys or free cities or trading companies like the English East India Company, these traditional bodies wanted to be governments. Within the sphere they indeed wanted to be sovereign. They demanded control of jurisdiction over their members. They aimed at having their own coinage. They tried to regulate trade and commerce within their boundaries. And in many cases they formed and ran their own armies.

The new institutions of the society of organizations have no interest in 'public power'. They do not want to be governments. But they demand – and, indeed, need – autonomy with respect to their function. Even at the extreme of Stalinism the managers of major industrial enterprises were largely masters within their enterprise, and the individual industry was largely autonomous. So was the university and the research lab, let alone the military.

In the pluralism of yesterday, the feudalism of Europe's Middle Ages, or of Edo Japan in the seventeenth and eighteenth centuries, all pluralist organizations, whether a feudal baron in the England of the War of the Roses or the *daimyo* – the local lord – in Edo Japan, tried to be in control of whatever went on

---

* The phrase is that of the American medievalist J. R. Strayer (1904–1987)

in their community. At least they tried to prevent anybody else from having control of any community concern or community institution within their domain.

But in the society of organizations, each of the new institutions is concerned only with its own purpose and mission. It does not claim power over anything else. But it also does not assume responsibility for anything else. *Who then is concerned with the common good?*

This has always been a central problem of pluralism. No earlier pluralism solved it. The problem is coming back now, but in a different guise. So far it has been seen as imposing limits on these institutions, that is, forbidding them to do things in the pursuit of their own mission, function and interest, which encroach upon the public domain or violate public policy. The laws against discrimination – by race, sex, age, education, health, and so on – which have proliferated in the United States in the last forty years all forbid socially undesirable behaviour. But we are increasingly raising the question of the 'social responsibility' of these institutions: 'What do these institutions have *to do* – in addition to discharging their own functions – to *advance* the public good?' This, however – though nobody seems to realize it – is a demand to return to the old pluralism, the pluralism of feudalism. It is a demand for 'private hands to assume public power'.

That this could seriously threaten the functioning of the new organizations the example of the school in the United States makes abundantly clear. One of the major reasons for the steady decline in its capacity to do its own job, that is, to teach children elementary knowledge skills, is surely that, beginning in the 1950s, the United States has made the school increasingly the carrier of all kinds of social policies, beginning with the elimination of racial discriminations, the elimination of discrimination against all other kinds of 'minorities', against the 'handicapped', and so on. Whether we have actually made any progress in assuaging social ills is highly debatable; so far the school has not proven a particularly effective tool for social reform. But making the school the organ of social policies has, without any doubt, severely impaired its capacity to do its own job.

The new pluralism has the old problem of pluralism – who takes care of the common good when the dominant institutions of society are single-purpose institutions? But it also has a new problem: how to maintain the performance capacity of the new institutions and yet maintain the cohesion of society? This makes doubly important the emergence of a strong and functioning social sector. It is an additional reason why the social sector will increasingly be crucial to the performance, if not to the cohesion, of the knowledge society.

The first new organization to arise, 125 years ago, was the business enterprise. It was only natural, therefore, that the problem of the emerging society of organizations was first seen as the relationship of 'government and business'. It was also natural that the new 'interests' were first seen as 'economic interests'.

The first attempt to come to grips with the politics of the emerging society of organizations aimed, therefore, at making economic interests serve the political process. The first to tackle this was an American, Mark Hanna, the restorer of the Republican Party in the 1890s and, in many ways, the founding father of twentieth-century American politics. His definition of politics as being a dynamic disequilibrium between the major economic interests – farmers, business, labour – remained the foundation of American politics until the Second World War. In fact, Franklin D. Roosevelt restored the Democratic Party by reformulating Hanna. The basic political statement of this philosophy is the title of the most influential political book written during the New Deal years – in 1936 – *Politics: Who Gets What, When, How*, by Harold D. Laswell.

Mark Hanna, in 1896, knew very well that there are plenty of concerns other than economic concerns. And yet it was obvious to him – as it was to Franklin D. Roosevelt forty years later – that economic interests had to be used to integrate all the others.

This is still the assumption underlying most analyses of American politics – and, in fact, of politics in all developed countries. But it is no longer a tenable assumption. Underlying the Mark Hanna formula of the 'economic interests' is the view of land, labour, and capital as the 'resources'. But knowledge, the new resource for economic performance, is not in itself economic.

It cannot be bought or sold. The *fruits* of knowledge, such as the income from a patent, can be bought or sold. The knowledge that went into the patent cannot be conveyed at any price. No matter how much a medical student is willing to pay a neurosurgeon, the neurosurgeon cannot sell to him – and surely cannot convey to him – the knowledge that is the foundation for the neurosurgeon's performance and for the neurosurgeon's income. The acquisition of knowledge has a cost, as has the acquisition of anything. But the acquisition of knowledge has no price.

Economic interests can therefore no longer integrate all other concerns and interests. As soon as knowledge became the key economic resource, the integration of the interests – and with it the integration of the pluralism of a modern polity – began to fall apart. Increasingly, non-economic interests are becoming the new pluralism, the 'special interests', the 'single-cause' organizations, and so on. Increasingly, politics is not about 'who gets what, when, how' but about values, each of them considered to be an absolute. Politics is about 'the right to live' of the embryo in the womb as against the right of a woman to control her own body and to abort an embryo. It is about the environment. It is about gaining equality for groups alleged to be oppressed and discriminated against. None of these issues is economic. All are fundamentally moral.

Economic interests can be compromised, which is the great strength of basing politics on economic interests. 'Half a loaf is still bread' is a meaningful saying. But 'half a baby', in the biblical story of the judgment of Solomon, is not half a child. Half a baby is a corpse and a chunk of meat. There is no compromise possible. To an environmentalist, 'half an endangered species' is an extinct species.

This greatly aggravates the crisis of modern government. Newspapers and commentators still tend to report in economic terms what goes on in Washington, in London, in Bonn, or in Tokyo. But more and more of the lobbyists who determine governmental laws and governmental actions are no longer lobbyists for economic interests. They lobby for and against measures they – and their paymasters – see as moral, spiritual, cultural. And each of these new moral concerns, each represented by a new organization, claims to stand for an absolute. Dividing their loaf is not compromising. It is treason.

There is thus in the society of organizations no single integrating force that pulls individual organizations in society and community into coalition. The traditional parties – perhaps the most successful political creations of the nineteenth century – no longer can integrate divergent groups and divergent points of view into a common pursuit of power. Rather, they become battlefields between groups, each of them fighting for absolute victory and not content with anything but total surrender of the enemy.

This raises the question of how government can be made to function again. In countries with a tradition of a strong independent bureaucracy, notably Japan, Germany, and France, the civil service still tries to hold government together. But even in these countries the cohesion of government is increasingly being weakened by the special interests and, above all, by the non-economic, the moral, special interests.

Since Machiavelli, almost 500 years ago, political science has primarily concerned itself with power. Machiavelli – and political scientists and politicians since him – took it for granted that government can function once it has power. Now, increasingly, the questions to be tackled will be: 'What are the functions that government and only government, can discharge and that government *must* discharge?' and 'How can government be organized so that it can discharge these functions in a society of organizations?'

Conclusion: the priority tasks – the need for social and political innovations

The twenty-first century will surely be one of continuing social, economic, and political turmoil and challenge, at least in its early decades. The Age of Social Transformations is not over yet. And the challenges looming ahead may be more serious and more daunting still than those posed by the social transformations that have already happened, the social transformations of the twentieth century.

Yet we will not even have a chance to resolve these new and looming problems of tomorrow unless we *first* address the challenges posed by the developments that are already accomplished facts, the developments reported in the earlier sections of this chapter.

They are the priority tasks. For only if they are tackled can we, in the developed, democratic, free-market countries, hope to have the social cohesion, the functioning economy, and the governmental capacity needed to tackle the new challenges. The first order of business – for sociologists, political scientists, and economists; for educators; for business executives; politicians and non-profit leaders, and for people in all walks of life, as parents, as employees, as citizens – is to work on these priority tasks for only a few of which we so far have a precedent, let alone tested solutions.

In sum, these priority tasks are as follows;

- We will have to think through *education* – its purpose, its value, its content. We will have to learn to define the *quality* of education and the *productivity* of education, to measure both and to manage both.
- We need systematic work on the *quality of knowledge* and the *productivity of knowledge* – neither even defined so far. On

those two, the performance capacity, and perhaps even the survival of any organization in the knowledge society will increasingly come to depend. But so will also the performance capacity and perhaps even the survival, of any individual in the knowledge society. And what *responsibility* does knowledge have? What are the responsibilities of the knowledge individual, and especially of people of high – and therefore highly specialized – knowledge?

- Increasingly, the *policy* of any country – and especially of any developed country – will have to give primacy to the country's competitive position in an increasingly competitive world economy. Any proposed domestic policy needs to be shaped so as to improve the country's competitive position in the world economy or, at the least, so as to minimize adverse impacts on it. The same holds true for policies and strategies of any institution within a nation, whether a local government, a business, a university, or a hospital.

- We need to develop an *economic theory* appropriate to the primacy of a world economy in which knowledge has become the key economic resource and the dominant – and perhaps even the only – source of comparative advantage.

- We are beginning to understand the new integrating mechanism: *organization*. But we still have to think through how to balance two apparently contradictory requirements. Organizations must competently perform the *one* social function for the sake of which they exist – the school to teach; the hospital to cure the sick; the business to produce goods and services and the capital to provide for the risks of the future. They can do so only if they single-mindedly concentrate on their own specialized mission. But there is also the need of society: that these organizations take social responsibility, that is, *work* on the problems and challenges of the community. Together these organizations are *the* community. The emergence of a strong, independent, performing *social sector* – neither public sector, that is, government, nor private sector, that is, business – is thus a central need of the society of organizations. But by itself it is not enough: the organizations of both the public and the private sector must share in the work.

- *The function of government* and its *functioning* will increasingly become central to political thought and political action The 'megastate' in which this century indulged has not performed, neither in its totalitarian nor in its democratic version. It has not delivered on a single one of its promises. And *government by countervailing lobbyists* is neither particularly effective – in fact, it is paralysis – nor particularly attractive. Yet effective government has never been needed more than in this highly competitive and fast-changing world of ours in which the dangers created by the pollution of the physical environment are matched only by the dangers of worldwide armaments pollution.

And we do not have even the beginnings of political theory or the political institutions needed for effective government in the knowledge-based society of organizations.

If the twentieth century was one of social transformations, the twenty-first century needs to be one of social and political innovations.

1994

22
It profits us to strengthen non-profits

America needs a new social priority: to triple the productivity of the non-profits and to double the share of gross personal income – now just below 3 per cent – they collect as donations. Otherwise the country faces, only a few years out, social polarization.

Federal, state, and local governments will have to retrench sharply, no matter who is in office. Moreover, government has proved incompetent at solving social problems. Virtually every success we have scored has been achieved by non-profits.

The great advances in health and longevity have been sponsored, directed, and in large part financed by such non-profits as the American Heart Association and the American Mental Health Association. Whatever results there are in the rehabilitation of addicts we owe to such non-profits as Alcoholics Anonymous, the Salvation Army, and the Samaritans. The schools in which inner-city minority children learn the most are parochial schools and those sponsored by some Urban League chapters. The first group to provide food and shelter to the Kurds fleeing from Saddam Hussein last spring was an American non-profit, the International Rescue Committee.

Many of the most heartening successes are being scored by small, local organizations. One example would be the tiny Judson Center in Royal Oak, Michigan – an industrial suburb of Detroit.

It gets black women and their families off welfare while simultaneously getting severely handicapped children out of institutions and back into society.

Judson trains carefully picked welfare mothers to raise in their homes, for a modest salary, two or three crippled or emotionally disturbed kids. The rehabilitation rate for the welfare mothers is close to 100 per cent, with many of them in five years or so moving into employment as rehabilitation workers. The rehabilitation rate for the children, who otherwise would be condemned to lifetime institutional confinement, is about 50 per cent: and every one of these kids had been given up as hopeless.

The non-profits spend far less for results than governments spend for failures. The cost per pupil in the New York Archdiocese's parochial schools – 70 per cent of whose students stay in school, stay off the streets, and graduate with high literacy and saleable skills – is about half that in New York City's failing public schools.

Two-thirds of the first-offenders paroled in Florida into the custody of the Salvation Army are 'permanently' rehabilitated – they are not indicted for another crime for at least six years. Were they to go to prison, two-thirds would become habitual criminals. Yet a prisoner costs at least twice as much per year as a parolee in the custody of the Salvation Army.

The Judson Center saves the state of Michigan $100 000 a year for each welfare mother and her charges – one-third in welfare costs and two-thirds in the costs of keeping the children in institutions.

Though the majority of the students in private colleges and universities get some sort of financial aid, their parents still pay more than do the parents of students in state universities and colleges. But the state-university student's education actually *costs* a good deal more (in some states twice as much) than that of the student in a private non-profit institution – with the difference paid by the taxpayer.

The non-profits have the potential to become America's social sector – equal in importance to the public sector of government and the private sector of business. The delivery system is already in place: There are now some 900 000 non-profits, the great majority close to the problems of their communities. About 30 000 of them came into being in 1990 (the latest year for which figures are available), practically all dedicated to local action on one problem: tutoring minority children; providing ombudsmen for patients in the local hospital; helping immigrants through government red tape.

Where twenty years ago the American middle class thought it had done its social duty by writing a cheque, it increasingly commits itself to active doing as well. According to the best available statistics, there are now some 90 million Americans – one out of every two adults – working as 'volunteers' in non-profits for three hours a week on average; the non-profits have become America's largest 'employer'.

Increasingly these volunteers do not look upon their work as charity; they see it as a parallel career to their paid jobs and insist on being trained, on being held accountable for results and performance, and on career opportunities for advancement to professional and managerial – though still unpaid – positions in the non-profit. Above all, they see in volunteer work access to achievement, to effectiveness, to self-fulfilment, indeed to meaningful citizenship. And for this reason there is more de-mand for well-structured volunteer jobs than there are positions to fill.

Some observers (such a Brian O'Connell, head of Inde-pendent Sector, the national association of the large non-profits) believe that, within ten years, two-thirds of American adults – 120 million – will want to work as non-profit volunteers for five hours a week each, which would mean a doubling of the person-nel available for non-profit work.

And the non-profits are becoming highly innovative. When some friends and I founded the Peter F. Drucker Foundation for Non-Profit Management a year ago, we planned as our first public event a $25 000 award for the innovation that 'creates a significant new dimension of non-profit performance'. We hoped to receive 40 applications. We received 809 – and most were deserving of a prize.

The actual award went to the Judson Center, But the big non-profits are as innovative as the small fry in many cases. With several billion dollars in revenue, Family Service America – headquartered in Milwaukee – has become bigger than a good many *Fortune* 500 companies; it now is probably the biggest American non-profit next to the Red Cross. It has achieved its phenomenal growth in part through contracting with large employers such as General Motors to help employee families with such problems as addiction or the emotional disorders of adolescent children.

For the non-profits' potential to become reality, three things are needed. First, the average non-profit must manage itself as well as the best-managed ones do. The majority still believe that good intentions and a pure heart are all that are needed. They do not yet see themselves as accountable for performance and results. And far too many splinter their efforts or waste them on non-problems and on activities that would be done better – and more cheaply – by a business.

Second, non-profits have to learn how to raise money. The American public has not become less generous – there is little evidence of the 'compassion fatigue' non-profit people talk about. In fact, giving has been going up quite sharply these past few years – from 2.5 per cent of personal income to 2.9 per cent. Unfortunately, a great many non-profits still believe that the way to get money is to hawk *needs*. But the American public gives for *results*. It no longer gives to 'charity'; it 'buys in'. Of the charitable appeals most of us get in the mail every week, usually just one talks of results – the one that gets our cheque.

The non-profits will have to get the additional money they need primarily from individuals – as they always have. Even if there is government money – mainly via vouchers I expect – and money from companies, it can supply only a fraction of what is needed.

Finally, we need a change in the attitude of government and government bureaucracies. President Bush has spoken glowingly of the importance of the non-profits as the 'thousand points of light'. If he really believes this, he should propose allowing taxpayers to deduct $1.10 for each dollar they give to non-profits as a cash donation. This would solve the non-profits money problems at once. It would also could cut government deficits in the not-so-very-long run. For a well-managed non-profit gets at least twice the bang out of each buck that a government agency does.

Instead of such a policy, however, we have the tax collector making one move after the other to penalize and to curtail donations to non-profits. Each of these moves is presented as 'closing a tax loophole'; in fact, none has yielded a penny of additional revenue and none is likely to do so.

The real motivation for such actions is the bureaucracy's hostility to the non-profits – not too different from the bureaucracy's hostility to markets and private enterprise in the former Communist countries. The success of the non-profits undermines the bureaucracy's power and denies its ideology. Worse, the bureaucracy cannot admit that the non-profits succeed where governments fail. What is needed, therefore, is a public policy that establishes the non-profits as the country's first line of attack on its social problems.

In my 1969 book *The Age of Discontinuity* I first proposed 'privatization', only to have every reviewer tell me that it would never happen. Now, of course, privatization is widely seen as the cure for modern economies mismanaged by socialist bureaucracies. We now need to learn that 'non-profitization' for modern societies may be the way out of mismanagement by welfare bureaucracies.

1991

23
Knowledge work and gender roles

In any work that requires skill or confers status, men's and women's jobs have been distinct and separate through all but the last few decades of history, in all cultures and civilizations. The belief that women's jobs and women's social status were always inferior to men's – practically an article of faith today – is a half-truth at best. Rather, men competed with men, women with women. In knowledge work today, however, men and women increasingly do the same jobs and are competing and working collegially in the same arena.

This is still an experiment – though practically all developed countries (beginning, of course, with the United States) are engaged in it. For all anyone can know so far, the experiment may fail and be abandoned or sidelined after a few decades. I consider this unlikely, but it cannot be ruled out. After all, the experiment preceding it, the feminist movement that began in the early nineteenth century and saw 'freedom for women' in their not having to work (its model being the 'cultured, middle-class housewife'), is now widely (though by no means generally) considered to have been both a mistake and a failure.

Historically, women have always worked as hard as men. A farmer had to have a wife, and she had to have a farmer husband. A craftsman had to have a wife, and she had to have a goldsmith husband or shoemaker husband. Neither could run the craft shop alone. The store owner had to have a wife. And, conversely, no woman alone was likely to be able to run a store.

But, historically, men and women did the same work only when it was menial. Men and women both dug ditches, and they worked together. Men and women both picked cotton in the fields. But any work involving skill, and any work conferring social status or providing income above minimum subsistence, was segregated by sex. A 'spinster' is a woman. Potters were always men.

In every primitive society studied by anthropologists, work requiring skill or giving social status is strictly separated by sex. In the Trobriand Islands in the Pacific Ocean – studied around the time of the Second World War by Bronislaw Malinowski (1884–1942) – the men built boats, manned them, and fished; the women tilled the land and grew yams. And then the men turned over half their catch to the women, and the women half their crop to the men.

Such sex segregation was still the rule in nineteenth-century Europe and America. The first of the new knowledge jobs was nursing, invented by Florence Nightingale in 1854, during the Crimean War. It was designed to be exclusively women's work. After the typewriter became all-pervasive in the office, the job of secretary soon became a female one. From the beginning, telephone operators were women; telephone installers were men.

Indeed, until recently, 'feminism' meant extending the separation of jobs by sex, all the way down to the menial work men and women traditionally had been doing together. From 1850 on, when agitation to limit women's hours of industrial work first began, the thrust of traditional feminism was to enlarge the scope of occupations in which there was men's work and women's work, with each sphere clearly defined and limited to people of one sex only.

But knowledge is gender-neutral. Knowledge and knowledge jobs are equally accessible to both sexes.

As soon as there were a substantial number of knowledge jobs, women began to qualify for them, reach for them, move into them. The movement began in the last decades of the nineteenth century – teaching came first. It gathered momentum after the First World War. In fact, the era of outstanding American women leaders is not today. In the 1930s and 1940s a galaxy of exceptional women bestrode the American stage. Eleanor Roosevelt and Frances Perkins in government and politics; Anna Rosenberg in personnel management and labour relations; half a dozen brilliant presidents of women's colleges; Helen Taussig in medicine; Lillian Hellman and Clare Boothe Luce as playwrights; Dorothy Thompson in foreign affairs and journalism. Margaret Thatcher and Hillary Clinton are very much throwbacks to this earlier generation.

The movement of women into the same kinds of knowledge work as men has become a flood since the Second World War, and a 'cause' in the past twenty years. Conversely, men, in increasing numbers, are moving into what, for more than a century, had been the one exclusively female knowledge profession: nursing. Two-fifths of the nurse-anesthetists in the United States – all of them RNs – are now men.

The higher up the ladder we go in knowledge work, the more likely it is that men and women are doing the same work. Being a secretary in an American bank still means being a woman, but a vice-president in the same bank may be a man or a woman. Increasingly, what an earlier generation of feminists saw as advancing the status and position of women – for example, prohibiting women from doing physically dangerous work – is now seen by feminists as discrimination against women, and possibly even as oppression of women.

Unless this movement fizzles out – or at least abates to where the 'career woman' is again the exception she was half a century ago – it will have tremendous impact, and not only on workforces and careers. The greatest impact may be on the family.

Throughout the ages, all attempts to take children away from their mothers and to bring them up in collective institutions – as was done in Sparta in Greek antiquity – were deeply resented and bitterly fought by women. They saw such moves as depriving them of their rightful sphere of power, of influence, and of contribution. Now the demand for child-care centres, to look after children while their mothers work, is seen as crucial to women's equality and as a woman's right.

Throughout the ages, it was axiomatic that the first task of the adult woman was to hold the family together and take care of the children. And the first responsibility of the man was to support wife and children. Today's feminism, especially in its radical form, fights as discrimination and as oppression woman's role as 'homemaker' and child-care provider. But at the same time, the 'single mother' who does not need a man to support her children releases the father from responsibility for the family. What, then, will family mean tomorrow, if these trends persist? And what will this mean for community and for society?

This is all still quite speculative. But this development, well outside of anything that traditional economics, sociology, and political science ever considered to be within their purview, may well be seen a century hence as the distinctive social innovation of the twentieth century. It is a reversal of all history and tradition.

In this century the workforce in the developed countries has shifted from manual workers doing and moving things – on the farm, in the factory, in the mines, in transportation – to knowledge work and services work. These are momentous shifts. But they are shifts in how we earn our living. The disappearance of sex roles in knowledge work profoundly affects how we live.

1994

24
Reinventing government

Vice-President Al Gore's promise to 'reinvent government', proclaimed with a great fanfare in the first year of the Clinton administration, produced only a nationwide yawn. (The similar promise made in the Republicans' 'Contract with America', last year, initially met with no better response.) There has been no lack of publicity about the Gore initiative since. Press release after press release has announced the reinvention of yet another agency or programme; big conferences, one chaired by the President himself, have been convened, and any number of TV appearances made. Of all the domestic programmes of the Clinton administration, this is the one in which there actually have been results and not just speeches. Yet neither the public nor the media have shown much interest. And last November's elections were hardly a vote of confidence in the administration's performance at reinventing government.

There are good reasons for this. In any institution other than the federal government, the changes being trumpeted as reinventions would not even be announced, except perhaps on the bulletin board in the hallway. They are the kinds of thing that a hospital expects floor nurses to do on their own; that a bank expects branch managers to do on their own; that even a poorly run manufacturer expects supervisors to do on their own – without getting much praise, let alone any extra rewards.

Here are some examples – sadly, fairly typical ones:

- In Atlanta, Georgia, six separate welfare programmes, each traditionally with its own office and staff, have consolidated their application process to give 'one-stop service'. The reinvented programme is actually getting phone calls answered, and on the first try.
- In Ogden, Utah, and Oakland, California, among other places, the Internal Revenue Service is also experimenting with treating taxpayers as customers and with a one-stop service, in which each clerk, instead of shuffling taxpayers from one office to another, has the information to answer their questions.
- The Export–Import Bank has been reinvented. It is now expected to do what it was set up to do all of sixty years ago: help small businesses get export financing.
- The US Geological Survey office in Denver is supposed to sell maps of the United States to the public. But it is almost impossible to find out what maps to order and how and where to order them, since the catalogue is carefully hidden. And the very fact that a map is in demand by the public all but guarantees that it will be unobtainable. It cannot be reprinted simply because the public wants to buy it; another government agency must order it for internal use. If the map sells well, it therefore immediately goes out of print. What's more, the warehouse is so poorly lit that when an order for a map in print comes in, the clerks cannot find the map. The task force that the Geological Survey created seven months ago to reinvent all this has succeeded so far in putting more lights in the warehouse and making a few other minor improvements.

For the future, however, more ambitious things are promised:

- The Department of Agriculture proposes to trim its agencies from 42 to 30, to close more than 1000 field offices, and to eliminate 11000 jobs, for savings of about $3.6 billion over five years.
- Of the 384 recommendations of ways to reinvent government identified by the Vice-President in 1993, about half are being proposed in the budget for the fiscal year 1995. If all these recommendations are accepted by Congress, they should result in savings of about $12.5 billion over two years.

But neither the trimming of the Department of Agriculture nor the Vice-President's 384 recommendations are new. We have long known that a great many agricultural field offices are in cities and suburbs, where few (if any) farmers are left. Closing them was first proposed in the Eisenhower years. And a good many, perhaps the majority, of Gore's 384 recommendations were made ten years ago, in the Grace Report, under President Ronald Reagan.

Nor is it by any means sure that all of these proposals and recommendations will become law. Mike Espy proposed large cuts in the bloated US Department of Agriculture on 6 December 1994. But he then resigned on 31 December, and there is no guarantee that there will be someone at the top of the department committed to these changes.

Even if all these proposals were to be enacted, the results would be trivial. The proposed Agriculture Department saving of $3.6 billion over five years works out to about $720 million a year – or around 1 per cent of the annual department budget of almost $70 billion. A saving of $12.5 billion looks like a lot of money. But over two years the federal government spends $3 trillion. An annual saving of $6 billion – and this is many times more than Congress is likely to accept – would thus be a cut of no more than two-tenths of 1 per cent of the budget. Surely the only way to describe the results of Gore's efforts so far is with the old Latin tag 'The mountains convulsed in labour only to give birth to a ridiculous, teensy-weensy mouse'.

Restructuring

The reason most often given for this embarrassment of non-results is 'resistance by the bureaucracy'. Of course, no one likes to be reinvented by fiat from above. But actually, one positive result of Gore's programme has been the enthusiastic support it has received from a great many people in the government's employ – especially the low-level people who are in daily contact with the public and are thus constantly frustrated by red tape and by such inane rules as those that prevent their selling the beautiful Geological Survey maps, of which they are justly proud.

Nor is lack of effort the explanation. Some of the most dedicated people in Washington meet week after week to produce these embarrassing non-results. They include the deputy secretaries of the major government departments. Vice-President Gore – an unusually energetic man – pushes and pushes. And the driving force behind the whole endeavour is the most knowledgeable of all Washington insiders, Alice Rivlin, formerly the director of the Congressional Budget Office, and now the director of the Office of Management and Budget.

These able people are getting nowhere fast because their basic approach is wrong. They are trying to patch and to spot-weld, here, there, and yonder – and that never accomplishes anything. There will be no results unless there is a radical change in the way the federal government and its agencies are managed and paid. The habit of continuous improvement has to be built into all government agencies, and has to be made self-sustaining.

Continuous improvement is considered a recent Japanese invention – the Japanese call it *kaizen*. But in fact it was used almost eighty years ago, and in the United States. From the First World War until the early 1980s, when it was dissolved, the Bell Telephone System applied 'continuous improvement' to every one of its activities and processes, whether it was installing a telephone in a home or manufacturing switchgear. For every one of these activities, Bell defined results, performance, quality, and cost. And for every one, it set an annual improvement goal. Bell managers weren't rewarded for reaching these goals; but those who did not reach them were out of the running and rarely given a second chance.

What is equally needed – and is also an old Bell Telephone invention – is 'benchmarking': every year comparing the performance of an operation or an agency with the performances of all others, with the best becoming the standard to be met by all the following year.

Continuous improvement and benchmarking are largely unknown in the civilian agencies of the US government. They would require radical changes in policies and practices which the bureaucracy, the federal employees' unions, and Congress would all fiercely resist. They would require every agency – and every bureau within every agency – to define its performance objective, its quality objective, and its cost objective. They would require defining the results that the agency is supposed to produce. Continuous improvement and benchmarking also need different incentives. An agency that did not improve its performance by a preset minimum would have its budget cut – which was Bell Telephone's approach. And a manager whose unit consistently fell below the benchmark set by the best performers would be penalized in terms of compensation or – more effective – in terms of eligibility for promotion. Non-performers would ultimately be demoted or fired.

But not even such changes, though they would be considered radical by almost anybody in Congress or the federal bureaucracy, would warrant being called a reinvention of government. By themselves alone they would probably even do harm. For what should not be done at all can always be improved the most and thus we usually see the greatest improvements in things that should not be done at all.

Any organization, whether biological or social, needs to change its basic structure if it significantly changes its size. Any organization that doubles or triples in size needs to be *restruc-*

tured. Similarly, any organization, whether a business, a non-profit, or a government agency, needs to rethink itself once it is more than forty or fifty years old. It has outgrown its policies and its rules of behaviour. If it continues in its old ways, it becomes ungovernable, unmanageable, uncontrollable.

The civilian part of the US government has outgrown its size and outlived its policies. It is now far larger than it was during the Eisenhower administration. Its structure, its policies, and its rules for doing government business and for managing people go back even further than that. They were first developed under William McKinley after 1896, and were pretty much completed under Herbert Hoover from 1929 to 1933.

In fact there is no point in blaming this or that president for the total disarray of our government today. It is the fault neither of the Democrats nor of the Republicans. Government has outgrown the structure, the policies, and the rules designed for it and still in use.

Rethinking

The first reaction in a situation of disarray always is to do what Vice-President Gore and his associates are now doing – patching. It always fails. The next step is to rush into downsizing. Management picks up a meat-axe and lays about indiscriminately. This is what both the Republicans and the Clinton administration now propose to do. In the past fifteen years one big American company after another has done this – among them IBM, Sears, and GM. Each first announced that laying off 10 000 or 20 000 or even 50 000 people would lead to an immediate turnaround. A year later there had, of course, been no turnaround, and the company laid off another 10 000 or 20 000 or 50 000 – again without results. In many if not most cases, downsizing has turned out to be something that surgeons for centuries have warned against: 'amputation before diagnosis.' The result is always a cripple.

But there have been a few organizations – some large companies (GE, for instance) and a few large hospitals (Beth Israel in Boston, for instance) – that quietly, and without fanfare, did turn themselves around, by *rethinking* themselves. They did not start out by downsizing. In fact, they knew that to start by reducing expenditures is not the way to get control of costs. The starting point is to identify the activities that are productive, that should be strengthened, promoted, and expanded. Every agency, every policy, every programme, every activity, should be confronted with these questions: 'What is your mission?' 'Is it still the right mission?' 'Is it still worth doing?' 'If we were not already doing this, would we go into it now?' This questioning has been done often enough in all kinds of organizations – businesses, hospitals, churches, and even local governments – that we know it works.

The overall answer is almost never 'This is fine as it stands; let's keep on'. But in some – indeed, a good many – areas, the answer to the question is 'Yes, we would go into this again, but with some changes. We have learned a few things.'

An example might be the Occupational Safety and Health Administration, created in 1970. Safety in the workplace is surely the right mission of OSHA. But safety in the American workplace has not improved greatly in the past twenty-five years. There may be slightly fewer disabling injuries now than there were in 1960 or 1970, and to be sure, the workforce has increased tremendously over those years. But considering the steady shift of the labour force from highly unsafe to fairly safe work (for example, from deep-level coal mining to the safer surface strip mining, and especially the shift from inherently dangerous manufacturing jobs to inherently safe office and service jobs), safety in the American workplace may actually have deteriorated since 1970. Such a result usually means that we have been going about the right task in the wrong way. In OSHA's case we actually understand the problem. OSHA runs on the assumption that an unsafe environment is the primary cause of accidents. It therefore tries to do the impossible: create a risk-free universe. Of course, eliminating hazards is the right thing to do. But it is only one part of safety, and probably the lesser part. In fact, by itself it achieves next to nothing. The most effective way to produce safety is to eliminate unsafe behaviour. OSHA's definition of an accident – 'when someone gets hurt' – is inadequate. To cut down on accidents the definition has to be 'a violation of the rules of safe behaviour, whether anyone gets hurt or not'. This is the definition under which the United States has been running its nuclear submarines. Anyone in a nuclear sub, whether the commanding officer or the most junior seaman, is punished for the slightest violation of the rules of safe behaviour, even if no one gets hurt. As a result, the nuclear submarine has a safety record unmatched by any industrial plant or military installation in the world; and yet a more unsafe environment than a crowded nuclear sub can hardly be imagined.

OSHA's programme should, of course, be maintained, and perhaps even expanded. But it needs to be refocused.

Rethinking will identify a number of agencies whose mission is no longer viable, if it ever was – agencies that we would definitely not start now if we had the choice.

The mission may have been accomplished, for instance. An example is that most sacred of cows, the Veterans Administration's 171 hospitals and 130 nursing homes. When they first became accredited hospitals, around 1930, competent hospitals were scarce in the rural areas and small towns where a great many veterans lived. Today a competent hospital is easily accessible to a veteran almost anywhere. Medically, most VA hospitals are, at best, mediocre; yet, they are extremely expensive. Worst, they are not neighbourhood facilities, and thus veterans – especially elderly, chronically ill ones – have to travel far from their communities and their families just when they most need community and family support. The VA hospitals and nursing homes long ago accomplished what they were set up to do. They should be closed and the job contracted out to local hospitals and Health Maintenance Organizations.

Or there may be no mission left. For example, would be now establish a separate Department of Agriculture? A good many Americans would answer with a loud No. Now that farmers are no more than 3 per cent of the population, and productive farmers are half that (and 'agribusinesses' to boot), a bureau at Commerce or Labour is probably all we need.

Some perfectly respectable activities belong elsewhere. Why, for instance, should a scientific agency like the Geological Survey run a retail business? Surely there are enough businesses around, map stores or book chains, to sell its maps. Or they could be offered in the catalogues of firms that sell outdoor gear.

Continuing with activities that we would not now choose to begin is wasteful. They should be abandoned. One cannot even guess how many government activities would be found to be worth preserving. But my experience with many organizations suggests that the public would vote against continuing something like two-fifths, perhaps even half, of all civilian agencies and programmes. And almost none of them would win a vote – that is, be deemed to be properly organized and operating well – by a large margin.

Abandoning

Together the qualified yea and nays are likely to be awarded in any organization to some three-fifths or two-thirds of programmes and activities. The thorny cases are the programmes and activities that are unproductive or counterproductive without our quite knowing what is wrong, let alone how to straighten it out.

Two major and highly cherished US government programmes belong in this category. The welfare programme is one highly visible example. When it was designed, in the late 1930s, it worked beautifully. But the needs it then tackled were different from those it is supposed to serve today: the needs of unwed mothers and fatherless children, of people without education, skills, or work experience. Whether it actually does harm is hotly debated. But few claim that it works or that it even alleviates the social ills it is supposed to cure. And then there is that mainstay of US foreign policy during the cold war years: military aid. If it is given to an ally who is actually engaged in fighting, military aid can be highly productive: consider Lend–Lease to Great Britain in 1940–1941, and military aid to an embattled Israel. But military aid is counterproductive if it is given in peacetime to *create* an ally – a proposition that Plutarch and Suetonius already accepted as amply proved 2000 years age. Surely our worst recent foreign-policy messes – Panama, Iran, Iraq, and Somalia are prime examples – were caused by our giving military aid to create an ally. Little, if any, military aid since the beginning of the cold war has actually produced an ally. Indeed, it usually produced an enemy – as did Soviet military aid to Afghanistan.

The favourite prescription for such programmes or activities is to reform them. President Clinton's welfare reform is one example, as is the welfare reform proposed by the new Republican majority. Both are quackery. To reform something that malfunctions – let alone something that does harm – without knowing why it does not work can only make things worse. The best thing to do with such programmes is to abolish them.

Maybe we should run a few – a very few – controlled experiments. In welfare, for instance, we might try, in some carefully chosen places across the country, to privatize retraining and placing long-term welfare recipients. Indianapolis Mayor Stephen Goldsmith has achieved promising results in this area. In health care we might try several different approaches in different states: for example, managed competition in California, home of the strong and experienced health-care wholesaler Kaiser Permanente; single-payer health care on the Canadian model in New Jersey, where there has been support for it; and rationing on the basis of medical expectations, which is now being tried in Oregon for the care of indigents.

But in areas where there are no successes to be tested – for example, military aid – we should not even experiment. There are no hypotheses to test. We should abandon.

Rethinking will result in a list that has activities and programmes that should be strengthened at the top, others that should be abolished at the bottom, and between them activities that need to be refocused or in which a few hypotheses might be tested. Some activities and programmes should, despite an absence of results, be given a grace period of a few years before they are put out of their misery. Welfare may be the prime example.

Rethinking is not primarily concerned with cutting expenses. It leads above all to a tremendous increase in performance, in quality, in service. But substantial cost savings – sometimes as much as 40 per cent of the total – always emerge as a by-product. In fact, rethinking could produce enough savings to eliminate the federal deficit within a few years. The main result, however, would be a change in basic approach. For where conventional policy-making ranks programmes and activities according to their good intentions, rethinking ranks them according to results.

An exception for crusades

Anyone who has read this far will exclaim 'Impossible. Surely no group of people will ever agree on what belongs at the top of the list and what at the bottom.' But amazingly enough, wherever rethinking has been done, there has been substantial agreement about the list, whatever the backgrounds or the beliefs of the people involved. The disagreements are rarely over what should be kept or strengthened and what should be abandoned. They are usually over whether a programme or activity should be axed right away or put on probation for two or three years. The programmes that people do not agree on are the ones concerned not with results but with 'moral imperatives'.

The best American example is the War on Drugs. After many years it has had little effect on substance abuse and addiction, and much of the effect it has had is deleterious. But it underlies the destruction of our cities in that addicts are prostituting themselves, mugging, robbing, or killing to earn enough for the fix that the War on Drugs has made prohibitively expensive. All the War on Drugs is actually doing, in other words, is enriching drug dealers and penalizing and terrorizing non-users, especially in the inner city. But the War on Drugs is a crusade. What lies behind it is not logic but outrage. Stopping the War on Drugs no matter how beneficial, would be 'immoral'. The smart thing to do is to exclude such crusades from the rational analysis involved in rethinking. Fortunately, there are never a lot of them. As for the rest – more than 90 per cent of all programmes and activities – rethinking will in all probability produce substantial agreement.

A government that is effective

Surely, it will be argued, even total agreement among highly respected people will be futile. Congress will not accept anything like this. Neither will the bureaucracy. And lobbyists and special interests of all persuasions will be united in opposition to anything so subversive.

Perfectly true: action on rethinking is impossible today. But will it be impossible tomorrow? In the last presidential election almost one-fifth of the electorate voted for Ross Perot, the man who promised to get rid of the deficit by slashing government expenditures. A substantial number – perhaps another fifth – agreed with his aims even though they could not bring themselves to vote for him. Just now the federal deficit is declining. But even without health-care reform or welfare reform, the deficit will again grow explosively, at the latest by 1997. And then the demand for cutting the deficit may become irresistible and overwhelm Congress, the bureaucracy, and the lobbyists. If no rational rethinking of government performance has yet occurred, we will in all likelihood do what so many large companies have done – apply the meat-axe and downsize. We will then destroy performance, but without decreasing the deficit. It is predictable that the wrong things will then be cut – the things that perform and should be strengthened.

But if we have a plan that shows how and where the government needs to be rethought, we have a chance. In a crisis one turns to people who have thought through in advance what needs to be done. Of course, no plan, no matter how well thought through, will ever be carried out as written. Even a dictator has to make compromises. But such a plan would serve as the ideal against which the compromises are measured. It might save us from sacrificing things that should be strengthened in order to maintain the obsolete and the unproductive. It would not guarantee that all – or even most – of the unproductive things would be cut, but it might maintain the productive ones. Within a few years we are likely to face such a crisis, as the federal budget and the federal deficit resume explosive growth, while taxpayers grow ever more resistant to tax increases and ever more contemptuous of government and its promises.

In fact, we may already be very close to having to reinvent government. The theory on which all governments in the developed world have operated at least since the Great Depression (Harry Hopkins, Franklin Delano Roosevelt's adviser, called it 'Tax and Tax, Spend and Spend') no longer delivers results. It no longer even delivers votes. The 'nanny state' – a lovely English term – is a total failure. Government everywhere – in the United States, the United Kingdom, Germany, the former Soviet Union – has been proved unable to run community and society. And everywhere voters revolt against the nanny state's futility, bureaucracy, and burdens. The landslide in which California's voters last November enacted Proposition 187, abolishing health care and even free public education for illegal immigrants, is but one example. But the countertheory that preaches a return to pre-First World War government has also not proved out – the theory that was first formulated in 1944 in Friedrich Hayek's *The Road to Serfdom*, and that culminated in neo-conservatism. Despite its ascendancy in the 1980s, despite Ronald Reagan and Margaret Thatcher, the nanny state has not shrunk. On the contrary, it is growing ever faster. As the new Republican majority is soon going to find out, neither maintaining nor curtailing the nanny state is acceptable to the public.

Instead we will have to find out what government programmes and activities in community and society *do* serve a purpose. What results should be expected of each? What can governments – federal, state, local – *do* effectively? And what non-governmental ways are there to do worthwhile things that governments do not and cannot do effectively?

At the same time, as President Clinton learned in his first two years, government cannot opt out of the wider world and become domestic only, as he so very much wanted it to be. Foreign brushfires – in Bosnia, in Rwanda, in the former Soviet Union – have to be attended to, because they have a nasty habit of spreading. And the growing threat of international terrorism, especially if used as a weapon by outlaw governments, will surely require more government involvement in foreign affairs, including military matters, and more international cooperation.

By now it has become clear that a developed country can neither extend big government, as the (so-called) liberals want, nor abolish it and go back to nineteenth-century innocence, as the (so-called) conservatives want. The government we need will have to transcend both groups. The mega-state which this century built is bankrupt, morally as well as financially. It has not delivered. But its successor cannot be 'small government'. There are far too many tasks, domestically and internationally. We need *effective* government – and that is what the voters in all developed countries are actually clamouring for.

For this, however, we need something we do not have: a theory of what government can do. No major political thinker – at least not since Machiavelli, almost 500 years ago – has addressed this question. All political theory, from Locke on through *The Federalist Papers* and down to the articles published by today's liberals and conservatives, deals with the process of government: with constitutions, with power and its limitations, with methods and organizations. None deals with the substance. None asks what the proper functions of government might be and could be. None asks what results government should be held accountable for.

Rethinking government, its programmes, its agencies, its activities, would not by itself give us this new political theory. But it would give us the factual information for it. And so much is already clear: the new political theory we badly need will have to rest on an analysis of what does work rather than on good intentions and promises of what should work because we would like it to. Rethinking will not give us the answers, but it might force us to ask the right questions.

Now is the time to start, when polls show that less than a fifth of the American public trusts government to do anything right. Vice-President Gore's 'reinventing government' is an empty slogan so far. Yet what the slogan implies is what free government needs – and desperately.

1995

25
Can the democracies win the peace?

Communism has lost the cold war. Now the democracies have to win the peace. That may be harder, as all history teaches. For forty years now it was enough that the democracies were infinitely – and visibly – better. Now they are expected to be good. They are being measured now against their *own* professions and their *own* performance. Now the democracies have to rethink and to reform.

Specifically, to win the peace, the democracies have:

- To regain control of their *domestic, economic,* and *fiscal policies*, both lost as a result of the bankruptcy of the Keynesian Deficit State
- To stop and reverse the corrosion and spreading decay of *domestic* society caused by the failure of the welfare state
- To promote worldwide *civil society* without which there can be neither political nor social stability, least of all in the former Communist countries. For we now know that the free market, however effective economically, does not by itself alone build and sustain a functioning society.

The bankruptcy of the Keynesian welfare state

For forty years the domestic policies of the developed countries have been dominated by two sets of beliefs, each considered self-evident:

- One is the Keynesian (or neo-Keynesian) belief in the 'Deficit State'. It rested on three *economic* assertions. Consumption automatically creates capital formation and capital investment (the Keynesian 'multiplier'). Savings are dangerous to economic health (Keynes' 'over-saving'). Government deficits stimulate the economy.
- The other set, the belief in the welfare state, rested on two *social* assertions. Government can and should redistribute income so as to promote greater income equality – an assertion which when first pronounced as government policy (by David Lloyd George when he became England's Chancellor of the Exchequer in the Liberal Cabinet of 1908), was considered the most radical of heresies but which became orthodoxy in the Great Depression. The second assertion: the only thing the poor need is money – what might be called the Social Worker's creed.

Both beliefs have been decisively disproven.

In the West all Democracies came to accept these beliefs – though West Germany accepted the Keynesian propositions only with great reservations. Japan – with its habitual preference for ambiguity in policies – never completely accepted nor completely rejected these beliefs and followed their prescriptions only intermittently.

Originally the two beliefs were opposed to each other. Keynes was outspoken in his contempt for the welfare state. He claimed that his economics would make unnecessary large-scale social spending. And he considered futile any governmental attempt to redistribute income. The proponents of the welfare theorem in turn had little use for the free market in which Keynes passionately believed. After the Second World War the two found, however, that they needed each other. Keynes' putting consumption over thrift and his advocacy of deficits, converted 'charity' into 'economic stimulus' and thereby enabled the middle class to accept welfare spending on the poor. In turn,

Keynesian economics, despite their middle-class and free-market bias, needed the political support of Progressives and Socialists. And so the two embraced each other, thus forming the *Keynesian welfare state*.

The Keynesian welfare state has ruled for forty years. Whatever differences there have been in the democracies on economic and fiscal policies – between Republicans and Democrats in the United States, between Tories and Labour in the United Kingdom, between Christians and Socialists in West Germany – were mainly differences in degree. Reagan's 'supply siders' fully subscribed to the basic tenets of the Keynesian welfare state for all their being considered arch-conservatives. Each side, the Right as well as the Left, boasted that it was better at building and running the Keynesian welfare state – which, by the way, largely explains why government deficits grew the fastest under supposedly Conservative governments, e.g. under Reagan in the United States, under Thatcher in the United Kingdom, under Kohl in Germany.

There was actually never any evidence to support the Keynesian propositions – as was pointed out by such eminent economists as Lionel Robbins in England and Joseph Schumpeter in America when Keynes first published his theses in the mid-1930s. By now these propositions are so completely discredited that economists hardly mention them. Nowhere has increased consumption led to capital formation and investment. On the contrary, the United States and the United Kingdom which have been pushing consumption most consistently and most thoroughly, have the lowest rates of capital formation. In the United States it has long been hovering around a dismal 4 per cent of disposable income. In the United Kingdom it plunged from 8 or 9 per cent to 5 per cent of disposable income in 1989 when Mrs Thatcher tried (unsuccessfully) to stimulate an ailing economy by (successfully) pushing up consumption. Conversely, as long as Japan discouraged consumption, it had a capital-formation rate of almost 15 per cent of disposable income. But when in the mid-1980s, Japan tried to fight a sudden recession by revving up consumption (with disastrous results, by the way), the capital-formation rate plunged at once to 9 per cent of disposable income, and has stayed there ever since.

Oversaving has proven to be pure myth. No one believes any more Keynes's assertion that it had anything to do with the Great Depression, let alone that it caused it. And far from oversaving having caused depression in Japan – as the theory would have had it do most assuredly – Japan's high rate of capital formation is universally considered a key factor in its economic success. The abundant supply of savings pushed interest rates so low that Japanese big business could obtain capital at almost zero cost while the Americans and the Europeans had to pay up to 15 per cent or more for their money. Japan thus had a 10 per cent cost advantage over its world-market competitors – and even a 5 per cent cost advantage is usually decisive.

There also has not been one single case of government spending stimulating the economy, let alone one of government spending turning around a recession or depression.

The one instance usually cited to the contrary, the so-called Kennedy tax cut of 1962, is a phony. The economy did indeed recover in 1962–1963. Only there was no Kennedy tax-cut. On the contrary, the US tax burden went up in 1962 and 1963 – in part because President Kennedy did not get through Congress his key proposal for a cut in the capital-gains tax, in part because states and cities raised their taxes faster and further than the federal government lowered its take.

Contrary to the promises of Keynesian economics, business cycles have not been eliminated. There is no difference either in frequency or severity between the recessions of the period since the Second World War (that is the period of the Keynesian welfare state) and those of the nineteenth and early twentieth centuries.

Had there been any validity to the basic theories of the Keynesian welfare state the democracies would be rolling in money.

Government spending would have so stimulated the economy that both capital formation and tax revenues would have sky-rocketed. In short order there would then have been huge budget surpluses. President Reagan's supply-siders still promised that. Instead, the democracies – except only Japan – are so deeply in debt that they can pay their daily bills only if their creditors lend ever more and more money. The proper term for this condition is *insolvency*.

The return of the panic

A few academic Keynesians – Robert Eisner at Northwestern University is an example – still argue that government deficits do not matter. But even they do not claim any more that they are beneficial. Outside of the economics departments everybody now knows: business executives, labour leaders, bankers, investors, the stock market, the bond market, that damage is all that deficits can do. At the first sign of an increase in the government deficit, stock markets drop, money flees the country and business investment dries up, and employment with it. Above all, there is no longer the slightest doubt that government deficits destroy capital formation. But this then means that to pay their bills governments which run continuous deficits cannot borrow at home to finance themselves. They become increasingly dependent on foreign money borrowed for shorter and shorter terms. This is extremely volatile money, easily scared, and prone to panic.

Financial panics were the bane of the nineteenth century. Keynes' claim that his economics would once and for all put an end to them was therefore a major factor in their acceptance. But panics have returned with a vengeance. They are as plentiful now as they ever were a century ago, and as destructive. A three-day flight of capital in 1981 devastated France's financial markets and threatened to turn into a run on the banks. It forced President Mitterand to jettison all the social promises on which he had won the election only a few months earlier. A few years later panic forced Sweden to raise interest rates overnight to a disastrous 30 per cent. Two years ago another panic caused by the flight of foreign money all but destroyed the Italian lira. And only last December panic brought on a run on Mexico's peso, devalued it overnight by 50 per cent, and in one fell swoop wiped out years of hard, painful work that had raised the economy to the threshold of being 'developed' (or at least 'emerging').

No country that practises Keynesian welfare economics can be considered immune from panic. Indeed, the list of countries that are on the brink is steadily growing – in Europe the worst cases are Italy (government deficit 9.7 per cent of disposable income; government debt 125 per cent of disposable income; rate of capital formation: zero, if not negative); and Sweden (government deficit 10 per cent of disposable income; government debt 100 per cent of disposable income; capital-formation rate no more than 2 per cent). Belgium, Holland, Spain, Denmark are not much better off; Britain and France only marginally so – and Canada is almost as close to bankruptcy as Sweden. The United States actually has a fairly low deficit in terms of its disposable income – around 2 per cent, or no more than Japan. But because its rate of capital-formation is totally inadequate, it is as dependent on short-term money from abroad as any of the Europeans – and thus equally vulnerable to panic. In fact the United States has already suffered two 'mini-panics'. The 1987 stock market crash was caused by the Japanese panicking and dumping huge quantities of US Treasury Bonds. And the 1993 crash of the bond market – also caused primarily by a sudden flight of foreign capital – forced President Clinton to scuttle his plans for stimulating the economy and to accept instead the priority of the Federal Reserve Board (led by a Republican Chairman!) to placate the foreign lenders, that is, to fight inflation even at the risk of domestic slump.

The worst consequences of the failure of the Keynesian welfare state are not economic. The increasing dependence on short-term and volatile foreign money impairs the ability of governments to set and to pursue policies. It increasingly subordinates sovereignty to the whims of an erratic world money market, driven by rumours, and with the next 'deal' as its long-term horizon. One recent example: to attract and keep the short-term money needed to finance Chancellor Kohl's (ultra-Keynesian) unification policy, Germany in 1993–1994 had to raise interest rates and keep them sky-high. This severely hurt Germany's neighbours in Europe who were already suffering from massive unemployment. They in turn had to push up *their* already high interest rates to prevent the flight of short-term money to high-interest Germany. Throughout Europe the Germans were berated for their 'selfishness'. Yet they had no choice. The global short-term money market was in control rather than the German government. The greatest damage was probably the blow the German policy inflicted on the support for political and currency union throughout Europe – Dr Kohl's own most cherished goals during his entire political life.

The Keynesian welfare state also did not deliver on its *social* promise to redistribute income and thereby to promote equality of income. There is, on the contrary, an almost perfect correlation among major democracies between welfare state spending and income *in*equality. The country with the lowest inequality of incomes is also the country with the lowest deficit, the lowest rate of social spending (only 12 per cent of disposable income), and the highest rate of capital formation: Japan. In the United States, in the United Kingdom, even in Germany (with social-spending rates of 15 per cent, 23 per cent and 27 per cent, respectively) income inequality has become greater rather than smaller, the more social spending has grown.

The entitlement crisis

Liquidating the deficit state can no longer be avoided. It cannot even be postponed much longer. It is clearly the number one *political* task faced by the democracies, and will be their political reality for the next decade. And it means the end of ever-increasing middle-class entitlements. A little over a hundred years old – they were invented in Bismarck's Germany in the 1880s – entitlements have now become a threat to the very survival of democracy, if not of the modern state altogether. The only way the democracies can regain control of their finances – and with them of economic, social and foreign policy – is to cut back sharply on entitlements, whether that be health care (spending on which is racing out of control in all developed countries rather than in the United States alone); on social security; on pensions; or, in Europe, on unemployment benefits.

That middle-class entitlements threaten the democracies' prosperity and health – and indeed their very survival – has been known for quite some time now. As early as 1988 it was proven with mathematical rigour by Peter G. Petersen (President Nixon's erstwhile Secretary of Commerce) in a book entitled *On Borrowed Time: How The Growth in Entitlement Spending Threatens America's Future*. But nobody was yet willing to listen.

Any attempt at cutting entitlements – or even at slowing their growth – is still bitterly resisted. Last year the voters in Sweden tossed out the incumbent Liberal government for proposing to cap a few entitlement programmes that had clearly gone out of control. Shortly thereafter, Italy's prime minister, Silvio Berlusconi, was kicked out of office for the same offence. A few months earlier he had been elected on the promise of reforming entitlements. But when he actually proposed taking a close look at the outrageous abuses of the country's pension system, his coalition partners deserted him. Everybody in Italy knows that hundreds of thousands of able-bodied people – some estimates say millions – are fraudulently receiving life-long disability pensions which are the main cause of Italy's financial troubles. They account for half of Italy's social spending, that is, for a full eighth of the country's disposable income and for all of its horrendous deficit. Cutting entitlements – even fraudulent ones – was, however, still not 'politically correct'.

That both Republicans and Democrats in the United States now agree that Medicare – long the most sacred of sacred cows – needs to be pruned back is thus a major change. It still remains to be seen, however, whether the Congress can get itself to do anything so unpopular. Actually, the middle class has no choice. Entitlements will be cut in all developed countries. The only question is by what method. The least painful way is to do it openly – e.g. by raising to seventy-five the age at which Americans get full social security benefits. If this is not accepted, middle-class entitlements will be cut by inflation, that is, by destroying the purchasing power of middle-class incomes. Or there will be draconian increases in taxation – in the United States most probably through substantial consumption taxes on top of already high income taxes.

And as soon as one major country cuts middle-class entitlements – e.g. if the United States were to accept more than token cuts in Medicare benefits – it will be the signal for entitlement reform in all the other democracies. This would herald the end of the Keynesian welfare state as surely as Mr Gorbachev's *perestroika* heralded the end of Communism.

To restore government to solvency – and with it restore its control of policy – requires that it be forced again to make priority decisions. It will again have to be forced to say 'No'. The first step might be a return to the way budgets were made before the advent of the Keynesian Deficit State: by beginning with the available *revenues*, that is, with how much money can be spent. This forces government to decide what can and should be financed within the limits set by the availability of money. What exceeds these limits has to be said 'no' to. Since the Second World War, however – or at least since Western Europe and Japan returned to prosperity in the late 1950s – all democracies start budget-making with the question: What do we want to *spend* money on? Spending beyond the available revenues, that is, deficit spending, was easy to finance. Above all, it was deemed beneficial. Indeed, the Keynesian postulates made saying 'no' appear heartless and almost immoral. Saying 'no' is indeed painful. For a politician it is risky. It is only necessary.

But that would only be the first step. The decisions on priorities would then still be ahead. They are likely – I would say, certain – to explode all existing parties everywhere. In fact, both 'Right' and 'Left' have already lost much of their meaning in the democracies. Who is on the 'right', for instance: people who want the pension age set according to life expectancies, that is, to be pushed up to seventy-five (sixty years ago when the United States embraced sixty-five as the social-security age, it was actually a good deal higher than average life expectancies at the time and chosen for that reason)? Or people who argue a duty of the young to support their elders? Traditionally both are 'Conservative' positions. What is 'Liberal': the argument that university education be free for all? Or the counter-argument that its recipients should repay from their greatly increased post-graduation earnings the cost of their schooling so that the next generation can have free access? These are new issues. They do not fit the existing mould of politics; they are neither *economic* nor *ideological*. In the democracies therefore more than political issues can be expected to be in transition; political structure will be in transition too.

Turning poverty into degradation

The *social axioms* of the Keynesian welfare state have worn no better than its economic axioms. Welfare has not ended poverty. It has instead turned it into degradation and dependence. It has done so in the domestic as well as the international society, that is, as much through domestic 'welfare' as through 'foreign aid'.

In the United States it is now generally accepted that neither of the two big welfare programmes works. Both Aid to Families with Dependant Children and Disability Aid are disasters. It is still widely denied, however, that they do damage. Rather, the dependence and degradation of long-term welfare dependents and the dreary squalor of their lives is being explained away.

In terms of income, America's welfare recipients are doing quite well. If non-cash benefits (e.g. food stamps or housing allowances) are included, the incomes of most are above the 'poverty line'. Yet they live in a squalor and degradation as bad as that of yesterday's worst slums, if not worse. The most common explanation asserts that the American 'welfare mess' is part of our racial problem. There are indeed proportionally many more Black unwed 'welfare mothers' who are permanently on Aid to Families with Dependent Children (37 per cent of the welfare population is Black, where Blacks are only 13 per cent of the population). And so one explanation is racial inferiority (no longer expressed publicly, as a rule, but surely held by a great many non-Blacks, whether Whites, Latinos or Asians). The other one is the legacy of discrimination and slavery. Both are equally racist and equally despicable. And both are patently wrong. There is the same 'welfare mess' – that is, the same turning of poverty into degradation – where the welfare recipients are purely white and indeed where they were competent, self-supporting middle-class until they became welfare recipients.

In Britain the 'welfare underclass' (what British statisticians classify as members of 'Class V') is now growing as fast as the same group in America. It suffers from the same social *anomie*, the same destruction of personality and competence and self-respect. Before 1950 illegitimacy in the British working class was no higher than it had been for centuries, i.e. around 4 or 5 per cent of births. It has now passed 25 per cent; and among chronic welfare recipients it is well past 30 per cent and already higher than among *White* welfare recipients in America. And it is climbing as fast as among America's Blacks. Unlike the United States, the British system also supports men on welfare through very high and long-term unemployment benefits. The dependency rate among young British males is climbing as fast as the welfare-dependency rate among American young women in the 'underclass'. The British on welfare and long-term unemployment payments are financially even better off than their US counterparts. Their pre-tax income is equal to that of the average *employed* blue-collar family but is tax exempt so that their net income on welfare is actually a good deal higher. Yet they display the same social pathology: dropping out of school; increasing illegitimacy rates; more and more fatherless families; increasing addiction – in Britain still primarily on alcohol though hard-drug use is growing fast. Britain's inner-cities – only thirty years ago among the safest in the world – are becoming jungles; the urban burglary rate is already higher in Britain than it is in America. Yet this British welfare underclass is almost totally white.

Across the Channel, in Germany, the welfare underclass consists of people – entirely white and predominantly male – who stay permanently idle because Germany pays unemployment compensation of 80 per cent of the employees' former wages for the rest of their lives. The recipients are graduates of the famed German apprentice training system and have grown up with the equally famous German work ethic. But welfare, within no time at all, converts growing numbers of them into what Germans call 'welfare cripples', with all the pathology of social disintegration and *anomie*: rising numbers of families headed by single, unwed mothers; sharp increases in alcoholism; and the young 'skinheads' and neo-Nazis who 'for kicks' set fire to tenement houses inhabited by Turks or other foreign workers. As a result, Germany now has one of the highest unemployment rates – even when the economy is booming – with an intractably high *permanent* unemployment.

In Italy, the welfare underclass consists of forty- to fifty-year-old males – all white, of course – who go on full or partial 'disability pension' and stay on it the rest of their adult lives. Most of them, it is generally known, are able-bodied; their disabilities are quite minor or totally fraudulent. That a great many of these people actually hold a job while claiming to be unable to do so mitigates the economic impact of their idleness. (In fact it is common knowledge in Italy that a fair number of the recipients of disability pensions actually hold *two* paid jobs: a patronage job in the public service where they only show up to collect their salary, and a paid job in the 'underground' economy.) But this does not mitigate the impact on Italy's government budget which is crippled by pension payments. And it aggravates the moral and psychological damage to society and individual alike. That Italy has become riddled with corruption from top to bottom is in large measure the result of pension fraud. It has made being on the take the accepted, indeed the proper, thing to do.

The evidence is thus crystal-clear. First, modern welfare destroys. It does not build competence; it creates dependence. It does not alleviate poverty even though it provides middle-class or near-middle-class incomes. And it does so irrespective of who the recipients are: black teenage girls in the United States; young, working-class white males in the United Kingdom; highly trained adult men in Germany; middle-class, mostly salaried men in Italy. The one thing these corrupted and poisoned people have in common is that they are being financially rewarded for staying on welfare and financially penalized for getting off it.

The failure of foreign aid

Internationally the failure of welfare has been just as great. Development aid was surely one of the most important political inventions of this century. The first attempt, the Marshall Plan, was successful beyond all expectations. There was thus every reason to expect great results from its two successors: President Truman's Point Four (1950) and President Kennedy's Alliance for Progress (1962). (No one expected greater things from both than I did; indeed I worked enthusiastically for both.) At best, neither plan did much damage. But neither did much good. The forty years since President Truman's proclamation have indeed brought more, and more widely spread, economic development than any earlier period in history. But the development was mainly in areas that received little or no aid – especially the countries of South-east Asia. Indeed, there is a near-perfect *negative* correlation between receiving development aid and development. The areas that received the *most* such aid either did not develop at all – India and Egypt are the prime examples – or actually lost ground as did most of tropical Africa. Just as with domestic welfare, the recipients of international welfare (we call it 'development aid') have little in common with each other except their developing the less the more aid they got. Nor do such popular explanations as the 'population explosion' hold water. Populations grew just as much in some of the fastest-developing countries in South-east Asia, e.g. Thailand, Malaysia, Indonesia, Turkey, or coastal China. The one factor that the non-developing countries share is their having received massive development aid. The one factor the fast-developing countries share is that they received little or no development aid.

Welfare and international aid which increases dependence or inhibits development – that is, a good many of the welfare and aid programmes of the last forty years – will be discontinued or, at least, be cut back sharply. But it is surely wrong to conclude – as a good many people now do – that the welfare concept, both domestic and international, was a mistake best to be forgotten. What is needed is to refocus welfare on creating independence, competence, responsibility.

The need for help – at least for temporary help – is surely going to grow. Developed and developing countries alike are undergoing major transformations of economy and society. There will therefore be massive dislocations in which well-established, competent, responsible people will find themselves uprooted. They may not need much – in many cases their main need is the assurance that help is available. But a society and economy in transition are a dangerous environment. There is need for what welfare was supposed to be: a 'safety net'. It must only be prevented from becoming instead a 'couch' and a permanent resting place.

A second reason for constructing an effective welfare system is that it would be total defeat for the democracies, and a denial of the very idea on which they are based, for affluence to lead to an erosion of compassion. In the not-so-long run, rising affluence does indeed most benefit those at the bottom of the income pyramid. It cannot be said too often that – contrary to everything Marx predicted – the 'proletarians' were the main beneficiaries of the enormous increase in wealth-producing capacity in the developed countries during the last hundred years. Their real income has risen at least three times as fast as that of the 'capitalists'. Contrary to the predictions of Marx's successors and disciples – e.g. Lenin and the other theoreticians of 'Imperialism' – the greatest increase in *national* prosperity and wealth in these hundred years were among 'colonial' and 'exploited' countries that have become developed countries. Japan's total national product has risen a good deal faster than that of the United States – but so also has that of South Korea and of the 'Tigers' of South-east Asia: Taiwan, Singapore and Hong Kong – all former colonies – and of such other former colonies as Malaysia and Indonesia.

But that the great majority in the developed and emerging countries is now so much better off only makes more visible and more painful the plight of the minorities who are left behind because of lack of competence or lack of opportunity. And this is just as true for the international society as for the domestic society. For their own self-respect the rich therefore need to help. But for the good of the poor it must be help that helps, help that creates competence, health, self-respect, rather than the help of the welfare state which creates dependence, destitution, incompetence, self-loathing.

Encouraging the competence of the poor and promoting their capacity to develop themselves is clearly in the self-interest of the affluent, that is, of the democracies. For their stability and social cohesion is increasingly threatened by the *anomie*, the degradation, the despair of the incompetent and dependent poor.

A hundred and sixty years ago an epidemic in London's East End made the wealthy in the West End realize for the first time that typhoid among the poor threatened them too. This was the beginning of public health – until then there had been only private health – and with it the beginning of the revolution in health and longevity which has benefited the rich surely as much as it has benefited the poor.

The *anomie*, the degradation, the lawlessness, the corruption caused among the incompetent poor by the failure of welfare – domestically and internationally – equally threatens the cities, the suburbs, the schools, the streets of the healthy, the competent, the affluent. It threatens to infect their children, above all. Surely, spreading contagion from the welfare underclass is heavily to blame for much of the coarsening and proletarization of middle-class life, middle-class culture, and middle-class values. The *anomie*, the degradation, the lawlessness of the non-developing 'Third World' equally threatens the safety, the peace, the affluence of the wealthy countries – if only through the increasing immigration-pressure of desperate and incompetent people fleeing to the developed world.

The final – and most compelling – reason for not giving up on development – whether at home or internationally – is that it is the wrong thing to do: there are enough successes to show that development out of poverty and into competence is possible, and also what it requires.

We know what made the Marshall Plan succeed – the world's biggest welfare programme ever, and its most successful one. Another – and equally impressive – success was the 'Green Revolution' in which new seeds and improved farming methods (financed and promoted by the Rockefeller and Ford Foundations, that is, by two non-governmental organizations) changed

India in the 1960s. From a country in which large-scale famines occurred every few years India has become one which in most years has an export surplus of cereal grains. Domestically there is the success of the Salvation Army in the United States in rehabilitating a large proportion of the worst losers – prostitutes; former convicts; alcoholics; hard-drug addicts – and turning them into competent, self-sustaining and self-respecting citizens. It is arguably the most successful social programme in any developed country today with, for instance, a 30 per cent rehabilitation rate for alcoholics and hard-drug addicts.

There is also the tremendous difference in results between two superficially very similar programmes: the European (both British and German) programmes of unemployment benefits and the one in the United States. The programmes in Britain and Germany turn self-respecting workers into permanent welfare dependants. In the United States there has been little chronic unemployment despite upheavals in the labour force which were considerably more drastic than anything Britain and Germany have experienced so far.

The Marshall Plan spent very, very little money by the standards of the 1900s; and it spent it sparingly. It liberally gave technical support and consulting help. But it gave money only as 'seed money' to businesses that had a convincing track record and submitted a realistic plan with clear performance goals. And both, support and money, were withdrawn the moment a business – whether private or government-owned – either diverted money from the agreed-upon plan or failed to meet agreed-upon performance goals. The Green Revolution spent even less money. Its agents – e.g. CARE, the American international relief organization – sought out competent Indian farmers and worked closely with them on trying out new seeds and new farming methods. The main use of money was as insurance against the risk of crop failure during the first two or three critical years. The Salvation Army spends practically no money at all. It explains its success as being based on discipline; hard work; minimum subsistence pay; a demanding programme of skill teaching, and unlimited *compassion*. And anyone who breaks the Salvation Army's draconian rules is out, no matter how needy. Unemployment compensation in the United States in the first weeks or months of unemployment is as high as it is in Europe – and for some workers, e.g. those in unionized car plants – even higher. It provides ample support for the period during which the newly unemployed is likely to be in a state of shock. But the money soon tapers off; and it stops altogether after two years. There is thus a powerful incentive to look for work. Even in cities or regions that have been heavily dependent on a single plant or a single industry which totally shut down, unemployment within two years or so drops to the national average. And national average in the United States, even in times of labour-market upheavals, rarely has stayed very long above the 'natural' rate of unemployment, that is, above the rate which expresses the normal in-between jobs turnover of the American economy.

Welfare can work, in other words. But only if the axiom is changed from 'All the poor need is money' to 'All the poor need is competence'. Of course there is need for money. But by itself alone money encourages incompetence and irresponsibility. Today's welfare focuses on *needs*. There will be true 'welfare', however, only if the focus is on *results*.

What welfare has to be

Major countries are now tackling welfare spending. In the United States, Aid to Families with Dependent Children is being sharply cut by some states, e.g. New York, California and Massachusetts; and for the United States altogether by the new, Republican-dominated Congress. Italy, as already mentioned, is at least talking about pension reform. Britain is about to enact cuts in the rewards for remaining permanently unemployed, as is Germany. These proposals penalize staying on welfare. This may do the trick where, as with German unemployment compensation and Italian disability pensions, the recipients are largely competent and healthy people whose main incapacity is welfare itself.

But for people who lack competence – the welfare recipients in the United States and largely in Britain – there may be need also for positive *incentives* for not going on welfare in the first place, and for not staying on it. Governments will surely have to pay for this at least in part (though, as in the Salvation Army programmes, rehabilitated recipients should routinely be required to become themselves donors or volunteers). We are unlikely to be able to depend for helping the less competent entirely on philanthropy, as the Victorians believed. But the *delivery* of welfare programmes should be contracted out to non-governmental, community organizations as much as possible. This is what the example of the Salvation Army teaches (but also many smaller and less conspicuous programmes in the United States – especially a good many church-run ones). What is primarily needed by the less competent and the wounded is not money – whether less money or more of it. It is what makes the Salvation Army successful: discipline; commitment; hard work; self-respect and a great deal of individual attention. And such intangibles a government bureaucracy, however well intentioned, cannot deliver.

In the present discussion of 'welfare reform' the emphasis in all countries is on money. It is the wrong emphasis. In the first place, welfare is a big-budget item only if it is 'entitlement' to the middle class as are German unemployment compensation and Italian disability benefits. Welfare to the truly less competent – the US and UK programmes – is a minor budget item in comparison to the entitlements to the competent middle class such as Medicare, social security, or the British National Health Service. Second, that welfare wastes money – and it does – is its least offence. *It wastes lives.* If welfare had results it would be cheap even if it cost twice as much. And the reason for welfare should not be, as the welfare state asserted, that the less fortunate and less competent deserve to be financially supported. The reason must be that they deserve to be restored to competence, self-respect and self-support – and those are the results welfare needs to aim for and to pay for.

Internationally too, welfare, i.e. foreign aid, is being pruned drastically. It should, however, in all probability be stopped altogether – except as disaster aid in an earthquake or to house and feed refugees from civil war. What is needed internationally – as the next section discusses – is Civil Society; and that money cannot buy.

But to develop policies that truly promote *domestic* welfare rather than create dependence and destitution will be the major *social* challenge for the democracies in the next decade, and a crucial test for them as functioning societies.

The free market's power and its limitations

Keynesian economics still underlie the *domestic* policies of the democracies. But only in the first half of the period since the Second World War did they reign unchallenged. In the second half, i.e. since the 1970s, Keynesian economics have come under increasingly heavy attack from what in the United States is known as 'neo-Conservatism' (elsewhere called 'neo-classic economics', the term I shall use). And in *international* economics, neo-classicism has come to reign supreme. It is the economics on which the international agencies – the World Bank and the International Monetary Fund – base themselves. And the same governments that are Keynesian at home – especially the US government – have also been turning neo-classic in their international economics. Whenever a foreign country gets into trouble, the United States advises it to accept, and fast, the neo-classic prescription.

Neo-classic economists, like their forebears in the nineteenth century, preach the superiority of the free market over any other system of economic organization. But they go far beyond their mentors. They claim that the free market by itself will create a functioning *society* and, indeed, even a stable democratic *political* system.

Neo-classicism goes back to Friedrich Hayek's 1944 book *The Road to Serfdom*. Hayek asserted that any tampering with the free market soon leads to destruction of political freedom and to tyranny. He also claimed – and that has proven eventually his most important thesis – that an economy based on the free market and unencumbered by government controls, regulations and interventions creates, by itself, an optimally free, just, and equal society. What to the nineteenth century had primarily been economic theory Hayek converted into social and political doctrine.

Hayek's book was an immediate sensation: though, for a long time, without much impact on government policy or on academia. But as the failure of Keynesian economics became more and more apparent, neo-classicism became increasingly respectable. It is still not domestic *government* policy – deficit spending is much too attractive for governments to embrace the neo-classics' austerity and self-discipline – and not only in the Anglo-American countries. But in the universities Keynesians are now a minority and are found mainly among the older economists. The younger ones have predominantly become 'neo-classics', even in such Keynesian strongholds as Harvard, MIT, or Cambridge University. Until the late 1970s and early 1980s the Nobel Prize for Economics went regularly to Keynesians, e.g. Paul Samuelson (1970) or Kenneth Arrow (1972). In the last twenty years it has gone increasingly to neo-classics (examples are George J. Stigler in 1981; James M. Buchanan in 1987, and Gary S. Becker in 1992). Neo-classic economics have become the standard prescription for turning around an economy; after it had floundered under the statist or neo-Keynesian economics of the 1950s and 1960s (e.g. the economies of Latin America); when it embarks on systematic economic development (e.g. the economies of South-east Asia, beginning with South Korea); and to bring back to life economies asphyxiated by Communism, e.g. the countries of the former Soviet Empire and post-Maoist China.

There can be no longer any doubt that neo-classics work as *economics*. In fact, they work like a wonder drug. As soon as an economy moves towards free-market policies – that is, cuts government spending and balances the budget; privatizes government-owned businesses; cuts back or eliminates government regulations and government controls of economic activity; opens its borders to imports and thereby allows competition; eliminates or at least cuts back government restrictions on the movement of money and capital – an *economic* boom gets going. At first it is accompanied by – often severe – dislocation. Inefficient enterprises go bankrupt as they are no longer kept alive by tariff walls or government subsidies. There is a drastic jump in unemployment. But this transition period should not last very long, as a rule no more than two years. Then unemployment, for instance, goes down again, and fast.

This has happened in quite a few countries. It happened in desperately poor Bolivia in the 1980s; in Chile a little later; in Argentina after 1989; in the Czech Republic in 1991–1992 and, most spectacularly, in the 'Tigers' of mainland Asia: Hong Kong, Taiwan, Singapore and, a few years later, in their neighbours, Malaysia, Thailand, and Indonesia.

But it did not happen in *all* countries. Except for the Czech Republic it has not happened so far in any of the countries of the former Soviet Empire, whether they had been incorporated into the Soviet Union or had been nominally independent. Free-market economics did not turn around the East German economy. To keep East Germany from dying, West Germany had to pour in larger amounts of government aid than has ever been poured into any area. Freeing the economy did indeed produce economic boom in China. But in inland China where most of the people live, the boom soon collapsed. And even coastal China has wild inflation rather than a stable economy. Mexico experienced tremendous economic growth as soon as it adopted free-market economics in 1987–1988. But this did not produce social and political stability. On the contrary, economic growth only activated the profound cultural, economic, social, and political seismic faults which economic backwardness had kept from producing earthquakes.

Economically neo-classicism has been fully proven. But its claims that it would also generate a functioning society and a stable polity – the claim that made it *neo*-classicism – has been fully disproven. The free market works only where there are effective institutional guarantees of property rights and, especially, effective protection of property rights against the powerful whether kings, nobles, bishops, generals, or parliaments – as shown by the American economic historian Douglass C. North, especially in his 1990 book *Institutions, Institutional Change and Economic Performance* (Cambridge University Press), for which he received the 1993 Nobel Prize for Economics. For the free market to work also requires a reliable legal system, an infrastructure of financial institutions and an adequate educational system. *The free market does not create a functioning society – it presupposes it.* Without such a functioning civil society a few speculators may get very rich. But the economy will remain poor. There may be tremendous economic excitement as there is in Mr Yeltsin's Russia, or in today's Shanghai. But unless there is the social infrastructure of a civil society this apparent economic turn around is likely to be short-lived. It will either collapse right away or swell into a speculative bubble and burst. Sustained economic development does indeed require the neo-classic economics. But there first have to be the legal, financial, educational institutions of a functioning *society*, and the human resources such a society produces, educates, develops, tests – and respects.

Before Hitler the Czech core of Czechoslovakia was one of the stablest, most solid, most *bourgeois* – and most productive –

societies in the world – next to Switzerland the stablest and most solid society on the continent of Europe. It was first brutally persecuted by Hitler and then totally suppressed by Stalin. But the foundations were still there; the traditions were there; the memories were there – and the people remained resolutely *bourgeois* in their values and commitments. In the Czech Republic the free market could and did indeed perform economically almost as soon as the Stalinist shackles were struck off. Hong Kong, Taiwan, Singapore – even South Korea – all inherited legal, financial, educational institutions from their former colonial rulers, as did Malaysia and Indonesia. For a century or longer Chile – with a stable society and stable politics – was considered 'the Switzerland of Latin America'; and thus the free market could produce a functioning economy despite a few years of Communist incompetence followed by a brutally repressive military dictatorship. But where no such tradition of civil society exists – in tropical Africa; in the former lands of the Tsar; in China which never knew civil law – the free market by itself is unlikely to create a functioning economy, let alone a functioning society.

Democracy – as the term is commonly understood, that is, free elections and a parliament or Congress – is by itself not the answer. Hong Kong knows neither. Neither does Singapore. Taiwan was a military dictatorship until fairly recently. Chile started its spectacular turnaround under a repressive military dictatorship. In fact, there is considerable evidence for the claim made by the authoritarian rulers of the rapidly developing economies of South-east Asia: political freedom and democracy *follow* economic development rather than *precede* it as US political dogma preaches. Indeed, except in the United States, political development has everywhere followed economic development. The enormous social, economic, and cultural development of major continental-European countries during the nineteenth century, for instance – Imperial Germany; the Austria–Hungary of Francis Joseph; France under Napoleon III – all took place under authoritarian political regimes. The Japan of the 'economic miracle' of the last forty years is in its political reality (e.g. in the supremacy of a politically uncontrolled bureaucracy) much closer to the authoritarian nineteenth-century continental-European countries than to Anglo-American 'democracy'. That the United States – alone of all countries in the world – achieved political development *before* it achieved economic development may thus be only another case of 'American exceptionalism'.

But what is absolutely essential – or otherwise the free market will not function even as an economic institution – is what nineteenth-century political theorists called by a German word: the *Rechtsstaat* (the Justice State), and what we now call *human rights*: a social and political order which effectively protects the person and the property of citizens against arbitrary interference from above. Human rights equally guarantee the citizen's freedom to choose their religion; to choose their professions or their vocations; to form autonomous social institutions and to read, speak, write, and think, free of dictation by any power whether party, church or state.

Whether democracy then actually emerges – as the nineteenth-century Liberal fervently believed – remains to be seen. But without human rights as its foundation there surely will never be political democracy. There can only be chaos or tyranny. Equally, without human rights there is unlikely to be lasting economic development, even with market freedom.

'Capitalism' and 'capitalists' we now know – thanks mainly to the work of a great French historian, the late Fernand Braudel – are not modern phenomena. Both have been common throughout the ages and are found in most cultures and countries of which we have any knowledge. What is 'modern' is the free market as an organizing principle of the economy. The neo-classicists are right: without the free market there will be no functioning modern economy and, in fact, no economic growth. But the free market is in turn dependent on a functioning civil society. Without it, it is impotent.

The nineteenth century European Liberal fervently believed that civilization – and that meant a stable government, political order, rapid economic growth, a thriving middle class, and political and religious freedom – would follow automatically upon the establishment of the political institutions of a constitutional monarchy: a hereditary monarch with limited powers; a parliament with political parties and an annual budget; a professional civil service; a small standing army with a professional officer corps; an independent judiciary; a central bank; compulsory public education; a German-style university; and a (substantially) free press. The nineteenth-century American Liberal believed in the same model with only one change: the substitution of an elected president for the hereditary king. And both, the European and the American version of the model, were exported to the four corners of the earth.

This nineteenth-century modernization through political institutions does not have a good press today. It did better, however, than is commonly believed. In two countries – nineteenth-century Japan and early twentieth-century Turkey – it worked and created a new and modern civilization. Elsewhere – in Romania, Bulgaria and Poland; in Brazil and Mexico; in Egypt; and even in the Tsar's Russia – it established an ideal to which an educated elite still aspires despite a century's frustrations and disasters. But the nineteenth-century political model failed overall to create the liberal, enlightened, peaceful civilization it promised. Even in Italy it had impact mainly in the north which had had civilization for many centuries. In the south – in Calabria, for instance, or in Sicily – political modernization brought railways and hotels but little civilization.

The neo-classic economics of today have done somewhat better than the Old-Liberal politics of the last century. The free market has been changing the lives of many more people. Telephone, film, television, computer, hit harder than did the steamship, the railway, and the factory-made goods, which accompanied political modernization and were its most visible symbols. Goods, no matter how greedily desired, change consumption; information changes the imagination. Goods change how we live; information how we dream. Goods change how we see the world; information changes how we see ourselves.

Still, the free market of the neo-classicists no more creates a civil society than did the political institutions in which the Old-Liberals of the nineteenth century so firmly believed. The free market thus finds itself very much at the same impasse. It will not work unless there is civil society. But it cannot by itself create a civil society – as little as did political Liberalism a hundred years ago. Yet for the democracies truly to win the peace in the post-cold war world they must bring forth civil societies, especially in the former Communist parts of the world, i.e. the successors to the Soviet Empire and the successors to Mao's (or Deng's) China.

Can civil society be exported?

The one public figure in the democracies who has so far asked this question has answered it with a 'yes'. When Jimmy Carter as President of the United States made establishment of 'human rights' a goal of American policy and a prerequisite to giving American aid, he in effect proclaimed the promotion of civil society to be a goal of American foreign policy on a par with the military and political goal of containing and outliving Communism.

Mr Carter was ridiculed as a 'dreamer'. Viewed twenty years later he may have been the realist, and the dreamers are the believers in the efficacy of the free market. But Mr Carter did not succeed in getting a single country to accept human rights nor in convincing the public in the democracies of the wisdom of his priorities. But that was then still at the height of the cold war – and in any war, winning it always comes first, and thinking about the peace is brushed aside as a dangerous diversion, and subversive. Now the democracies need to reconsider; to win the peace in today's post-cold war world they have to establish civil society as a policy goal of its own. The failure of the free market to deliver on its economic promises, especially in the former Communist countries, may otherwise destroy the credibility of freedom and again endanger world peace.

At the least, governments will have to learn that it is futile, folly, and, predictably, a waste of money, to invest – whether through a World Bank loan or through a Stabilization Credit – unless the recipient country establishes a truly independent and truly effective *legal* system. Otherwise the money will only make the wrong people rich: political bosses; generals; con-artists. Instead of enriching the recipient country it will impoverish it. The same lesson needs to be learned by businesses: to invest in a country – like today's Russia or today's China – which has not even started building a legal system means, with near-certainty, to lose one's money, and in fairly short order. The experience of the last decades is crystal-clear: the free market will not produce a functioning and growing economy unless it is embedded in a functioning civil society, with effective human rights a minimum requirement.

It is often said today that the democracies have lost their bearings with the collapse of Communism. They no longer have a policy, no longer have priorities, no longer have criteria for what to do and what not to do. To be sure: the old policies, priorities, criteria do not make sense now that there is no longer a 'public enemy'. But there is a new policy, a new priority, a new necessity: the promotion of civil society as a goal of international policy. A civil society is not a panacea. It is not the 'end of history'. It does not by itself guarantee democracy, and not even peace. It is, however, a prerequisite to these, and equally to economic development. Only if civil society worldwide becomes their goal, can the democracies win the peace.

1995

Conclusion

Interview: Managing in a post-capitalist society
An interview with *Industry Week*
Conducted by Tom Brown

*One of the downsides of what passes as contemporary manage-
ment thinking is that too many managers venerate 'newness' and
nothing else. The latest-fad authors, whether there's substance to
their claims or not, too often become the hot ticket for a month
or two and then fade. But then there's Peter Drucker. He wrote
his first book,* The End of Economic Man, *in 1937 and in more
than half a century, the steady stream of rock-solid management
books that he has written are, in and of themselves, a complete
management library. His analysis is consistently on point, his
conclusions well reasoned, his counsel worthy of any manager's
consideration. Peter Drucker refuses to become outdated. So far
anyone who overlooked or ignored the best management book
published in 1993,* Post-Capitalist Society *(Harper-Business),
missed a very great deal indeed. In this relatively short book,
written in the clear and cogent style that Peter Drucker is
famous for, he asserts that we are in a period of immense social
transition. Then he handily interprets the consequences of the
transformation we're living through as it applies to business,
labour, and, of course, management. He also re-evaluates how
the politics of nations must be accounted for in future business
planning; here, too, he shares his insights about the role of
workers, managers, and plants in the larger context of citizenship.*

And in an age when everything seems to be in flux, he affirms that flux is the right word for our age and that success can only come through deliberate, constructive action. But the most cogent theme throughout the book, a theme that is consummated in the final section, is that knowledge needs to be better understood, measured, and managed. As you will see in this interview, far from dismissing the important role of management and manufacturing in the future of the United States, Peter Drucker affirms them. He cautions, however, that executives had better understand that there will be both informed and uninformed management and manufacturing – and only the former will be competitive enough to survive. By my count, Post-Capitalist Society is Peter Drucker's twenty-seventh book, but I found no pretence or self-importance in the man. To meet him in his neighbourly California home, to see him most comfortable in sports shirt and casual walking shoes, to hear him cite facts, figures, names, and anecdotes without strain, and to note that he shares his thinking with courtesy and good humour – this is the Peter Drucker that still remains in many ways hidden from even his most avid followers. If there ever was a master of management, then Peter Drucker is the genuine article.

Industry Week: Peter, let me start this interview at a strange place – at the last chapter of your book, in which you discuss 'the educated person'. Just how educated are most of us, in terms of being prepared to deal with the society and the workplace of the future?

Peter. F. Drucker: You know, we have a very peculiar situation. Young people, when they are in school, are extremely excited by the humanities, even the most traditional subjects. And five years after graduation, they will reject them, basically, and become totally vocational in their orientation. This imbalance isn't healthy in a long-range sense. As I look at our executive-management people who started out twenty or thirty years ago, I thought that these just-turned-45-or-50-year-old managers would ultimately come back to their schools and say, 'Now we need to understand a little bit about ourselves and about life!' But the postgraduate education of our managers, from this perspective, has been a total flop.

A flop?
Almost a total fizzle. But more and more are coming back, and they always want to come back to this vocational or their professional area. They start to see the humanities or the world of history as a way to reflect on their business experiences and to judge how they might have thought or acted differently, to look at their lives from whole new perspectives.

What does this mean, that too many of us blur the world of work and the world of 'life'?
It's deeper than just that. For most of history, earning a living was something you had to do because, after all, you had to eat. Life did not have that much leisure at all, in our sense of the word. Now, many people allow their work to consume their lives totally: that's what they enjoy. But in the past for people to admit that they enjoyed their work was simply – I wouldn't say it wasn't done – it wasn't expected. . . . The idea that your work was supposed to be meaningful was not a topic of discussion in the past. That's much different from today and even more different from the world of the future. Today more and more people simply expect and demand that their work and their jobs should be meaningful. I don't think it would ever have occurred to most people a hundred years ago.

So this, of course, has management and business implications, no?
I think the growth industry in this country and the world will soon be continuing education of adults. Nothing else is growing as fast, whether you are talking physicians, or engineers, or dentists. This is happening in part because things are changing so fast in every field of every business or occupation.

Let me personalize this for you. There's a young man I know – at least he's a young man to me; he's in his forties – he's probably the leading radiologist on the East Coast. I've known him since he was a child. He heads up the radiology, now 'imaging', department at a major medical school. I was heading to the East Coast to do some speaking, so I called him up, to arrange a get-together. His response: 'Peter, I am sorry. I'll be out of town that week. I'm going to Minnesota for a course.' And I asked, 'What are you teaching?' And he said, 'Peter, I'm not teaching. I'm going for a week to study new aspects in ultrasound technology. You know, I should have gone to study this last year, but I had some surgery, and I couldn't go. Now I'm way behind.'

And so I think that the educated person of the future is somebody who realizes they need to continue to learn. That is a new definition, and it is going to change the world we live and work in.

That brings me to the management implications. I had the feeling in your book that you felt that a lot of companies forced people, or encouraged people, to be too narrowly focused.
Not just companies. Almost the only organization that is different is the military. Check it out, and you'll see that practically all the senior military people have been back to school numerous times. Now when they go to the command and general staff school, that's very narrow. But when the Air Force or Army sends them to the university to get their master's or PhD, then they've pushed them to be more broad, to get some new perspectives.

So how does a company broaden its managers?
A good many companies today are encouraging their people to work in the community with non-profit organizations, which is perhaps the best educational experience I could advise for a thirty-five-year-old manager.

Peter, I feel that I'm almost grasping the significance of what you're driving at. Your book extols how the shrinking world will

increasingly be the reality for everyone in business. Are you saying that we need to learn more about how the world works?
One hundred years ago, people did not travel as much, but many talked more to each other about the nature of being human and about life. I can't explain to my children or my grandchildren, in a way that they can appreciate, that when I was growing up, my father had a dinner party every Monday. There were economists, ranking civil servants, a major international lawyer. And about every week there were other dinners when my parents would invite medical people. My mother and father were very interested in mathematics and philosophy – so they invited folks to dinner from these fields once a month. This is unthinkable today.

The reason that your words are so important is that your book makes many forceful points about the increasing importance of knowledge as a commodity in and of itself. You say that 'knowledge is the only meaningful resource today'. You also state that 'knowledge employees cannot, in effect, be supervised'. Will managers be needed in the future?
Managers will still be needed. But fewer will be needed than we see today. A lot of people who now have the title *manager* don't manage a damn thing. We have all these corporate layers for a variety of reasons. One is that when big organizations came into existence, the only model we had was the army. The Prussian army was at that time at the peak of its renown, right after 1870, and – like all armies – they had to have a lot of redundancy. So corporations built in a lot of redundancy. No one under sixty can possibly imagine how denuded we were of people after the Second World War. As the economy began to expand right after the war, you needed people and you had none, because the baby boomers didn't join the workforce until twenty-five years later. And so the available young people had to be promoted very fast. Before 1929 you didn't become a full professor anywhere until you were fifty. When I first taught in a business school, enrolments

were exploding: for five years, we doubled each year. When I joined it in 1949, it had 600 students. When I left, it had 6500. And it reached that in ten years!

During this time, I once studied the management of a bank, at one point reporting to the chief executive officer the average age of the bank's senior managers. 'Your vice-presidents,' I said, 'have fewer years of age than your predecessor's vice-presidents had years of seniority.' It traditionally took thirty years to become a vice-president at a bank. Traditionally, you could come into a bank during this tough time, say at age twenty-one and if you were very, very, very good, you became an assistant vice-president in your mid-forties. Then suddenly, because of man-power shortages, you had twenty-six-year-old vice-presidents. You had to! And we made jobs very small.

There will, to be sure, be less of a need for this many levels of management and for this many managers in the future. The nature of work – and of workers – is such that oversupervision can become a drag on the productivity of the firm. But as I say in the book, management is needed in all modern organizations; it's a generic function of all organizations, whatever their specific mission. And you could say that management is the generic organ of the knowledge society.

Yet I noted the importance you attached to teams in your book – and how they can manage themselves. It is one of the most powerful and useful parts of your book.
A team is one of the most difficult things to run. Look, I've done a lot of work with baseball teams. They are very peculiar organizations. They are among the most difficult things to run. Very few coaches do a good job, precisely because you are dealing with a team, but your best pitcher is either a prima donna or he's no good. In baseball, average pitchers need not apply.

In corporations, you are also often dealing with prima donnas, yet it is a team where people often don't perceive that they have to work together. Think of almost any design team you know.

I happen to know Toyota quite well. A couple of years ago, I asked one of their senior executives, just retired, 'How long did it take you before your design team performed well?' He laughed and said, 'In the first place, it doesn't perform yet. And in the second place, we began in 1950.' Donald Petersen of Ford started in the early 1970s and retired in the mid-1980s; he worked very hard to get teams going, but you hear constant complaints at Ford that their teams don't work.

It takes a really superb manager to build that kind of team where people really work together and adjust and take their cues from the others and move ahead as a unit. That's not easy. That takes time and nerve and a very clear mission and a very skilful leader . . . perhaps 'skilful' isn't the right word. You need a very focused, a very clear kind of leadership. So what's needed in the future may not be 'a manager' in the typical sense. Many executives I meet are totally baffled by what I'm talking about. They don't know how to build a team. And not because they don't try it, but because it's got to be built. You manage to build a team, and yet you work each day with individuals.

Peter, the time when I have seen managers get the most bothered by your writing is when you talk about the move to knowledge work as part of a 'a knowledge society', and they say – perhaps without reading you closely – 'Does Drucker believe we in the United States won't manufacture things anymore, that our economy will be solid enough without a manufacturing base?' How do you answer them?

That's nonsense. Look, most people believe that American manufacturing has been in decline. There isn't the slightest reason for that belief. Manufacturing has grown as fast as the economy, that is, very fast. It has expanded two-and-a-half times in the last, well, since the late 1960s – the last twenty, twenty-five years. Same as GNP. But people still identify manufacturing production with manufacturing and blue-collar employment. Big mistake.

Explain, please.
Blue-collar employment has grown less fast than manufacturing volume since 1900, which nobody seems to know, even though it's in every statistical yearbook. It has been declining: the unit of blue-collar labour needed to make an additional unit of manufacturing has been going down at 1 per cent compounded for more than ninety years – for almost a century!

Manufacturing production has been going up steadily and shows every sign of continuing to grow, and the share of manufacturing in GNP has remained steady since about 1890 – for one hundred years – between 21 per cent and 23 per cent. The entire growth of services is at the expense of agriculture. Agriculture in 1900 was still 50 per cent; it is now 3 per cent. Manufacturing has remained constant. But blue-collar employment – not total employment – has come down and will continue to go down. We are not at the bottom yet, though we are getting there. We're down to 18 per cent. It'll bottom out at around 10 per cent or 11 per cent, which doesn't mean that you have another cut of 50 per cent, because manufacturing production is steadily growing. But you have another cut of maybe 2 per cent to 4 per cent of the present workforce. But this trend represents an enormous shift.

What caused the shift?
There are two or three key things we could talk about. Let me talk about the biggest single factor: the emergence of new manufacturing industries that are not blue-collar labour-intensive, but knowledge-intensive!

So it's knowledge in the form of . . .
Re-engineering! It's the steady re-engineering of the manufacturing process. Most people think of automation as the reason for the lower demand for labour; automation is almost irrelevant. Take, for example, making blue jeans. That's a sewing operation. Even thirty years ago, blue jeans came in three sizes – that was it – and in one colour and in one style.

Today, blue jeans come in about sixteen sizes and twice as many styles. But the process has been organized so that the burden of adjustment is not at the beginning of the process, but at the end. It's at the very end: you go right through to the final sewing stage with one length, one width, and maybe one colour. The burden of adjustment to styles and sizes is all at the end, the culmination of a continuous and uniform process. It costs a little extra cloth to do it this way, but you basically have a flow process in which practically all the work can be programmed. It's not machine work; there's still a lot of handwork, but it is programmed and very well engineered. And so the labour needed is probably one-fifth of what you had even twenty years ago, but not just because they've automated anything. We have cut cloth by machine for sixty years; this is nothing very new. It's the re-engineering.

That doesn't sound all that radical.
It's not. Any good engineer was probably taught to approach production this way since 1940. But the last ones to actually do it will probably be the car manufacturers, because they had the fantastically efficient system based on a minimum number of models. Once you have locked into a model for the year, you didn't do anything to it. Well, that's gone. So they have to relearn the process. The Japanese have led the way, but there's still more to be learned.

So knowledge is absolutely key.
It's as I say in the book: A country that has the knowledge workers to design products and to market them will have no difficulty getting those products made at low cost and high quality. But narrow-mindedness and narrow perspectives are not going to make any business in any country more competitive in the future.

I was amazed at how I misunderstood F. W. Taylor, the pioneer business thinker of the early 1900s. You have given me a new

appreciation for him. Do you think, given your awesome stretch of books, that you have been understood?
I think I have been understood in different ways in different parts of the world. For example, in Japan people seem to note that I made businesses and managers much more aware of the need to understand marketing in the truest sense: you have to let the market drive your business; you have to listen to customers and heed their wants and needs.

The Japanese also seem to appreciate my words on price-controlled costing: that you have to design products to the price that the marketplace is willing to pay.

I also believe the Japanese heeded first and best my point of view that people must be viewed as your colleagues and one of your prime resources. It is only through such respect of the workers that true productivity is achieved.

And, lastly, the Japanese seemed to take to heart that there really is such a thing as a world economy and that trying to sell only within your national borders is provincialism when it comes to business.

How about in Europe?
I think they see me as a pioneer of the counterculture. During modern times, most of European management (and Europe is, after all, where my own roots are) had what I would call a 'Krupp' mentality, where the manager projects the attitude that 'I *own everything*' and that everyone who works within a company is no more than a 'helper'. I'm afraid to think how many managers of this ilk are still around, all over the world.

The problems with this attitude are many. It blocks out the kind of communication and dialogue that you need to run a business. It doesn't allow for the possibility that lots of people need to make decisions if a business is to be dynamic. In fact, a lot of European managers were reduced to counting pencil stubs or meaningless stuff like that.

Well, European managers who have followed my books and my thinking right away saw my advocacy of management as a profession, as something that was a bit subversive, a bit revolutionary, and – in short – countercultural. In fact, in this light my book *The Practice of Management* was, and is, a sort of a manifesto in Europe.

What about the United States?

My impression is that managers in the United States derived two major points from my writing and my counsel. First, they at least started to understand that people are a resource and not just a cost. I think that the most enlightened managers have started to understand what could be realized by managing people towards a desired end or goal.

Which raises the second major point that managers here seem to note about my work, that I helped them start to *see* management. In other words, for a long time, the impact – plus or minus – of management was invisible to most Americans. I think that many credit me with discovering the discipline and insisting that businesses take management seriously – as a profession that can make a difference in the life of the business.

I would hope that American managers – indeed, managers worldwide – continue to appreciate what I have been saying almost since day one: that management is so much more than exercising rank and privilege; it's so much more than 'making deals'. Management affects people and their lives, both in business and in many other aspects as well. The practice of management deserves our utmost attention; it deserves to be studied.

1994

Index